College Autonomy in India
Performance and Prospects

Abraham George

AUTHORSPRESS
Publishers of Scholarly Books

Worldwide Circulation through Authorspress Global Network
First Published 2011
by
Authorspress
E-35/103, Jawahar Park
Laxmi Nagar, Delhi-110 092
e-mail: authorspress@yahoo.com

College Autonomy in India:Performance and Prospects
ISBN 978-81-7273-569-2

Printed in India at Tarun Offset, Delhi.

Dedicated to

Ann

An inspiration always

Foreword

Over the years attempts to bring about reforms in higher education sector often got defeated due to the rigidity in the structure of university education in the country. This has been particularly evident in the affiliating system that exists in most of the universities. The concept of college autonomy is expected to raise the academic standards of the higher education institutions selected for autonomy.

Three decades have passed since autonomy was first granted to a few colleges in some of the states of India. In spite of the efforts of the UGC and the success of the scheme wherever it has been implemented, the number of autonomous colleges in the country is relatively low even today. Further, some more states are yet to grant autonomy to any of their colleges.

In order to implement qualitative reforms in the institutions of higher learning, reputed colleges which are capable of performing better than others, need to be granted academic autonomy. They may be thus given the freedom and flexibility to experiment with academic innovations in pursuit of academic excellence.

Beyond the traditional functions of teaching, research and innovation, universities are expected to fulfil new roles and tasks and respond to new challenges in an increasingly complex and global environment. I firmly believe that increasing institutional autonomy is a key to enabling universities to respond to these new demands. The book which contains articles by prominent academicians of the country strongly recommends for the granting of autonomy to more higher education institutions. While delineating the advantages of the system, it also makes significant observations regarding the practical problems and issues related to its implementation and also make valuable suggestions for improvement. Moreover, the volume provides useful tips regarding the preparations to be done by an institution which is planning to become autonomous. A few articles are exclusively devoted to Kerala state where autonomy is yet to be implemented. I congratulate Dr. Abraham George for his efforts to bring out this valuable piece of academic content.

I am hopeful that the book will ignite greater enthusiasm among the academicians and policy makers in propagating autonomy and enhancing the number of autonomous institutions across the country.

Dr. V. N Rajasekharan Pillai

Vice-Chancellor, IGNOU, New Delhi

Preface

The Indian higher education sector is predominantly characterized by the affiliating pattern. The affiliating system worked well so long as the number of colleges affiliated to a university was relatively less. However, with the proliferation of colleges during the post-independent era, affiliating universities found it increasingly difficult to fulfil effectively the role expected of them. Various attempts to reform the university education in India have also not met with considerable success due to the existing rigidity in the structure of the affiliating system. Individual colleges which have the potential for considerable quality enhancement are incapacitated by the affiliating system as these institutions do not have the freedom to make their own academic development initiatives.

The idea of college autonomy aims at giving freedom to colleges to determine their own courses of study and syllabi, rules of admission and methods of evaluation within the framework of the rules and regulations of the university and the state government. The concept received serious attention in India only after it was given specific recommendation in the Education Commission Report (1964-66). After prolonged discussions and deliberations, academic autonomy was granted to colleges in India for the first time in 1978. However, the number of autonomous colleges has not increased during the last three decades as was originally envisaged. Although the University Grants Commission (UGC)has proposed to grant autonomy to ten per cent of the eligible colleges by the end of the Eleventh Plan period, there are at present only 314 autonomous colleges in India spread over sixteen states, the maximum number being in Tamil Nadu.

While a good number of states in the country have experimented with autonomy and found it successful, a few states like Kerala have shied away from introducing the scheme for one reason or another. Today, Kerala does not have a single college which figures among the best higher education institutions at the national level. It is high time the state experimented with this time-tested concept so that at least a few higher education institutions in the state are enabled to grow in an atmosphere of academic freedom and excel at all India level. It is in this context that the present volume on autonomous colleges which includes a special section on Kerala is brought out.

There are altogether twenty-five articles included in this volume. Most of them deal with the evolution, growth, performance, challenges, prospects, etc., related to the autonomous colleges in India as a whole. Apart from analyzing the general issues related to autonomy, the last six articles of the book give special emphasis to the need for granting autonomous status to colleges in Kerala.

The idea to bring out this volume was mooted a few years ago when I was the Principal of Mar Thoma College, Tiruvalla, Kerala. The College had then applied for autonomous status and autonomy was granted provisionally by the UGC subject to the concurrence of the state government and the university. Since the concept of autonomy had not found favour with the state government, such an effort did not bear fruit for Mar Thoma College, Tiruvalla and a few other colleges in Kerala which had also been granted autonomy provisionally by the UGC. However, as part of preparing the College for autonomy, a Natonal Seminar on Autonomy was organized at Mar Thoma College, Tiruvalla in 2006. In the same year, the Staff Council members and the IQAC steering committee members of the College were taken on an educational tour to visit three autonomous institutions in Tamil Nadu - American College, Madurai, Lady Doak College, Madurai and Bishop Heber College, Thiruchirappally. Over the past few years, as a member of the National Asessment and Accreditation Council(NAAC) Peer Team, I had the privilege and opportunity to visit several autonomous colleges in different states in India. The performance of these institutions really convinced me about the potential of autonomy and also the need for granting academic autonomy to leading colleges in all the states of India including Kerala.

I express my profound gratitude to the United Board of Christian Higher Education in Asia (UBCHEA) for providing the financial assistance to conduct the National Seminar on Autonomy at Mar Thoma College, Tiruvalla, and also for facilitating the faculty visits to three autonomous colleges in Tamil Nadu. My special thanks to Dr. Betty Cernol McCann, Vice President, UBCHEA, for her support and encouragement.

This volume includes articles by some of the leading educationists of our country. Each of them is in one way or the other related to the scheme of academic autonomy. In spite of their preoccupations, it was their academic interest and eagerness for quality enhancement in the higher education sector in the country which motivated them to graciously contribute articles for this volume. With great appreciation I thankfully acknowledge their valuable contribution.

My deepest gratitude to Prof. V.N. Rajasekharan Pillai, Vice-Chancellor of Indira Gandhi National Open University (IGNOU) for writing the 'Foreword' for the book.

I am indebted to Dr. Mani Jacob, (General Secretary of All India Association for Christian Higher Education (AIACHE), New Delhi, for his constant encouragement and guidance in bringing out this volume.

I am grateful to my colleagues Smt. Remani George and Dr. Icy K. John for the help and assistance they rendered.

I owe much to my beloved wife Ann (who passed away last year) and my daughter Rini for their encouragement and support in all my academic endeavours including the publication of this volume. This book is dedicated to Ann.

My sincere gratitude to Authorspress, New Delhi, for bringing out this volume elegantly.

This volume is presented before for all the stakeholders in the higher education sector of the country, particularly those in Kerala and other states where autonomy is yet to be introduced, who look forward to quality enhancement in the institutions of higher learning, and who perceive education as an instrument of social and economic change.

— ***Abraham George***

Contributors

1. **Dr. Abraham George,** Former Principal, Mar Thoma College, Tiruvalla, Kerala.
2. **Dr. Xavier Alphonse S.J.** UGC Member & Former Principal, Loyola College, Chennai.
3. **Dr. Mani Jacob,** Chancellor, Allahabad Agricultural Institute Deemed University & General Secretary, AIACHE, New Delhi.
4. **Dr. S. Ignacimuthu S.J.** Former Vice Chancellor, Bharathiar University & University of Madras.
5. **Dr. Francis Soundararaj,** Former Principal, Madras Christian College, Chennai.
6. **Prof. S.P. Thyagarajan,** Former Vice-Chancellor, University of Madras.
7. **Prof. Mariamma A. Varghese,** Former Vice Chancellor, SNDT Women's University, Mumbai.
8. **Dr. A. Sukumaran Nair,** Former Vice-Chancellor, Mahatma Gandhi University, Kerala.
9. **Dr. D. Peter Jayapandian,** Former Principal, American College, Madurai.
10. **Dr. S. John Britto S.J.** Former Principal, St. Joseph's College, Tiruchirappalli.
11. **Sri. B.S. Ponmudiraj,** Assistant Adviser, NAAC, Bangalore.
12. **Dr. Sr. Annamma Philip & Dr. Ordetta Mendoza,** Former Principal, Stella Maris College, Chennai & HOD, Bioinformatics, Stella Maris College, respectively.

13. **Dr. Nirmala Jeyaraj,** Former Principal, Lady Doak College, Madurai.
14. **Dr. A. Albert Muthumalai S.J.,** Principal, Loyola College, Chennai.
15. **Dr. K. Nirmala Prasad,** Principal, MOP Vaishnav College for Women, Chennai.
16. **Dr. M. Thavamani,** Principal, Ethiraj College for Women, Chennai.
17. **Sr. Philomena Cardoza,** Principal, Jyoti Nivas College, Bangalore.
18. **Prof. S. Sivasubramanium,** Former Vice-Chancellor, Bharathiar University.
19. **Dr. R.B. Lal,** Vice-Chancellor, Allahabad Agricultural Institute Deemed University.
20. **Prof. M.V. Pylee,** Former Vice-Chancellor, Cochin University.
21. **Dr. B. Ekbal,** Former Vice-Chancellor, University of Kerala.
22. **Prof. Ninan Abraham,** Former Vice-Chancellor, Kanpur University.
23. **Dr. Cyriac Thomas,** Former Vice-Chancellor, Mahatma Gandhi University.
24. **Dr. J.V. Vilanilam,** Former Vice-Chancellor, Kerala University.

Contents

1

Introduction

— Abraham George

Higher education the world over at present is passing through a crucial phase. The higher education sector in India is also faced with a number of challenges. Several steps have been initiated in recent times to improve the quality of education imparted through India's higher education institutions. The qualitative changes that take place in this sector are going to play a major role in the future development of the country. In this context, granting academic autonomy for higher education institutions assumes great significance considering its potential for quality enhancement and academic excellence.

Academic autonomy is expected to enable higher education institutions to achieve academic excellence in an atmosphere of freedom. It has the potential to make the educational process more dynamic and more adaptable to contemporary conditions. According to the UGC document on the Eleventh Plan profile of higher education in India, "The only safe and better way to improve the quality of undergraduate education is to delink most of the colleges from the affiliating structure. Colleges with academic and operative freedom are doing better and have more credibility." Autonomy gives a college freedom and opportunity to experiment and innovate in areas like curriculum, courses, teaching methods, evaluation, etc. The UGC aims at granting autonomy to 10 per cent of the eligible colleges by the end of the Eleventh Plan period.

Evolution of Autonomous Colleges in India

The concept of academic autonomy for colleges started receiving serious attention only after the Education Commission (1964-66) under the chairmanship of Dr. D.S. Kothari made specific recommendations in its report for the establishment of autonomous colleges. According to the Kothari Commission report:

"We should like to refer to the question of 'autonomous' colleges which has been under discussion for many years. Where there is an outstanding college (or a small cluster of very good colleges) within a large University which has shown the capacity to improve itself markedly, consideration should be given to granting it an autonomous status. This would involve the power to frame its own rules of admission, to prescribe its courses of study, to conduct examinations and so on. The parent University's role will be one of general supervision and the actual conferment of the degree. The privilege cannot be conferred once and for all. It will have to be continually earned and deserved and it should be open to the University - after careful scrutiny of the position, to revoke the autonomous status if the college begins to deteriorate in its standards. We recommend that provision for the recognition of such autonomous colleges be made in the constitution of the Universities. It should be possible in our opinion, by the end of the Fourth Five Year Plan, to bring about fifty of the best colleges under that category" (*The Education Commission Report,* 1964-66, p.286).

Among the different states of India, it was Tamil Nadu which took the early lead in granting autonomy to affiliated colleges. During 1978-79, eight affiliated colleges belonging to the University of Madras and four colleges of Madurai Kamaraj University were granted autonomous status. Since 1978, the UGC has taken special interest to grant autonomy to larger number of colleges. But the progress has been rather slow. By 1988 only 50 colleges had been granted autonomy in the entire country out of which 43 were in Tamil Nadu. At present, there are altogether 314 autonomous colleges in India spread over 16 states. The following Table reveals that even today the largest number of autonomous colleges (116) are in Tamil Nadu.

Statewise List of Autonomous Colleges in India (as on March 2009)

1	Andhra Pradesh	47
2	Chhattisgarh	10
3	Gujarat	1
4	Himachal Pradesh	5
5	Jharkhand	4
6	Karnataka	41
7	Madhya Pradesh	31
8	Maharashtra	14
9	Nagaland	1
10	Orissa	31
11	Pondicherry	2
12	Rajasthsan	2
13	Tamil Nadu	116
14	Uttar Pradesh	5
15	Uttarakhand	1
16	West Bengal	3
	ALL INDIA	314

Source: UGC Website

Need for Granting Autonomy to Colleges

The system of affiliation was started at a time when the number of colleges was less and manageable. During the six decades after independence, there has been a significant growth in the number of colleges in the country. Under the affiliating system, universities continue to exercise rigid control over the affiliated colleges with regard to courses, syllabi, examinations, etc. Even academically strong colleges which have the potential to offer higher quality education do not have the freedom to innovate or improve. The university treats all the affiliated colleges in the same way and there hardly exists any incentive for better colleges to innovate or improve. Broadly speaking, there will always be a few affiliated colleges under every university that are academically weak. Quite often it is these institutions which set the standard in the common system of the university.

The Committee on Standards of University Education (1965) under the Chairmanship of Prof. S. K. Sidhanta had made the following observation way back in1965: "In an affiliating system, the weak colleges tend to determine the policy of the University with regard to the course of study, teaching requirements, examination, etc. The good colleges which are capable of rising to much higher standards are consequently not allowed to do so. Unless these colleges which can do better than the rest are permitted to go ahead with their plans for modernizing and improving their academic programmes, they will not be in a position to hold on to their superior standards infinitely."

Committed teachers also feel frustrated and dissatisfied. According to the Report of the Expert Committee constituted by the Kerala Government (1987), "Most of the teachers in an affiliating University have passive role to play....They feel frustrated and alienated from the system of which they should be the main priests." Since all important decisions are taken by the university, affiliated colleges do not have much accountability either. For any failure, they can get away by blaming the university.

Another major drawback is the interference of non-academics in the decision-making bodies of the affiliating universities. Professional competence is often overlooked while constituting bodies like boards of studies, senate, syndicate, etc. It not only affects the smooth functioning of the university, but also stands in the way of the efforts for quality enhancement.

In order to free the colleges from the stranglehold of the affiliation system, autonomous status may be given to the leading colleges in every university. Granting autonomy to better institutions provides opportunity for them to grow further and it will also motivate other institutions to improve their academic performance.

Major Advantages of Autonomy

It is now more than thirty years since college autonomy was introduced in India. It would be useful to look back and evaluate the performance of the system and examine whether it is worthwhile to grant autonomy to more higher education institutions. When we take into account the performance of the autonomous colleges in different states in India during the past three decades, it becomes clear that autonomy has provided ample opportunities for many colleges to introduce significant academic and administrative reforms. Some of the important advantages of the scheme are given below.

a) Autonomy provides an atmosphere of freedom and flexibility for the colleges which enables them to make innovations and experimentations. As the autonomous colleges no longer need to wait for decisions to be made by the university, majority of them are able to introduce several innovative programmes and courses. The quality of education imparted could be improved by introducing innovative changes in the courses offered as well as in the teaching and evaluation methods.

b) Under academic autonomy, colleges have the freedom to redesign and update the course curriculum and syllabi. Autonomous colleges can restructure the existing traditional courses to make them more relevant and up-to-date. Moreover, many of them have started diverse job-oriented new generation courses. Most of the autonomous colleges have introduced project work at undergraduate and postgraduate levels. Several vocational and socially relevant job-oriented courses, add-on / certificate / diploma programmes and courses to suit the needs of the locality could also be introduced.

c) Innovative and diversified teaching methods like project work, field surveys, group discussions, seminars, book reviews, on the job training, etc. could be introduced by the autonomous colleges without much problem. ICT-enabled teaching methods are also more effectively introduced in autonomous colleges compared to colleges under the affiliating system.

d) Although semester system has been introduced by many universities in the affiliated colleges by now, undue delays in completing the semesters and announcing the examination results on time (even at the postgraduate level) is a major problem faced by them. However, autonomous colleges are able to implement the semester system efficiently and systematically.

e) Compared to affiliated colleges, autonomous colleges are found to implement the choice based credit system (CBCS) more smoothly and effectively. Autonomous colleges provide relatively greater freedom for students to choose their subjects according to their preferences under the CBCS.

f) Autonomous colleges have successfully introduced several examination reforms like semester examinations, continuous internal assessment (CIA), improved question patterns, provision for student appeal, evaluation by internal and external examiners, etc. Many of them have developed their own question banks also. Autonomous colleges are able to adhere to the time schedule for the conduct of examinations as well as for the announcement of results which most of the affiliating universities find hard to observe. Several instances have been reported where students have lost up to a year due to the delays in examinations and announcement of results by the affiliating universities.

g) Making use of the freedom and flexibility under autonomy, several colleges have introduced extension activities and community work as a component of the syllabi in order to improve social awareness among the students. It is easier for autonomous institutions to establish linkages with the local community, NGOs and other agencies and to effectively implement them.

h) In the affiliating system, several working days are often lost every academic year due to strikes, agitations, etc. However, autonomous colleges are able to adhere to their annual academic calendar without loss of any teaching days.

i) Compared to affiliated colleges, autonomous colleges have achieved greater degree of decentralization and delegation of responsibilities, making the system more participatory. Academic planning relating to courses, curriculum, evaluation, etc. requires great deal of involvement and participation of the entire faculty. The administrative structure in the autonomous colleges involves better sharing of power and responsibilities among the faculty and other staff members. Further, teachers are given representation in all the important bodies like the Governing Body, Academic Council, Board of Studies, etc. as per the UGC guidelines. Students are also given representation in the Academic Council.

j) Autonomy has given not only greater academic freedom, but also greater responsibility, particularly for the faculty members. The teacher's role is most crucial as his / her responsibilities range from developing the course and syllabus to choosing the teaching methods to assessment and evaluation of the students. While designing and updating the curriculum, the teacher needs to give due consideration for the employability and usefulness of a course for the students.

k) Under the affiliating system, teachers have only a passive secondary role where one teaches the syllabus set by the university and trains the students for evaluation by others. Whereas under autonomy, the teacher has a primary role as he/she develops the syllabus, makes decisions regarding the teaching method, learning materials, reference books and evaluation.

l) The participation of faculty in professional development programmes, seminars, workshops and conferences is found to be much higher in autonomous colleges than in affiliated colleges.

m) An autonomous college has more flexibility to develop a research culture in the institution. Compared to affiliated colleges, autonomous colleges have been more successful in obtaining funds for research from various national and international level funding agencies and research organizations.

n) Since classes and examinations are held as per schedule, students belonging to autonomous colleges are generally found to be relatively more regular in their studies compared to their counterparts in affiliated colleges. As part of the continuous internal evaluation system under autonomy, tests, assignments, project work, etc. are conducted regularly which keep the students more engaged and systematic. The semester system and continuous internal assessment in autonomous colleges have also been instrumental in promoting better discipline and peaceful atmosphere on the campus.

o) By providing relevant, up-to-date and need based courses, autonomous colleges can ensure increased employability for their students. The flexibility available in designing the curriculum and course content enable the autonomous colleges to foster all round personality development of the students more effectively than under the rigid affiliation system. They can also ensure involvement of larger number of students in the co-curricular activities of the institution.

p) In contrast to the affiliating system, there is greater scope for joint academic activities between institutions and for better interaction among teachers belonging to different disciplines under the autonomous scheme. Facilities available in partner institutions can thus be shared effectively by both students and teachers.

q) In recent times great emphasis has been given for value based education at all levels. By virtue of the inherent flexibility of the system, value based education can be effectively incorporated in the syllabi of autonomous institutions.

r) Funds available for academic activities including course development, research, infrastructural development and the like from the UGC and other funding agencies for an autonomous college is much higher than that for an affiliated college. Moreover, autonomous colleges have greater freedom to offer various self-financing programmes in order to generate additional revenue for the institution.

s) The system of autonomy is found to promote healthy competition among different colleges. The demand for any course in any subject will depend primarily on the standard maintained by the concerned department in that particular course. Consequently, every autonomous college and every department in an institution will have to strive continuously to improve quality for their survival, thus leading to academic excellence.

Some Limitations of the Scheme

When we take into account the performance of all the autonomous colleges in different states in India during the past three decades, we come across considerable variations in the achievements of different institutions. Many autonomous colleges have made remarkable progress and have performed much better than they otherwise would. At the same time, some of them have not fared well enough.

It has been observed that the curricular innovations made by some of the autonomous colleges have not been as significant as it was expected to be. Autonomous institutions still face several problems and challenges, especially during the early stages of implementation. They include lack of training for the faculty and other staff in the new academic and administrative functions which were earlier done by the university, difficulty in getting funds for infrastructure and other facilities and for starting innovative courses, delays in receiving grants from the UGC and the government, etc. It has been pointed out that the government workload norms for the staff stand in the way of offering enough number of electives under the choice based credit system (CBCS). The internal system of examinations of some of the autonomous institutions is yet to gain full credibility among other institutions. However, if the authorities and the institutions make a genuine effort, most of these constraints could be mitigated.

Generally speaking, the merits of autonomy far outweigh the deficiencies of the system. As a departure from the redundant affiliating system, autonomy is definitely a positive move towards quality enhancement and academic excellence. Therefore in order to bring about a qualitative change in the higher education scenario of the country, the scheme of college autonomy need to be assiduously promoted.

An Overview of the Articles

The present volume is a collection of twenty five papers contributed by different authors dealing with different aspects of autonomy. The articles in this book have been arranged in two parts. Part I contains majority of the articles and they analyse mainly the historical evolution of autonomous colleges in India, their growth, performance, challenges, prospects, suggestions for improvement and the like.The four articles included in Part II of the volume give special emphasis to the need for implementing the scheme in Kerala in addition to the discussion of the general issues related to autonomy at the national level.

In his article 'The History, Evolution and Relevance of College Autonomy in India', Xavier Alphonse S.J. gives a brief historical evolution of college autonomy in the country. He highlights autonomy as a corrective to the existing affiliating system. After delineating the objectives and advantages of autonomy, he gives specific suggestions to achieve further improvements in the functioning of the autonomous colleges. Mani Jacob's article 'College Autonomy—A Historic Educational Innovation' traces the development of the concept of autonomy in the country. He describes college autonomy as the most significant innovation introduced in the Indian higher education sector during the latter part of the twentieth century and analyses the strategies adopted while switching over from the affiliating system to autonomy. In his article 'Advantages of Autonomous Colleges', S. Ignacimuthu S.J. expresses his firm conviction that India requires a good higher education system to build a modern knowledge society and that if educational standards have to improve, autonomous colleges need to be encouraged in a big way. How a college stands to benefit from the introduction of autonomy is the main focus of the article.

Francis Soundararaj in his paper 'Academic Autonomy for Change Towards Quality' articulates the need for effective implementation of autonomy as a vehicle for a qualitative transition in Indian higher education. Of the five areas of academic autonomy which the UGC has identified (academic, social, pedagogic, technological and community development), the article concentrates on the academic dimension alone and provides a detailed account on the construction of an integrated curricular model in an autonomous institution as part of the strategy for academic development and quality assurance. S.P. Thyagarajan's article 'Autonomous Colleges and Relationship with the University, State Government and the UGC' highlights the role of the university, state government and the UGC in relation to autonomous colleges. He stresses the need for achieving autonomy with accountability and the importance of a code of ethics to ensure the ethical standards of the members of the university community. In the article 'Autonomous Colleges – Prospects and Challenges', Mariamma A. Varghese suggests college autonomy as a partial solution to the general problem of universities lagging behind in the pursuit of academic excellence. She explains the academic, administrative and financial dimensions of autonomy and analyses the different aspects of the working of autonomous colleges in the backdrop of the existing policies of the UGC. A. Sukumaran Nair in his paper titled 'Institutional Autonomy for Quality Improvement of Higher Education' argues that giving greater freedom to educational institutions and making them socially accountable is a better method of ensuring quality than exercising rigid controls over them. The paper discusses the meaning, scope and possibilities of academic autonomy and highlights the need to frame a common code of conduct and operational procedures at the national level with regard to granting autonomy along with adequate safeguards against the misuse of autonomy.

D. Peter Jayapandian's paper 'College Autonomy' starts with a discussion about the need to grant autonomy to colleges in the country. To him, under the affiliating system the teacher plays only a secondary role in the whole process of teaching, learning and evaluation whereas the primary role of the teacher is restored under autonomy. He observes that adequate preparation and training are essential for the proper implementation of autonomy. Through the article 'Teaching, Research and Extension in Autonomous Colleges', S. John Britto S.J tries to establish that by redesigning their academic strategies, autonomous colleges have the potential to make significant contributions in the domains of teaching, research and extension. Teachers need to be most resourceful and innovative in ensuring the optimum implementation of these strategies so that not only teaching, but research, consultancy and extension activities also could be strengthened leading to overall quality enhancement in higher education. B.S. Ponmudiraj in his article 'Autonomous Colleges in India – A Step Towards Quality Assurance' outlines the development of the concept of autonomy in a historical perspective and appraises its importance. He explains how autonomy can help an institution to improve quality through reforms in curriculum, teaching-learning, leadership and governance and particularly in evaluation systems. The assessment and accreditation process also stregthens the quality sustenance and quality enhancement efforts of autonomous colleges.

Annamma Philip and Ordetta Mendoza in their article 'College Autonomy - A Privilege to Practice' observe that autonomy provides an institution remarkable academic freedom particularly for curricular revision and examination reforms. According to them, it is for the teachers that the scheme gives maximum autonomy and the teachers enjoy greater freedom to be innovative and to make classrooms vibrant by using technology-based teaching and learning methods. In the article titled 'College Autonomy – Gains and Constraints' , Nirmala Jeyaraj states that autonomy involves academic freedom coupled with responsibility requiring self-regulation. Autonomy gives not only academic freedom, but also several challenges for the teacher in the areas of curriculum framing, teaching and evaluation. Besides analyzing the main benefits and constraints of autonomy, she puts forward a few suggestions for the improvement of the scheme. A. Albert Muthumalai S.J, in his article 'Academic Autonomy', provides an account of the opportunities and constraints of autonomy from the experience of Loyola College, Chennai, and traces the efforts undertaken by the College towards quality enhancement through curriculum modification, skill formation, value education and outreach programmes. He also discusses the steps to be initiated in order to make the teaching-learning process more meaningful and purposeful.

In her article 'Challenges and Problems of Higher Education in India—The Role of Self-Financing Autonomous Colleges' , K. Nirmala Prasad takes stock of the reality of the Indian higher education as it exists today and stresses the need for reforming the system through new initiatives. She elaborates the freedom under autonomy to reform teaching, learning and evaluation mechanism and gives special emphasis to innovative practices like skill learning, industry-institution interface, optimum use of information and communication technology, etc. in the context of an autonomous self-financing institution. M. Thavamani in her article 'Autonomy – An Analysis' describes autonomy as a healthy way to reform higher education in the country. The article focuses on what to be expected of the institutions which would like to become autonomous and highlights the importance of accountability in the autonomous scheme. In the article 'Autonomy for Colleges in the 21st Century—Relevance, Challenges and Suggestions', Philomena Cardoza stresses the need for granting autonomy as the affiliating system has become irrelevant and decadent. She highlights the importance of promoting human, ethical, social and spiritual values for the overall quality improvement of the education imparted through autonomous colleges. S. Sivasubramanium's paper 'Some Glimpses on the Style and Functioning of Autonomy in Colleges' presents the author's observations regarding the working of autonomous colleges. To him, total team work by all the stakeholders is essential for the successful functioning of an autonomous institution. R.B. Lal in his article 'Autonomy: Prospects and Challenges' discusses mainly about university autonomy which involves both administrative and academic freedom. He believes that continuous evaluation system for students as well as teachers will help improve the quality of higher education in autonomous institutions.

As has been pointed out earlier, the articles included in Part II of the volume highlight the need for introducing autonomy in the state of Kerala besides dealing with the salient attributes and issues related to academic autonomy in India. M.V. Pylee's article 'College Autonomy, A Must for Higher Standards' briefly traces the history of the concept of autonomy and explains the importance of the scheme in the changed higher education scenario. He emphasizes the need for the state government to take the initiative for its implementation in Kerala. B. Ekbal, in his article 'Autonomous Colleges', gives a brief sketch of the evolution of the concept in India and the experience of Kerala with the scheme. He analyses the relevance of college autonomy for the state and gives an account of what to be done for its introduction at the college, university and state government levels. In the article 'The Autonomous College' , Ninan Abraham discusses the benefits of shifting from affiliation to autonomy and analyses the major issues involved. The article tries to allay the apprehensions and arguments raised against the introduction of autonomy in Kerala. Cyriac Thomas's paper 'Autonomy for Colleges in Kerala' gives a detailed account of the major problems afflicting the higher education sector of Kerala and of the initiatives already taken for the introduction of autonomy in the state. The paper cautions the policy makers that the unique social and political realities of the state have to be considered while implementing autonomy. J.V. Vilanilam in his article 'Why are We Still having the Burden of Affiliation in the 21st Century? Why Not Autonomy?' advances a forceful argument in favour of introducing academic autonomy in Kerala. He stresses the need for utilizing autonomy to meet the challenges faced by the higher education sector in the present century. In the concluding article 'Academic Autonomy for Colleges in Kerala—Proactive Initiatives and Planning Need of the Hour' , the editor of the volume discusses the significance of granting autonomy in Kerala and attempts to provide clarification to the major apprehensions and issues connected with the implementation of autonomy in the state. The paper also provides broad guidelines with regard to the planning and preparation to be undertaken by the colleges which aspire to become autonomous.

The book has also incorporated the UGC Guidelines for Autonomous Colleges during the Eleventh Plan Period (2007-2012) and the Statewise and University-wise List of Autonomous Colleges in India as Appendices.

This volume seeks to promote the concept of college autonomy in India, especially in Kerala and a few other states where autonomy is yet to be implemented. It brings into focus the major advantages of this educational innovation which has the potential to bring about significant qualitative transformation in the higher education sector of the country. Many of the academics who have contributed to this volume have also put forward varying suggestions for improvement in the functioning of the existing autonomous colleges, based on the experience during the past three decades. It is our fervent hope that this attempt will be appreciated by the academic community which would like to see positive changes in the Indian higher education system.

2

The History, Evolution and Relevance of College Autonomy in India

— Xavier Alphonse S. J.

The Origin and Evolution of the Concept of College Autonomy

Autonomy for colleges is not a new idea. The colleges were virtually autonomous universities since 1817 until the birth of the three affiliating universities of Calcutta, Bombay and Madras in 1857. The concept of autonomy was revived by the Principal of Presidency College, Calcutta, at the beginning of this century in the context of postgraduate studies (1921). But the effort failed. In 1953 the idea of autonomous colleges was revived by the Principal of Balwant Rajpur College, Agra. The amendment was passed by the senate of the Agra University in 1954 and it was also passed by the UP legislature. It was unfortunate that not a single college in the university applied for the autonomous status. In 1965 Prof. S.K. Sidhanta Committee proposed the Autonomous scheme as an alternative and as a corrective to the affiliating system.

The first formal and specific recommendation on college autonomy appeared in the Kothari Commission report 1964–66. In 1966 the UGC Committee expressed a keen interest and the earnestness of the UGC is evident in the promotion of the autonomous scheme from this committee report. Dr. P.B. Gajendragadkar Committee (1969) suggested that the concept of autonomy be extended to the departments or units of the university and changes in the statutes of the universities to accommodate autonomous colleges. In 1973, the UGC sent a circular to all universities recommending that they should set up autonomous colleges. This circular entitled 'Autonomous Colleges: Criteria, Guidelines and Pattern of Assistance' highlighted the objectives of autonomy, the distortions and consequences of affiliation system, the relationship of autonomous colleges with the parent universities, the procedure to be followed for the conferment of the autonomous status and the pattern of assistance given by the UGC to autonomous colleges. The circular attributed the failure of all attempts at the reform of university education to the existing rigidity in the structure of university education and the lack of academic autonomy.

The All India Association for Christian Higher Education organized a consultation at New Delhi during March 1974. The consultation was attended by a group of principals and professors from 27 Colleges. A number of senior educationists, members of the UGC and the Chairman of the UGC were present at the consultation. The consultation examined in depth various aspects of autonomy and considered in detail the problems and opportunities that autonomy might produce.

In 1975, the University of Madras urged several colleges to prepare and submit proposals for autonomy. More than 12 colleges responded from which eight were selected and recommended to be given autonomous status. Subsequently, three more colleges in Madurai Kamaraj University submitted proposals for autonomy. The UGC sent an inspection team to visit all the 12 colleges, inspect the facilities and discuss the proposals with the faculty and others concerned. In August 1977, the Tamil Nadu state legislature amended the University Act providing for autonomous colleges. All the 12 colleges, eight in Madras University and four in Madurai Kamaraj University started functioning as autonomous colleges from June 1978. Thus the Government of Tamil Nadu was a pioneer in accepting and implementing the concept of college autonomy. Tamil Nadu can boast of having the lion's share of autonomous colleges in the country even today.

In 1978, the UGC again emphasized the need for the development of autonomous colleges. In a policy framework published by it, the UGC observed, "It is equally essential to move away form the existing system of the affiliating university or centralization of academic authority and external examinations.

The system as it works creates very dilatory procedures. The rigidity of the affiliating system also deprives the good teachers of the opportunity to take initiative for creative, imaginative and more fruitful action. It is therefore absolutely essential to decentralize authority and confer autonomy, from the university administration to the university departments and from the universities to colleges. The existing bureaucratic and centralized structures of the universities have to be radically altered to avoid delays, to evade attempts at rigid uniformities, to create an elastic and dynamic system and to promote innovations and reforms."

In May 1979, at the end of the first year of autonomy, a consultation on the functioning of college autonomy was held at Madras. The consultation brought to light some of the lacunae and difficulties in the functioning of autonomous colleges which were promptly set right. In 1981, a UGC team conducted a mid-term evaluation of all the 12 autonomous colleges and was satisfied with the progress. It recommended continuation of autonomous status for the first full term of five years. Some colleges had done their own evaluation of their functioning. At the end of the first five-year term, in 1983, all the autonomous colleges were subjected to detailed review and evaluation.

The National Policy of Education (1986) expressed the need for providing autonomy to colleges to undertake innovations, designing curricula, evolve methods of teaching and learning, frame own rules of admissions, prescribe its own course of study and conduct of examination. The Programme of Action (POA) of the NPE (1986) specified the details of the development of autonomous colleges. It went even a step further to confer Deemed University status on autonomous colleges. Though it was targeted to make 500 colleges as autonomous by the end of the Seventh Plan period, there were only 127 colleges spread over seven states by that time.

In 1991, Prof. Iqbal Narain Committee did an excellent job in reviewing the implementation of autonomous colleges. It published in its report 'The Academic and Management aspects of the working of Autonomous Colleges', the position and perception of the state governments of Andhra Pradesh, Bihar, Delhi, Gujarat, Himachal Pradesh, Karnataka, Maharashtra, Manipur, Orissa, Punjab, Rajasthan, Tamil Nadu and Uttar Pradesh. It also published the views of the universities, the

Principals of autonomous colleges and the organisations of teachers.

In 1993, UGC issued the *Revised Guidelines*. This document had the usual features of the previous documents published by UGC in 1973 and 1987 such as the need for autonomy, objectives of autonomy, relationship with the parent university and other educational institutions, award of degrees, criteria for identification and conferment of autonomous status. In the part on governance, there was a clear and lucid exposition of the composition and function of the Finance Committee. The pattern of financial assistance with its specificities were also mentioned. *The Revised Guidelines of the UGC* (1998) published in 1998 made several additions to the documents published by UGC on the Scheme of Autonomous Colleges in 1973, 1987, 1993 and 1995. It was a comprehensive document covering all the aspects of college autonomy.

College Autonomy – A Corrective to the Affiliating System

"Autonomous colleges represent a very radical departure from the existing structure of the university system—a system which is a product of distortions and consequences of an outmoded affiliation system zealously guarded, preserved and nurtured by the Indian universities" (Sankar Narayanan,1984). The concept of autonomous colleges is of special significance in this context. Autonomy for a college implies that the college and its teachers assume full responsibility and accountability for the academic programmes they provide, for the content and quality of their teaching and for the admission and assessment of their students. Unless this basic condition is first met, it will not be possible to tackle the problem of relevance satisfactorily or to diversify and relate curricula to local needs and conditions and what is even more important, to give greater individual attention to the students on the basis of their needs and aptitudes.

The Ills of the Affiliating System

a) Promotion of uniform mediocrity.

b) Lack of diversification of courses and customisation of syllabus to meet the demands of a changing society.

c) Affiliating university changed into a mere examination conducting body.

d) Conversion of colleges into tutorial institutions and academics into tutors.

e) Rigid and archaic atmosphere.

f) Teaching-learning process becoming mere examination qualifying process.

g) The antiquated university Act.

h) Infiltration of party and partisan politics into the university policy making bodies.

i) The university and the colleges by virtue of their insularity and legislative autonomy being outside the scope of public accountability.

The Objectives of College Autonomy

An autonomous college will have the freedom to:

a) Determine and prescribe its own courses of study and syllabi.

b) Prescribe rules for admission in consonance with the reservation policy of the state government.

c) Evolve methods of assessment of student work, the conduct of examinations and notification of results.

d) Use modern tools of educational technology to achieve higher standards and greater creativity.

Objectives of an Autonomous College

a) A primary objective of an autonomous college should be the pursuit of knowledge which serves the development of its neighbouring community and the country.

b) A second primary objective of an autonomous college is to ensure the employability of its students.

c) A secondary objective of the autonomous college should be the individualization of its teaching and learning programme.

d) Another secondary objective of the autonomous college is the promotion and development of research capability and involvement of its staff and students.

e) A tertiary objective of an autonomous college is to develop in its members a sense of integrity.

f) A second tertiary objective for the autonomous college is humanism. (Malcom S. Adiseshiah, 1974).

Achievements of College Autonomy

a) The ongoing restructuring of courses and innovating new courses to suit the local needs.

b) In the whole area of admission, many efforts have been made to change the concept of higher education from being elitist to democratic, including the disadvantaged without compromising quality and standards. Preferential option for the poor.

c) It is an encouraging fact there is a lot of relevant research done by the staff members of autonomous colleges. The increase in the number of Ph. Ds in the different disciplines in autonomous colleges is a proof of the above fact.

d) Evaluation, internal assessment has gone through ups and downs, trial and error, a lot of experimentation done. There have been efforts to improve the efficiency and objectivity. By and large the autonomous colleges have established the credibility for assessment and a lot of evidence can be found in the evaluation of 27 colleges by Dr. Mani Jacob (AIACHE) and the various studies of NIEPA during the last 15 years by Dr. K. Sudha Rao and her team.

e) Extension service aimed at the holistic formation, value education, responding to the social environment through outreach programmes, working in villages, making oneself relevant to the society in which one lives, human rights education. There has been an active promotion of all these schemes to develop the fourth dimension of education in autonomous colleges.

f) Administration has been de-centralised by the constitution of various committees and the participation of teachers directly in the administration of the college has been encouraged as per the UGC Guidelines.

g) The merits of autonomous colleges are innovation in teaching and learning, customisation and restructuring of the course content and accountability in the delivery of higher education.

h) "College autonomy is a challenge to the teacher. Autonomy means self-governance and in the realm of higher education it connotes a teacher oriented system. Functionally the autonomy of a college ultimately percolates to the teacher" (Raman,1998).

i) In the methodology of NAAC, the assessment of higher education institutions is done in the following aspects: (i) Curriculum Aspects, (ii) Teaching, Learning and Evaluation, (iii) Research, Consultancy and Extension, (iv) Infrastructure and Learning Resources, (v) Student Support and Progression, (vi) Organisation and Management (vii) Healthy Practices.

   "Our analysis of the assessment reports indicated that the autonomous colleges that have been rated high have proved their ability to innovate in all the seven criteria and more so in the first three".

j) "The general criticism that autonomy may lead to dilution in the standard of quality has been found to be baseless in the light of the innovations we could observe in these institutions. Most notable are the differences that could be seen in the curricular aspects, internal as well as external components of the evaluation of student progress, improved teaching methods, quality culture and participative management style" (Antony Stella, 2000).

k) Some express apprehension that autonomy may adversely affect standards. Tamil Nadu has nearly 86 autonomous colleges, the highest number for a state. The state also has 70 accredited colleges; the highest in the country and many of them are autonomous colleges. It can be seen therefore that autonomy has done no harm; it is really welcomed by the public, by the faculty and the students" (Kulandaiswamy, 2003).

Best Practices in Autonomous Colleges

a) Examination Reforms

b) Quality Assurance – IQAC

c) Project Work
d) Students' Feedback Mechanism
e) Choice Based Credit System
f) Extension Work
g) Curriculum Reforms
h) Teaching Methodologies and Innovations
i) Admission Reforms
j) Innovation in Curricular and Extra Curricular Activities

Recommendations to Autonomous Colleges

a) Choice Based Credit System to be followed in letter and spirit.
b) It is highly recommended that there is an active and ongoing networking of autonomous colleges where resources are shared and these colleges could have credit transfer facility.
c) In order to make the credit transfer networking a reality there should be a flexi-time in the colleges so that students can move from one autonomous college to another for various courses.
d) Autonomous colleges must promote multi entry system. The students can enter and leave the system in the first year or in the second year with a diploma at the end of first year and with an associate degree at the end of the second year and with a full degree at the end of the third year. There should also be a provision for lateral entry and vertical mobility.
e) Autonomous colleges have to introduce skill based and job oriented courses within or outside the curriculum which should be made mandatory to a student before he/she leaves the college in terms of employability.
f) There should be greater emphasis on value based education with life coping skills which certainly would create responsible citizens who are other centred, who will become catalysts of social transformation and harbingers of communal and religious harmony.
g) The autonomous colleges could move towards degree awarding status colleges.

3

College Autonomy—
A Historic Educational Innovation

— **Mani Jacob**

College autonomy which could be considered as a package of innovations in higher education capable of transforming the college system, encompassing its aims and objectives, courses, curricula, teaching strategies and evaluation pattern, took 12 years, after it was originally proposed by the Education Commission (1964-66), to germinate and sprout up in 12 colleges of Tamil Nadu in 1978. This experiment in academic freedom and institutional accountability, though much misunderstood and maligned, struck roots and continued to grow in inclement conditions.

Development of the Concept of College Autonomy

The Education Commission (1964-66), with a view to raising the standards and social relevance of college education, made the following proposal: "We should like to refer to the question of 'autonomous' colleges which has been under discussion for many years. Where there is an outstanding college (or a small cluster of very good colleges) within a large university which has shown the capacity to improve itself markedly, consideration should he given to granting it an autonomous status. This would involve the power to frame its own rules of admissions, to prescribe its course of study, to conduct examinations and so on. The parent university's role will be one of general supervision and the actual conferment of the degree. The privilege cannot be conferred once and for all—it will have to be continually earned and deserved—

and it should be open to the university, after careful scrutiny of the position, to revoke the autonomous status if the college at any stage begins to deteriorate in its standards. We recommend that provision for the recognition of such autonomous colleges be made in the constitution of the universities. It should be possible in our opinion, by the end of the Fourth Five Year Plan, to bring at least fifty of the best colleges under this category".

The University Grunts Commission, in October 1966 constituted a Committee (1966-67) to study the feasibility and practical steps for implementing the proposal for autonomous colleges. The Committee suggested certain practical steps to be taken to implement the proposal:

a) The autonomous college is an important concept which can be implemented for raising standards and encouraging the pursuit of excellence in carefully selected institutions. A modest beginning may be made to implement the principle, in some universities. To begin with, the experiment would be tried in one or two colleges in each university willing to undertake this. In the first instance, the possibility of establishing autonomous colleges within the framework of the existing University Acts should be explored.

b) The criteria for the selection of colleges as autonomous institutions have to be carefully worked out. The basic prerequisites are good students, good staff, good facilities and good management. The constitution of the colleges concerned should be carefully considered. The Board of Governors and other academic bodies in an autonomous college should be properly constituted with suitable external representation. In case government colleges are to be admitted to the privileges of autonomy, they should have proper Boards of Management bodies fulfilling other essential criteria.

c) The proposal for the conferment of autonomy on any institution should originate with the university and college concerned. The UGC may be associated with the process of selection, but the primary responsibility has to be undertaken by the university. The University Grants

Commission may constitute a standing committee to examine the proposals for the conferment of autonomy and if necessary, send the visiting teams to the institutions concerned in consultation with the parent universities. The universities concerned may periodically review the functioning of autonomous institutions. That could be done in consultation with the UGC.

d) Autonomous colleges may be permitted to modify the syllabus in the light of the facilities and staff available and prescribe their own admission policy and devise their own assessment procedures.

e) The approach has to be flexible and there may be a graduated scale of autonomy for institutions depending on their performance and achievement in various fields. If an institution has been doing outstanding work in all of the vast bulk of courses run by it, the entire institution being treated as one unit could be given an autonomous status. This, it was felt, would have administrative and academic advantages. However, even partial autonomy in which the institutions concerned have been doing very good work could be bestowed upon two or more outstanding colleges in close proximity which agree to coordinate their efforts and pool their resources and talents.

f) The degree in an autonomous college should be awarded by the parent university, but the name of the college should be specifically mentioned. Autonomous colleges should not be separated entirely from their parent universities at present.

g) Development grants on a liberal basis should be provided for the development of autonomous colleges.

Subsequently the Committee on the Governance of Universities and Colleges (1969-71) lamented the fact that no headway had been made in initiating the experiment as no provision for autonomy had been made in the legislative enactments governing most of the universities. The committee recommended that in future, in such Acts, provision should be made not only for autonomous colleges but also for autonomy to teaching departments, or the units of departments, in particular the Centres of Advanced Study.

The University Grants Commission advised the universities, in October 1973, to confer autonomy on selected colleges and announced the 'criteria, guidelines, and pattern of assistance' relating to autonomous colleges. Later, the Commission in the publication *Development of Higher Education in India: A Policy Frame* (1978), repeated its call for moving away from the rigidity and centralised academic authority, and external examinations obtaining under the affiliating system; and creating a flexible and 'dynamic system' promotive of innovative attempts and reforms. The Commission pointed out the significance of autonomous colleges:

'Autonomy for a college implies that the college and its teachers assume full responsibility for accountability for the academic programmes they provide, for the content and quality of their teachings and for the admission and assessment of their students. Unless this basic condition is first met, it will not be possible to tackle the problem of relevance satisfactorily or to diversify and relate curricula to local needs and conditions, and what is even more important to give greater individual attention to the students on the basis of their needs and aptitudes. This alone will make it possible for institutions of higher education to become communities of teachers and students engaged in an agreed and mutually satisfactory joint pursuit of truth and excellence. However, it would be necessary to ensure that the terms and conditions of service for teachers prescribed by the Government and the University Grants Commission continue to apply to these institutions, and that the institutions continue to subserve the needs of national integration and development. The concept of autonomous colleges does not imply permanent categorisation of an institution under a separate label for a higher formal status. It requires an institution to be continuously subjected, in order to justify its recognition as an autonomous college, to periodic reviews and should be liable to lose its recognition if the conditions of higher academic excellence as well as its contribution to society are not maintained at the expected level. In short, such a privilege will have to be continuously earned and sustained through performance. Over the years, we should move in a direction where autonomy becomes, not a reward for excellence, but the minimum conditions also be emphasized and in the larger interest of society itself, each institution has to seek its identity in its own unique fashion, consistent with its local situation and the academic perspective of the local community.

"As a step towards the development of this programme it is necessary to survey carefully all the colleges in a district and to identify one or two colleges which can become academically viable through guidance, planning and financial assistance. These colleges should be assisted to realise their potential and given autonomy to develop new courses in relation to the needs of the local region and its development. The programme can, over the years, be a desire and potential to develop on these lines".

Model of Change

It will be useful to look at autonomy, not merely as an ad hoc experiment, but as a well- planned innovation for change in higher education. In terms of the process of change involved, college autonomy has exhibited certain special characteristics:

a) It was a comprehensive innovation, embracing various facets of college life such as management and administration, courses, curricula, teaching methods, evaluation, relations with the university; and affecting the entire college population, students, faculty and administrators.

b) It was internally planned and executed; however the college system had a definite interface with the resource systems such as the university and the University Grants Commission. Without the active involvement of the resource system, the innovation would not have become possible.

c) The University Grants Commission was mainly responsible for the development or the innovation. The research dimension was present in the recommendations on college autonomy made by the Education Commission (1964-66) and the various subsequent committees. The design, engineering and packing of the innovation was also performed by the University Grants Commission. The diffusion of the innovation involving its promotion, information campaign, offer of support for initiation, also was accomplished by the commission to a great extent; and partly by the parent university which got a provision for autonomy inserted in the University Act and fabricated the necessary rules and regulations for the functioning of autonomous colleges within the framework of the affiliating system.

d) Even though the 'research, development and diffusion' functions were performed by the University Grants Commission and the parent university, the innovation was not imposed on colleges by administrative authority. It was offered to those colleges which fulfilled certain criteria of selection in terms of resources, personnel and performance; and it was optional for colleges to apply.

e) The 'research, development and diffusion' processes were rational processes with sequential activities moving from one stage to another. There was planning on the national, state and university levels. There was division of labour and careful selection of roles and functions with the university delegating all academic functions to the college and retaining only the right to award the degree and the right to withdraw autonomy if the terms and conditions of its conferment were breached. The clearly defined audience to which the innovation was communicated was the colleges in the university. Its validity and viability were examined by various expert committees and its impact assessed. Its institutional feasibility was assessed by getting detailed proposals formulated by the intending colleges. Widespread awareness was created by communication of the innovation through circulars and conferences.

f) At the level of the adopter college, the desirability, feasibility and operational details of the innovation were examined by the faculty in successive meetings. Attempts were made to build up conviction among the staff about its quality, value, fitness and utility in the institutional context. It was installed and integrated into the college system as an ongoing programme by dovetailing its characteristics with those of the college.

Strategies for Change

Multiple strategies of change were employed at the two levels of the innovation process. At the 'research, development and diffusion' level, the UGC which was the prime mover of the process of change used the empirical-rational approach to diffuse the innovation. Through the committees it had constituted the Commission which refined and sharpened the concept of autonomy and expounded rationally its justification and utility to the higher education system, through policy statements and announcement of its intention to implement the innovation. Since initially the user systems (universities) were not willing or ready to accept the package, public information campaigns were launched through workshops and conferences. The state government which brought the necessary legislative modification in the University Act facilitated the innovation's coming into being and legitimised it. The university through the required legal and procedural modalities rendered the innovation's adoption by colleges a practical possibility, Therefore the state government and the university used mostly the power-oriented strategies minus the element of coercion because no college was forced to accept autonomy; on the other hand the selection of colleges was based on very strict criteria and the autonomous status was considered by the college to be a privileged status. On the part of the university it was an administered change, sans the component of compulsion.

At the college level the value, rational, didactic, psychological and authority strategies were used at the various stages of the adoption and installation process.

A Critical Appraisal of the Innovation

After the process of development involving its clarification, expansion, engineering and package, the concept of college autonomy was diffused to the universities and colleges by the University Grants Commission for adoption and installation. The state government of Tamil Nadu pioneered in applying its political will and administrative impetus to the proposal by making the necessary legislative provisions in the University Acts and gave the green signal to the universities of the state to proceed with its implementation. Meanwhile the adopter colleges planned and prepared for the administrative, curricular, methodological and evaluational changes attendant on autonomy. The change agents from various areas participated in the colleges' efforts by training the teachers, solving in process problems and linking it with outside resource systems. In 1978, the universities took the decision to confer autonomy on the selected colleges and these colleges adopted the innovation by a collective decision of the staff and the governing council.

The objective of the innovation was to enable the colleges to exercise freedom in framing courses of study and syllabi; devising appropriate teaching methods; conducting evaluation and assessment independently; and developing principles of admission of students. Action was taken to frame new courses with excellence, social relevance, socio-ethical values and employability of students as guiding principles. Evaluation and assessment mechanisms based in the colleges were established with the course teachers in charge of them and with safeguards against subjectivity and unfair practices. The administrative structures provided for the participation of teachers and students in decision-making,

Many of the functions which were hitherto performed by university were transferred to the colleges. Needs of social justice and service to the local community were guiding concerns in organising remedial programmes for students from deprived sections of society, preferential admission of the poor, and community service programmes. With regard to the admission no alterations were effected and the norms prescribed by the university for admissions continued as before.

The programme was evaluated internally, and from outside by the university periodically and the feedback was used for corrective action. The consequences of the innovation were largely functional and positive.

Some critical observations on the innovation are called for. Judging from the performance of the student body no major change seemed to have taken place in the traditional worry and stressful concern over examination results. In fact the number of tests and examinations had increased and they were held according to schedule with little time left for creative pursuits. The teachers were burdened with excessive work due to the new responsibilities thrust on them. How the teachers could handle such accumulation of responsibility for planning, teaching, controlling and administering, was a serious problem to be solved. The intended new emphasis on work experience and orientation to application and employability were still very tenuous and the major concern was still academic. Doing more of what was being done still seemed to be in progress. There was also a trend of educational programmes getting eclipsed by the bureaucratic controls and administrative activities.

On the whole, the concept and practice of autonomy seemed to have been accepted by the college community and the parents. Another sign of its acceptance by the universities and the society as a whole was the fact that it was being extended to other colleges and that by 2009 the number of autonomous colleges in Tamil Nadu was 116.

Autonomy was an experiment in combining freedom with responsibility. As the principal of a college observed: "the right use of freedom is not an easy thing indeed; the ultimate purpose of the autonomous college is the creation of autonomous individuals."

Conclusion

It would not be an exaggeration to describe college autonomy as the most significant innovation introduced in Indian higher education since the publication of the *Education Commission Report* (1964-66). This would be amply proved by the testimony on accomplished changes and actualised impact of autonomy given by the principals of autonomous colleges. In a very exceptional way over 300 autonomous colleges, their managements, principals, teaching and non-teaching staff and students have worked relentlessly as a team during the span of the last 30 years since 1978 to bring about a major systematic change in college education. It has produced considerable qualitative improvements in administration, academic work, teaching–learning process, examination procedures and the employability of the students. In spite of certain weaknesses and shortcomings in some institutions or in some areas of activity, on the whole the impact of college autonomy has been salutary for the teachers and the learners. The centre of gravity of college education has shifted to the college campus, thanks to college autonomy. It is for the academic community to make or mar this creative change in coming years.

4

Advantages of Autonomous Colleges

— S. Ignacimuthu, S.J.

Introduction

Higher education is the foundation of a society's intellectual standards and the reservoir of future developments. We need a very good higher education system to build a modern knowledge society.

The higher education sector in India is considered to be the third largest in the world, which caters to approximately 106 lakh students and 4.6 lakh teachers in institutions of higher education through over 450 universities and more than 20,000 colleges. It is observed that after independence, a massive growth has taken place in higher education resulting in big increase in the number of universities and substantial increase in the number of colleges, while students' enrolment has gone up in a very big way. Every year, a number of new institutions and colleges start functioning. This obviously causes a considerable concern for the nation, particularly to the planners and administrators.

With the increase in the number of institutions, there is also an increase in expectations of the public in terms of quantity, quality, organization and purpose. The existence of a large number of affiliated colleges in a university has become a drag on the process of standards (UGC, 1987). The more we probe, the deeper aspects or its complexities come to the surface. The country's population, its socio-economic scenario, its obligations towards its people and in turn their expectations, political structure, manpower, employment status and the educational preparations, resource conditions, are only a few factors that have direct or indirect influence in shaping the structure and functions of the present Indian higher education institutions.

A college is a place not merely for courses of varied teachings but one for imparting education. College education to be true to itself should have a purpose and it should make the mind productive. It is really a growth of the consciousness of the mind. Education does not begin and end with learning the contents of a few books, but is directed to the mind and its development. It leads to the building up of character and finally to social adjustability. The student who undergoes true education is not only well-read but also well-bred.

The Education Commission (1964-66) has observed, "Where there is an outstanding college or a small cluster of very good colleges within a large university which has shown the capacity to improve itself markedly, consideration should be given to granting it an autonomous status".

The UGC Eleventh Plan Guidelines on 'Scheme of Autonomous Colleges' says: "The affiliating system has now become unwieldy and it is becoming increasingly difficult for a university to attend to varied needs of individual colleges. They do not have the freedom to modernize their curricula or make them locally relevant. The regulations of the University and its common system, governing all colleges alike, irrespective of their characteristic strengths, weaknesses and locations, have affected the academic development of individual colleges. Education Commission (1964-66) pointed out that the exercise of academic freedom by teachers is a crucial requirement for development of the intellectual climate of the country. Unless such a climate prevails, it is difficult to achieve excellence in our higher education system. With students, teachers and management being co-partners in raising the quality of higher education, it is imperative that they share a major responsibility. Hence the Education Commission (1964-66) recommended college autonomy, which, in essence, is the instrument for promoting academic excellence".

The above view of the Education Commission and the Scheme of Autonomous Colleges clearly emphasize that deserving colleges should be given autonomy. The emphasis laid on academic freedom of institutions of higher learning by UGC and the Education Commission led to the creation of autonomous colleges in 1978. An autonomous college is free to start a new degree or post graduate course with the approval of the Academic Council of the college.

The Concept of Autonomy

As early as in 1964, the Education Commission had emphasized that deserving colleges should be made autonomous so that their performance would be outstanding and they would develop into centers of excellence in the field of education. These colleges would evolve methods to impart knowledge, skills and values in order to make the minds productive and build up character. The country started experimenting with autonomous colleges from 1978.

Objectives

The objectives of autonomous college are to give opportunity to the teachers and students to make innovations in teaching, improve the standard of teaching, examination and research and respond quickly to societal needs. Accordingly, it is visualized that autonomous colleges will have the freedom to:

i) Determine their own courses of study and syllabi; restructure and redesign the courses.
ii) Prescribe rules for admission accommodating the reservation policy.
iii) Evolve methods of evaluation and conduct of examinations and notify results.
iv) While degree continues to be awarded by parent universities, the name of the college will remain in the certificate.
v) Use modern tools of educational technology.
vi) Promote healthy practices such as community services, neighbourhood programmes.

Advantages of Autonomy in Colleges

Innovation

Autonomous colleges have been very successful in introducing innovation in higher education by introducing new courses relevant to the needs of students and society. Some of the colleges have restructured the courses in such a way as to include skill oriented and job oriented training as envisaged by the vocational subjects of UGC.

Initiation

Review and redesigning of programmes are found to be systematically done through the boards of studies and academic council, which are established in the colleges themselves for the proper management of academic affairs.

Academic Councils

These bodies are actively represented by the faculty of the college at all levels along with experts from the industry, representatives of the university and the government. These bodies have adequately been empowered under the UGC guidelines so that their decisions will not be subject to any further ratification by the executive council or universities.

Choice Based Credit System

Autonomous colleges have successfully designed the model of choice based credit system which provides a wide choice of courses to suit the aptitude, interest and career plans of every student. The success of this concept has encouraged other colleges to opt for autonomy along with the credit system. However, due to tight-jacketed work load norms, choice based credit system has not been practiced to its full extent.

Value-based Education

Autonomous colleges have been able to introduce compulsory course on value education thereby moulding both character and personality development of the student at the most "vulnerable stage" in their development. This is an essential component of the learning processes for the harmonious development of the human personality. Autonomous colleges have the unique liberty to inculcate the vision and mission of integrating this with the introduction of relevant, ethical and socially harmonious value education to their students thereby imparting a holistic approach for teaching. This is done under foundation courses which are also part and parcel of the degree programme.

Challenges in Life

Autonomous colleges have an equally impressive record of enriching the syllabus to prepare the students for various competitive examinations in addition to preparing them to meet the challenges of life.

Computer Skill

Functional computer skills may be introduced to the discipline of study providing enhanced placement and self-employment opportunities, meaningful interaction between institution and industry and thereby widening the contacts for job opportunities are other positive features found in well established autonomous colleges.

Overall Development

Autonomous colleges have proved that there is no limit to the creativity of pedagogical techniques and the teaching-learning process is substantially enriched by creating a challenging, participative and highly interactive learning environment. The use of hi-tech teaching aids, interactive methods, imparting of self study techniques, etc. have been successfully adopted with great advantage to the students in autonomous colleges. Further, opportunities which enhance employability like on-the-job experience, project work, study circles have helped equip the student to assimilate skills equivalent to the earned degree and converted the process of learning and acquiring knowledge into a very satisfying experience.

Evaluation

Autonomous colleges have successfully implemented various evaluation techniques in the examination system which properly evaluates the student's intellectual ability and creative skill. The continuous assessment, which is an integral part of the autonomous system, has heightened the seriousness for study on the part of the students and enhances opportunities for continuous learning. Apart from this, the teachers themselves can set question papers and evaluate the students even in the final examinations. Unfortunately, not many colleges are ready to take this step due to some lingering doubts about our own ability to trust ourselves, our ability, our honesty, our sincerity and our integrity. The best method is the one in which the teacher prepares the syllabus, sets questions, conducts exams and awards the mark or grade.

There are several ways by which the potential of academic autonomy may be utilized by higher education institutions for improving the overall quality of the education imparted.

Urge for Excellence

Higher education has to enhance human capability through empowerment that knowledge gives. The managements have to assure that the academic inputs are correlated to meet this instinctive competitive urge for excellence in the world.

Upgradation of Skills through Vocationalisation

Upgradation of skills of the students is the need of the hour. This is critical for development and goes to meet the requirements of emerging occupational patterns. Vocational courses offered by the UGC are a laudable initiative to be grabbed by the enterprising Principals to prepare graduates with market sensitive competencies enabling them to take up careers and fill immediate job positions in local and regional markets.

Increased Selectivity

This gives the students a chance to opt for combinations of their own choice, keeping in view their interests, career orientation and aptitudes. The present challenges lies in optimizing the use of the available time to the best possible advantage of the students with enough time to spare for library and home study.

Professional Empowerment of Teachers

Teachers are the backbone of the collegiate system. Functional autonomy is the key to their professional empowerment. Allowing them opportunities of exposure through participation in academic workshops, seminars, conferences at the national and international levels, grants for minor research projects and other curricular activities, etc. will bring them closer to their subject and mainstream issues with genuine interest in their teaching. In fact teachers' empowerment is the right road to institutional pride and power. Academic Staff Colleges supported by the UGC are precisely a step in this direction and participation in them should be made more open-ended rather than the present day compulsions for entitlement to higher scales.

Appraisal Requirements

There has to be a transparent system of appraisal which enables the teachers to know themselves in most unerring terms with a chance to improve, if so required. The peers and the students should be allowed to give opinion on the performance of each teacher. The teacher's autonomy and his integrity should be respected, since the future of the students and the institution, depend on the effectivity of the teacher; each teacher should be ready for self-evaluation, student evaluation and peer evaluation. This will help the teacher to know the strengths and overcome weaknesses.

Students Support System

There has to be some guidance procedures for participation in social action and extension programmes and classes for the marginalized and weak students to bring them to the mainstream academics. This means that there has to be a procedure for the removal of difficulties and social disparities. For this, teachers have to be involved and made responsible.

Social Expectations and Obligations

Society has certain expectations from each institution of higher education. Needless to add that it is not restricted to the success of its students who are the future citizens and leaders of the country. Each institution is a school for their training and righteous conduct. For this, the management and the principal have to set standards and the students have to emulate them.

Conclusion

I have personally worked in three autonomous colleges from the inception of autonomy in 1978 and have found how wonderful it is to have such academic freedom. What I have enumerated above is a reflection of my own positive experiences. Autonomy gave ample opportunity to introduce new courses and concepts and it is my firm conviction that if standards of education have to improve, the only solution is autonomy. I have even suggested to the UGC to allow the individual college to issue the degrees. It is my firm belief that if educational standards have to improve in our country, we should encourage autonomous colleges in a big way with proper checks and balances. As a next step these autonomous colleges should be made into universities.

5

Academic Autonomy for Change Towards Quality

— Francis Soundararaj

Change for Transition

"Change" - the Watchword for Qualitative Progression

The word "change", used as a verb, has become an alarm bell to those who have hitherto sworn by obsolete systems that blocked the development of a better humanity. Far from expressing a desire for change, it has become an urgent call to mend ways towards qualitative progression, especially from the moment when Barak Obama used it to confirm such a progression before the American public. It seals the historic achievement of that people to bury the hatchet in order to affirm a better humanity among them. History records similar reversals incidental to change in ideas, movements, forms of government and beliefs. But for change, humanity would have missed the progression towards a juster and more equitable society through revolutions, reforms and peaceful transitions. Qualitative change is what we need today in order to work towards establishing dynamic systems that break free from the heresies of the past. This applies to all our concerns, including those about higher education in our country.

Change Needs Working for It

Positive change is often difficult to achieve. Conformity, compromise, complacency and prejudice perpetrate existing, but unhelpful, institutions and practices. It is a common human tendency to justify discriminatory bad practices in the name of ever so many labels such as "tradition", "the beaten track" and even "values"! While one cannot deny their salience in warning humanity against error or judgement, they cannot be idolized, if one has to make way for best practices and qualitative progression. What matters is "the presentness of the past" (as T.S. Eliot terms it) and not an uncritical acceptance of tradition as a "bolus" (the sum total). It is nevertheless equally important not to favour extreme liberalism which shows a disregard for anything old. As said earlier, it requires enormous effort to maintain this equilibrium. One needs to work strenuously for positive change. Whether it is building a new nation or ushering in a new beneficial system, one is required to work for it, and work for it sacrificially, not minding discomfiture or criticism.

Refusal to Change is Suicidal

The SOS received from deteriorating systems and institutions to ring the alarm bell, "change", in order to rescue them cannot be taken lightly. Men, institutions, cultures, languages and traditions which have done so in the past are lost for ever. Flexibility to accommodate positive change alone can pave the way for survival, and through it, for qualitative progression. It is easier to save an obsolescent or decaying system or practice with change than to revive an obsolete one. Before we begin to grieve over loss, let us seek ways of revival in order to avoid it. And this is true of every situation today. Peaceful transitions save bitterness and conflict that revolutions cannot avoid.

Need for Qualitative Progression in Indian Higher Education

A Brief Retrospect since 1947

The makers of our nation after Independence were part of the Western-educated Middle Class elite and they took important decisions that prevail to this day. They determined that governance should be through the system of parliamentary democracy based on the constitution that protects civic rights and privileges; that the country should be a socialistic welfare state; and that its economy should be liberal[1]. As a natural corollary, therefore, the system of higher education in the country adopted, through 'Macaulay's Minute', the Western (English) model. The curriculum replicated the London model and the affiliating system of higher education institutions got itself established. Nevertheless, it responded to national needs expressed through the early Five Year Plans, more by compulsion than by deliberate planning. Science, technology, commerce and management found their way into an otherwise linguistic and humanities curriculum. The curricular structure and transactions still remained essentially the same, summative terminal examinations being the only method of assessing students' work.

Such a system was challenged to cope with the quantitative expansion of Indian higher education in the sixties. The sudden growth in the number of colleges and universities (to about 6,000 colleges and 400 universities) made the affiliating system too unwieldy to address concerns of quality. The undergraduate was left to drift with an obsolete system of higher education with little hope of rising to levels of excellence in either leadership or performance.

Most recommendations of various education commissions appointed to review higher education after Independence were outcomes of micro-management. Changes made were by and large structural, not qualitative. The pre-university course was attached to the high school which adopted the 10 + 2 model of secondary and post-secondary education. Similarly M.Phil. was introduced in the limbo of academic study and research replacing the older more demanding M.Litt. Bureaucratic control was reinforced with newer institutions such as the UGC, AICTE, NBA, IMC and others. New types of institutions emerged with the entry of private agencies to manage education. Public, aided, unaided (or self-funded), partially aided and other types prevailed under the control of affiliating universities that were merely examining bodies for a large number of colleges. In all these and more, qualitative change was not contemplated. With the establishment of the University Grants Commission, however, the promise of such change became evident. The introduction of autonomous colleges in 1978 and the creation of more academic space for them to try out qualitative reforms with the launching of the National Policy of Education (1986-1992) initiated qualitative change. It articulated, for the first time in the history of education in this country, the principles of qualitative change to be achieved through limited academic autonomy conferred on select colleges with a reasonably good academic record. The concern for raising the quality of undergraduate and postgraduate education in Arts and Science colleges became the responsibility of the UGC-sponsored National Assessment and Accreditation Council since 1990. Such a retrospect, skeletal no doubt, makes it clear that the need for change is both recognized and acted upon as the following note quoted from the UGC Eleventh Plan Guidelines, "Scheme of Autonomous Colleges", confirms:[2]

"The (affiliating) system has now become unwieldy and it is becoming increasingly difficult for a university to attend to varied needs of individual colleges. They do not have the freedom to modernize their curricula or make them locally relevant. The regulations of the university and its common system, governing all colleges alike, irrespective of their characteristic strengths, weaknesses and locations, have affected the academic development of individual colleges. The 1964-66 Education Commission pointed out that the exercise of academic freedom by teachers is a crucial requirement for development of the intellectual climate of the country. Unless such a climate prevails, it is difficult to achieve excellence in our higher education system. With students, teachers and management being co-partners in raising the quality of higher education, it is imperative that they share a major responsibility. Hence, the Education Commission (1964-66) recommended college autonomy, which, in essence, is the instrument for promoting academic excellence."

Qualitative Progression

What Constitutes Quality?

Quality is a highly debatable theme. Definitions of quality in higher education defy a consensus-based specific statement about what constitute it. Most writers on quality have had exposure to industry and their definitions are couched in industrial language. Some equate quality with processes of production which include management of the human resource: they recommend a person-oriented approach in which the worker owns the processes in order to be able to give of his or her best to their efficient management. Others attach greater importance to the product and they recommend quality control with an eye on the market. Still others follow a customer-oriented approach and they recommend stakeholder satisfaction. All these definitions have far-reaching implications for the academic world. Yes, processes of imparting education need involvement of both the teacher and the taught in them, with neither superseding the other. It is also true that quality is linked to product: our graduates should be saleable in the job market. It is equally true that quality education should satisfy stakeholders, who are as many as we try to associate with higher education. This may be an oversimplification of the sophisticated nuances that quality *gurus* have brought to bear upon their definitions of quality. Essentially, however, the discussion of quality depends on concepts and processes of industry.

It seems to me that quality progression in higher education is much more than these. Whereas human resource is managed, if not driven, by industry to achieve assumed short-term or limited ends, it is self-created and self-driven in academics for long-term, even permanent, benefits to humanity. Whereas process, product and customer in industry are caught in business relations for mutual material benefit, the student, the teacher, the parent, the employer and the society are involved primarily, in a more altruistic relationship where ethics and values manifested in leadership matter more than material returns, and where disinterested creativity thrives. Moreover, human relationships are made, more than merely 'managed'. Quality higher education makes sound personalities shaped by ideals of integrity, character, transparency, forthrightness and compassion for the helpless, all of which take a back seat in industrial and business management. One need not look for proofs; they are around us everywhere. The primary concern of quality higher education is, therefore, the shaping of leaders with a specific call "to serve, and not to be served" alone. This is the crucial task necessary for community and nation building, for institutional and global welfare and for one's own personal development in the interest of offering effective service.

Unlike in industry, where academic interests are confined to R & D for developing products to be patented for monopoly and profit, the college and the university are wedded to academics and research for their own sake. Academic excellence, in terms of creativity marked by the best-ever with unique creations of the mind—whether it be fresh insights into language and literature, or qualitative research in science and technology aimed at making life on this planet better, or creations of life-energizing strategies in social sciences that stand up against social injustice—is the cornerstone of qualitative progression in higher education. It is greater than mere utility, material benefits notwithstanding.

This does not mean, however, that concepts of quality built upon insights into performance in industry are unhelpful. Far from it, some models of quality improvement offered by quality *gurus* admirably suit qualitative progression in higher education. The TQM (Total Quality Management) and the CMM (Capability Maturity Model), to name just two of the many, offer achievable goals through qualitative progression in institutions of higher learning. They are particularly noteworthy for the rigorous process check with instruments to measure concrete progress. Quality, therefore, serves the creation of leadership for service; it includes rigorous processes, sound output and stakeholder satisfaction as well. Only the former, namely, leadership for service, exists for the latter and not the other way round, and it is of supreme value.

The Urgent Need for Qualitative Transition in Indian Higher Education

UGC's Scheme of Autonomous Colleges

The emphasis laid on academic freedom of institutions of higher learning by public bodies such as the UGC and the Knowledge Commission of India is quite welcome, and timely. The creation of more autonomous colleges, clusters of autonomous colleges and central universities is the beginning of the long expected academic freedom from the affiliating system, thanks to the UGC for enlarging this freedom, as it is evident in the Tenth and Eleventh Plan Guidelines for Autonomous Colleges. Colleges hitherto prevented from offering degree programmes on their own can now offer them: and grants have been correspondingly liberalized.[3]

"An autonomous college is free to start a new degree or postgraduate course with the approval of the Academic Council of the College. Such courses shall fulfil the minimum standards prescribed by the University / UGC in terms of number of hours, curricular content and standards, and the university shall be duly informed of such courses."

This is great news to colleges on which autonomy has already been conferred since 1978, when autonomous colleges were first introduced in the country. Those known for outstanding performance, during the past thirty years, can legitimately pursue academic reform independent of the affiliating university. Many of them have been elevated by the UGC to the status of Centre of Excellence. They can play a creative role in changing the "intellectual climate" of the country as envisaged by the UGC. The charter of academic freedom, articulated in terms of the National Policy of Education is broadly indicated in the guidelines and it includes the freedom to:[4]

a) determine and prescribe (the college's) own courses of study and syllabi, and restructure and redesign the courses already offered in order to suit local needs;
b) prescribe rules for admission of students accommodating the reservation policy of the state government;
c) evolve methods of assessment of student performance, conduct examinations and notify results;
d) use modern tools of educational technology to achieve higher standards and greater creativity; and
e) promote healthy practices such as community service, extension activities, projects for the benefit of society, neighbourhood programmes, etc. [*paraphrase mine*].

This *academic panchasheel,* if one may so call it, has far reaching enabling implications to address academic, social, pedagogic, global and quality concerns of higher education in India, if only institutions could be diligent to perceive and internalize them in their own systems of operation.

Transition from the Obsolete Affiliating System

To offer academic autonomy is one thing but to appropriate it optimally is totally another. As the explicitly stated purpose of academic autonomy is the mandate, "Change", i.e. a qualitative transition from the obsolete or obsolescent affiliating system now in virtual practice, identification of the dead forms and practices of the former system is a pre-requisite for a qualitative transition. A few of the continuing constraints of the affiliating system are identified below:

Infringement of Freedom in the Name of Conformity

Curricular and governance practices, which are dead and gone elsewhere, are insisted upon by many affiliating universities in the country for no sound reason. Some universities in the South, for instance, doggedly hang on to colonial forms and structures of the college curriculum. When one of the colleges sought to radically alter the traditional tripartite model of Part I (language), Part II (English) and Part III (Major) which have lost their colonial logic long time ago (and are uncritically retained for no good academic purpose), the parent university turned down the proposal without a hearing and directed the college to conform to the age-old model for no specific reason. That such a model thrusts upon institutions an incoherent curriculum with neither of the three parts having any relevant connection to each other and that they do not give the undergraduate any help in cultivating skills in an area of specialization with support from the other parts, did not receive even a passing attention. On the contrary, the proposed model of an integrated curriculum with a more useful definition of "Foundation Courses" which reinforce major specializations—courses which impart foundation skills relevant to a more meaningful pursuit of specializations under the Major component of the curriculum—and with other inter-disciplinary and "life-frontier" engagement components was summarily rejected. Many an autonomous college is forced to conform to such obsolete colonial practices.

The freedom of academic governance is again infringed upon by replicating the university model of governance which was designed to administer hundreds of colleges with uniform procedures and practices which disable dynamic decision-making. For instance, syllabi are revised once in three years, local relevance is sacrificed in the name of universally applicable syllabi and examinations alone determine assessment. For this reason, the affiliating university prescribes three terminal examinations as the essential core of the so called "continuous assessment" (a contradiction, absurd and *naïve*) leaving other forms of skill assessment to be paper exercises with no credit attached to it. Assessment of skills is yet to be better organized.

Other colonial practices thrust upon autonomous colleges are:

a) the rigid compartmentalization of departments with no provision for formal inter-disciplinary cooperation;
b) absence of any arrangement, under the affiliating system, to incorporate internship, entrepreneurial training and other such strategies in order to enhance employability of learners, which adversely affects the university's attitude to them, especially, when colleges which take them seriously, are either not encouraged or when they are ignored.
c) the imposition of the university pattern of the Choice Based Credit System on autonomous colleges lands them in the absurd practice of conferring "credit" upon teachers thus preventing learners from "earning" it. The affiliating university calculates credits on the basis of the number of contact class hours totally ignoring student work. The most beneficial "American Credit Hour" which gives equal weight to teacher input and student output is not in practice in the Indian affiliating system. Student work—in seminars, assignments, etc.—is taken for granted but never systematically measured for continuous assessment.
d) Affiliating universities, having been examining bodies for centuries expect examination-driven academic systems to be followed by colleges it affiliates, whether they are autonomous or non-autonomous.

The Lukewarm Attitude to Teacher Accountability under the Affiliating System

Affiliating universities in India have no quality checks to ensure teacher development or teacher accountability. Teacher development is sought to be achieved with arbitrarily organized general orientation and refresher programmes which do not meet specific needs of teachers in their contextual areas of functioning. Neither the teachers nor the Academic Staff Colleges take them seriously. That a certain number of them should be undergone for fulfilling monetary requirements compel teachers to attend them. Neither the content, nor the execution of these programmes contributes to a qualitative exercise that results in substantial teacher development. The only appearance of teacher accountability is the much abused "self-appraisal" left to the whims and fancies of whoever designs the instrument and whoever uses it. The outcome of such a practice is never known to have helped in monitoring teacher accountability. It is unfortunate that these are imposed on autonomous colleges.

More innovative methods of teacher development—external peer appraisal that enhances teachers' professional practice in teaching, research and institutional involvement; consultations organized according to perspective plans of teacher development in response to feedback obtained; student assessment of teacher support, not teacher performance; incentive schemes for young faculty to prepare and present papers of high quality subject to a scholarly screening committee; appraisal of teachers by industry, community and alumi; and others—tried out by some autonomous colleges receive no encouragement because they are expected to conform to practices of the affiliating university. Even an organization like the National Assessment and Accreditation Council insists on only self-appraisal of teacher performance without consequences and ignores other better forms of teacher development and appraisal.

Affiliating universities are often intimidated into soft-pedaling by teachers' associations in an area of deep concern such as this. Only in our country can ineffective teachers thrive on lifetime tenure without any sign of accountability. Neither industry nor the global academia can tolerate the denial of the legitimate right of the stakeholders to quality input. Teachers who are not accountable cannot deliver it.

Absence of Strategies of Learner-Development under the Affiliating System

"Hungry sheep look up but they are not fed", said the British poet Milton in another context but this is unfortunately true of the affiliating system which has failed to equip learners with either the skill to perform or the personality to offer leadership and altruistic service. The ills of the system in this area are only too well known to be recapitulated.

Failure to impart study skills to find and react to sources of knowledge; encouragement of rote learning by exam-driven academics; poor or no academic counselling to the learner for self-management of his or her knowledge acquisition; perpetuation of the culture of teacher-dependency; denial of skills of oral and written communication in English; and failure to monitor continuous skill-progression through a programme are some.

Change Inevitable

Educators, educational experts, educational administrators and providers of education unanimously agree that our educational system has lost its robustness and that it is incapacitated to help the nation to sustain its momentum of growth. It has failed to reach peaks of academic excellence in knowledge creation and knowledge management. It stands low in global ratings. That which is worse is the deterioration of the human material in terms of moral robustness. This decline has cast aspersions on the credibility of persons shaped by education, and the consequent breakdown in leadership. We cannot any more justify the maintenance of our affiliating system although it has failed to produce reliable human and knowledge capital. Hence the mandate, "Change" and "Change at once". The transition from maintenance of dead-wood to radical recreation lies through the path of achieving and sustaining quality, not just in academics but in the creation of individuals who are sound in knowledge, reliable in character and integrity, effective in leadership and performance, and above all, zealous in offering service to the neglected sections of humanity everywhere.

Towards a Qualitative Appropriation of Academic Autonomy

Academic autonomy, as it is articulated within the framework of the UGC Guidelines, is a helpful strategy that facilitates colleges to move out of academic slavery to an obsolete system. The transition to a more dynamic system that is qualitatively more holistic is a great challenge indeed. Some possibilities of such a change may be explored in this section. It explores only the academic dimension implied in the five areas of academic autonomy, leaving the social, pedagogic, technological and quality dimensions to the reader's own comprehension of their implications, because of constraint of space.

The Academic Dimension

Vision

This is identified by the UGC in its first guideline:[5]

"Freedom to determine and prescribe (the college's) own courses of study and syllabi, and restructure and redesign the courses already offered, in order to suit local needs." [*paraphrase mine*].

This involves the vision of an educational agency and also the mission of its units. The vision, by and large, is the purpose for which an agency offers education. It may be anything ranging from the aspiration of the agency (such as serving a social cause, or an egalitarian ideal, or shaping youth for a desired goal) to upliftment of specific target groups such as women or specific professional or regional groups. This of course, does not exhaust the scope of vision. Unless an educational agency precisely states the purpose underlying its curriculum, the nature, type and expected outcome of its component courses can never be visualized. In fact, one may not know what courses should constitute the curriculum without it. Random selection of courses to either serve a popular craze or pursue a merely material purpose, sometimes against the very ideals with which an agency has been founded, is a wrong curricular policy.

There can be no curriculum without a specifically stated vision. Two illustrations will make this clear. One of our own colleges in the North was founded by the farming community of a specific region. Thousands of farmers had forgone their dividends for a certain period of time to establish a college to raise the quality of life of the community. Its specific vision was to raise the quality of life of the farming community through appropriate higher education. The mission to achieve this vision was also specific: lab-to-land skill transfer. Accordingly, the curriculum was determined to comprise courses, among others, intended to develop nuances of agricultural skills from microbiology, soil chemistry, entomology, marketing, management, communication, etc. No other courses were accommodated except those which, directly or indirectly, advanced the vision of the agency.

The Mission Statement

While the vision statement (often brief, and no longer than a sentence or two) describes the goal of an agency broadly, the mission statement spells out the strategy to achieve the goal in abstract terms, with minimum specific details. Some institutions club the vision and mission together as, for instance, the University of Virginia School of Nursing:[6]

"The University of Virginia School of Nursing is committed to educating future leaders, extending the boundaries of nursing and health care knowledge through research, and providing high-quality and compassionate health care in service to the citizens of the Commonwealth of Virginia, the nation, and the world."

Such a succinct statement makes the goal clear, namely, education to create leaders, and not workers; the means to achieve the goal, namely, research into health care knowledge; and the expected outcome of the course, namely, providing high-quality health care to the country, and, through outsourcing, to the world at large.

Learning Outcomes

Before courses are determined, departments are expected to spell out their mission, each of them in its own mission statement, based on consensus among its faculty, about the chosen three to four anticipated learning outcomes that are practical and achievable through the courses of the department. The School of Engineering and Applied Sciences of the same university has the following "Programme Outcomes / Objectives".[7]

A graduate (postgraduate) in civil engineering)

i) Can design a component of civil engineering system, incorporating social, economical, ethical and contractual considerations.

ii) Can develop a major research or design proposal for an engineering problem, complete the analysis, and prepare and present results, while demonstrating an understanding of the role and impact of engineering research and practice in society.

iii) Will demonstrate both leadership and teamwork capabilities.

Curriculum Development

After these preliminaries have been gone through, the department may begin exploring the number, the nature and the type of courses that should make the curriculum subject to the following conditions:

i) the courses should be compatible with the vision of the agency;

ii) they should be designed to fit the curricular model or design adopted by the institution;

iii) they should serve student needs as well as social and national purposes; and

iv) the faculty of the department takes the responsibility to implement the programme designing appropriate strategies to impart the necessary skills and to assess continuously the learning outcomes identified.

The Curricular Model

The courses thus identified may then be accommodated in a suitable curricular model. The model adopted by the affiliating universities is the same as that of the colonial curriculum no longer in use anywhere in the world except perhaps in former colonies like India, Pakistan and Bangladesh. The colonial model is that of the London University based on the ancient *trivium and quadrivium* with a focus on language and rhetoric, in addition to courses in the humanities. The three parts of the Indian curriculum, Part I (regional language / mother tongue), Part II (English) and Part III (Major and Ancillary) exist in isolation from each other without any mutual support. The content of Parts I and II, being literary studies, does not in any way directly help to offer a foundation in communication skills at the tertiary level. A more integrated model is followed by liberal arts and science colleges in most global frontline institutions, which have made remarkable facilities available to incorporate inter-disciplinary studies in the curriculum, including a journal dedicated to promote inter-disciplinary studies and web-contacts for mutual consultations on the matter. An autonomous college may devise a good model. The one suggested here has the following essential components:

a) Foundation Component

The concept of foundation is laying the foundation for a competent and purposeful study of subjects in the core curriculum. They are in the nature of providing basic skills of communication, forming the right attitudes to the outcomes and uses of the programme, creating awareness of the contextual use of the curriculum in community and nation building and sensitizing learners to the needs of the neglected sections of society.

Foundation courses are varied but specifically appropriate to the needs of the learner. For instance, a vague course in moral or social science may not be suitable to those who study business and management. Business Ethics in practice may be more ideal. A general course in grammar or phonetics may not be as useful as a practical course in the use of oral and written cornmunication in presentation, public speaking, group discussion, etc. A general course in Indian Constitution may not be as ideal as Women's Rights and Privileges in the Eyes of the Law, in a women's college.

Foundation Courses aim at nurturing the cognitive perception of moral, social and citizenship responsibilities the learner will shoulder in the adult world of tomorrow. These courses are end-oriented and the means, therefore, should enhance deeper involvement of learners in quality enhancing processes. Case studies, discussion of contextually relevant problems, debates on polarities of burning social, political and economic issues and such other effective pedagogic strategies will no doubt lay the desired foundation for a learner to take off into the core of the discipline with improved awareness, cognitive perception and communication of ideas. The student should have a range of options including information communication-technology in the foundation component to choose from.

A corollary to such foundation courses, specifically relevant to the Indian context is the inclusion of Bridge and Remedial Courses in this component. The mixed-ability groups a teacher is confronted with in an Indian classroom, especially among freshmen, who are from either a regional medium or a flawed school system, need to be helped to cope with the demands of university education. Such courses will be offered with the same care required for others, with well defined objectives, syllabi, time schedules and assessment practices. Whereas the purpose of the Bridge Course is spanning the transition from school to college within a timebound scheme at the beginning of the semester or academic year, remedial programmes are longer, as long as the learners require them to acquire minimum competence to handle communication or a difficult subject. Remedial programmes also need careful planning and implementation. Both these will be offered to learners screened after well-constructed diagnostic tests.

b) The Support Component

Support courses are specifically academic. Known as "ancillaries", or "subsidiaries" or "Minor" or "Auxiliaries", they offer the background necessary to pursue a Major. They comprise a whole range of options in a liberal curriculum of arts and science. The nature of these courses will be determined by the use the learner will put his or her specialized knowledge to in a specific context or background. One who majors in English literature *per se* in India, for instance, will be a poor exponent of that literature because it is made by native writers or NRIs saturated in the culture of the West and it is made for the aesthetic sensibilities of specific target audiences, not necessarily Indian.

While one can endorse the universal appeal of a Shakespeare or a Milton or a Faulkner or of classics that have endured the test of time, one cannot do so with most others, which do not satisfy sensibilities of other audiences. It is here the body of excellent Western literature, acknowledged for its excellence on its own artistic merits, should be put to optimal use by the Indian learner of English literature. It should be seen through the background of creative writing and critical theories of ancient and modern national and regional literatures. It should be appropriated for creative use to project the values of these to the Western world. Courses like A History of Indian Literatures, An Appraisal of Indian Poetics, Comparative Literature, Translation, English Language Teaching for Specific Purposes, or general backdrops such as the Philosophy of Language, Western Poetics and Critical Theories to Understand Genres of Literature may also help to understand the nuances of English literature. Texts from both streams may be prescribed for study. This is just one illustration. Other possibilities may be explored for other subjects keeping in mind the creative utility of pursuing a major.

c) The Inter-Disciplinary Component

No university or college worth its name in almost all global institutions is without a deep concern for promoting inter-disciplinary studies in the liberal arts and science curricula. The rigid compartmentalization of departments and the consequent absence of any formal arrangement to extend curricula across disciplines, not to speak of the fanatic ownership of departments by heads of departments, have denied learners through generations the opportunity to acquire inter-disciplinary knowledge, insights and skills. Therefore, this component becomes all the more important for an autonomous college.

Some leading autonomous colleges in the country have taken the right step forward by combining related disciplines to form "Schools" such as The School of Life Sciences, The School of Social Sciences with inbuilt facility for mutual cooperation for common utilization of available talent and expertise. Such a strategy is unimaginable under the affiliating system. This component may comprise both formal and non-formal modes of learning so long as they are accommodated into the curriculum instead of leaving them to an extra-mural arrangement. Credits may be additionally given for quality performance in this component. So long as undergraduate education remains liberal, inter-disciplinary studies are indispensable. Vocational programmes that promote horizontal mobility belong here.

d) Life-Frontier Engagement Component

This is the final test of the soundness or otherwise of all the knowledge that an undergraduate or postgraduate is reported to have acquired through an academic programme, however rigorous it may be... "to be useful"... the value of knowledge and information as well as skills learners acquire through a programme, "they must be connected to issues or questions that people (the stakeholders) really care about".[8] Unless higher education prepares learners to handle an issue, problem or critical situation in real life, the training they receive would be merely academic, without any potential for direct engagement of challenges in real life. For this reason this component of the core discipline becomes all the more significant. It is not a window on life but a door to go out to acquire practical wisdom from treading the hard road of life. The forms of such engagement are many. On the job-training picked up as internees, projects, preferably group projects, to study burning issues in an institution or social segment, a case analysis relevant to a situation related to major studies, a live-in experience resulting in a term paper, public or private net-worked effort to plan development of a region, etc., may form part of this component.

e) Core

Core or the Major component comprises 75 per cent of the courses in a curriculum. It may be organized into three compartments:

Core I: Courses (50% of the total number) with a deep study of the area of specialization which may be 10 including the two required application-oriented courses leading to constructive and usable proposals as outcomes and they account for 54 credits.

Core II: Strategies of 'Life-Frontier Engagement' such as internship or group projects on neighbourhood community needs, etc., constituting 15 per cent of the total number of courses, three of which are required from a choice of six or more, earning a total of nine credits.

Core III: Inter-Disciplinary Courses which constitute 10 per cent of the courses to earn nine credits. A regular non-vocational inter-disciplinary course of three credits and four modules of vocational study and training of two credits each may come under this component. Provision may be made to earn two additional credits outside the schedule by advanced learners.

A curricular model with these five essential components, besides any others found to be strategically necessary for an integrated holistic development of learners, should ensure the qualitative academic transition being discussed here. Extra-academic components conducive to holistic development of learners such as sports, culturals, community service, etc. are part of a holistic assessment of learners. Strictly speaking they do not form part of a curricular model, which deals with academics alone. They belong to the extra-curricular area and may be assessed accordingly, assigning them due credit.

Curricular Organization or Design

The vision of an agency states its goal; the mission outlines the strategy to achieve it; the objectives enumerate concrete steps to realize the mission and the curricular model provides an integrated picture or ground plan to make an ideal learner who would respond to all these. Finally we should make the curriculum work with appropriate courses chosen under each of the five components. That is an area where faculty and subject experts work together in Boards of Studies in order to help learners to be at the knowledge frontier and enable them to self-manage continuous acquisition of it by going to the right source and creatively interacting with them. Curricular organization enables implementation of the curriculum. Implementation has two dimension: temporal and quality.

The Temporal Dimension of Curricular Implementation

A degree programme should ideally span four years of three semesters each and this plan is adopted by most frontline institutions of higher learning in the world. Such a system can do full justice to the learners' need for time to do a good job of learning, while, at the same time, it enables teacher-mentors to be with learners long enough to motivate and assess them holistically through both course-embedded and direct assessment methods. The subtraction of one year from our earlier degree programme for transfer to the school has strengthened the school system without leaving a temporal alternative for colleges to cope. The abridged three-year degree programme, therefore, has certain inbuilt handicaps. Nevertheless, the curriculum has to work within the allowed timespan. A trimester plan may help enhance student curricular options but, perhaps, in the context of freshers' inability to take on university work straight on, the present two-semester plan for a year may be ideal until the feeder systems provide quality entrants or until an extra year is added. Annual systems are unhelpful for quality-driven curricula based on skill-development, and not on memory.

The Quality Dimension and Curricular Transaction

The temporal dimension of the curriculum is closely integrated with its qualitative dimension. It is nothing but the progressive development of learner-skills from the first year to the third year of a degree programme. The Foundation and Support Courses are often scheduled for the earlier part of the programme and the core (including support and Life-Frontier) for the latter half of it. If assessments are to be continuous, as they should be, then lower-order skills are mastered earlier in the course before learners are taken through progressive higher order skills of application and problem-solving. This is facilitated by the temporal upward phasing of courses of study. Fundamentals of the core discipline, foundation courses and some support courses may be offered in the first two years while advanced core and inter-disciplinary programmes may be offered in the third. Vocational and para-curricular courses may span the whole programme.

Measurement of quality by credits with the help of the Choice Based Credit System should respond to quality more than to mere quantum. It is not the number of credits that matters but the manifestation of skills that should underlie certification. The only way to do this is to adopt a strategy like that of the "American Credit Hour" which, as said earlier, gives equal weight to teacher input and learner output. A credit hour should, therefore, be calculated taking both into account. One hour of credit, accordingly, equals one hour of contact in class plus two notional hours of student work. In actual practice a student cannot complete all the work arising from one hour of classroom contact in two hours; he or she may need more than two, sometimes even more than ten, if the work involves reference, downloading, drafting and presenting or if it involves a set of practicals on that one lecture. Hence three hours (1 hour of contact + 2 hours of student output notionally calculated) equal one credit. Under the present system student work is taken for granted without meticulously measuring it for certification.

Conclusion

Academic autonomy envisaged by the UGC is so designed as to help institutions part ways with the dead academic practices of an obsolete system of higher education discarded by many countries long time ago. Parting ways does not imply a total severance from the system that has been salvaged from time to time by educators and educational planners. What is required is to obey the urgent mandate to facilitate a smooth transition from the rituals, dead forms and bad practices to which the system has succumbed over the past 60 years. The mandate to change is urgent because our education system should keep pace with the fast economic development of the nation and be a robust support to it.

The UGC Guidelines of both the Tenth and the Eleventh Plans have set forth five areas of academic, social, technical, pedagogic and community development. Of these the present paper attempts to examine strategies of the first parameter, namely, academic development outside the affiliating system. After a brief retrospect of Indian higher education since independence, the pre-requisites of designing new courses of study are detailed. The vision of the educational agency, its mission statement, expected learning outcomes and objectives have to be briefly but specifically stated. A curricular model may be designed to incorporate the essential components under which courses may be organized. A design of curricular organization is necessary to quantify courses and to devise qualitative strategies through the Choice Based Credit System. Other areas remain to be explored for want of space here. It is believed that the discussion, the curricular model and the curricular organizational model suggested here will help autonomous colleges to take the road to become universities. If change is dodged or ignored now, quality transition in our higher system will remain a remote possibility.

References

1. John Hariss, "The Onward March of the New Great Indian Middle Class", "Independent India at 60", *The Hindu,* p.18.
2. University Grants Commission, *Guidelines for Autonomous Colleges during the Eleventh Plan Period (2007-2012),* Introduction, p.1.
3. Ibid., p.10.
4. Ibid., pp.1-2.
5. Ibid., p.1
6. University of Virginia, *Assessment Guide,* Office of Institutional Assessment and Studies, p.7.
7. Ibid., p.23.
8. Indiana University Kokoma, *Indiana University Kokomo Assessment Policy,* Center for Teaching, Learning and Assessment, 9 *Principles of Good Practice for Assessing Student Learning,* p.2.

6

Autonomous Colleges and Relationship with the University, State Government and the UGC

— S.P. Thyagarajan

Introduction

Knowledge can be created, absorbed, and applied only by the educated mind. Universities and colleges will play increasingly important roles as our societies enter the knowledge driven twenty-first century. In a sense, knowledge should be the medium of the university education. Through the activities of discoveries, shaping, achieving, transmitting and applying knowledge, the university serves society in a myriad of ways: educating the young, preserving our cultural heritage, providing the basic research so essential to our security and well-being, training our professionals and certifying their competence, challenging our society and stimulating social change.

Higher education institutions (HEIs) are to be expected to build in the following seven principles of good and quality practices if they are to answer professionally the above requirements of modern higher education system:

i) Encouraging contact between students and faculty.

ii) Developing reciprocity and cooperation among students.

iii) Encouraging to achieve learning with advanced teaching tools.

iv) Giving prompt feedback.

v) Emphasising time on task.

vi) Complying with high expectations.

vii) Respecting diverse talents and ways of learning.

If these good practices are to be implemented visibly, a healthy approach of the government has to be created with the sole aim of transforming universities and colleges to become student-centric rather than teacher/administrator-centric. The qualities of this environment could be:

i) A strong sense of shared purposes.
ii) Concrete support from administrators and faculty for those purposes.
iii) Adequate funding appropriate for the purposes.
iv) Policies and procedures consistent with the purposes.
v) Continued monitoring and evaluation of how well the purposes are being achieved.

The facilitating/influencing factors of building and sustaining such environment are governments at the central and state level and the accrediting organizations by:

i) updating policies that are consistent with the good practices developed in HEIs.
ii) holding high expectations and recognitions for institutional performance.
iii) keeping bureaucratic regulations to a minimum that is compatible with public accountability.
iv) guarantee the principle of accountable autonomy and self-organisation of universities and HEIs.
v) provide statutory frameworks to allow universities and colleges to design decision-making structures that are congruent with their specific missions and goals and to enable them to develop long-term vision strategies and human resource policies in the Indian and global context;
vi) continue to support higher education as a public responsibility requiring long term commitments, stable legal and funding environments in spite of the emerging trends of privatization in higher education.

It is under this paradigm of higher education, the present day autonomous college system has to be introspected.

The concept of autonomous college system gained momentum after the Kothari Commission's Report of 1964-66 which was adopted by UGC in the Fifth Five Year Plan itself. In spite of continuous policy and financial support at the Government of India and the UGC levels, only 14 states in India had introduced the autonomous college system as of 4 October,2006 in a total of 233 colleges through 49 universities.

The Objectives of the Autonomous College System as Envisaged by the UGC

i) To determine and prescribe its own courses of study and syllabi; and restructure and redesign the courses to suit local needs;

ii) To prescribe rules for admission in consonance with the reservation policy of the state government;

iii) To evolve methods of assessment of students' performance, the conduct of examinations and notification of results;

iv) To use modern tools of educational technology to achieve higher standards and greater creativity; and

v) To promote healthy practice such as community service, extension activities, projects for the benefit of the society at large, neighbourhood programmes, etc.

It is anticipated that the parent university and state government would nurture the autonomous college system in the following manner.

The Role of the Parent University

i) To bring more autonomous colleges under its fold;

ii) To promote academic freedom in autonomous colleges by encouraging introduction of innovative academic programmes;

iii) To facilitate new courses of study, subject to the required minimum number of hours of instruction, content and standards;

iv) To permit them to issue their own provisional, migration and other certificates;

v) To do everything possible to foster the spirit of autonomy;

vi) To ensure that degrees/diplomas/certificates issued indicate the name of the college;

vii) To depute various nominees of the university to serve in various committees of the autonomous colleges and get the feedback on their functioning; and

viii) To create separate wings wherever necessary to facilitate the smooth working of the autonomous colleges.

Conferring Autonomous Status

Autonomous status covers certificate, diploma, undergraduate, postgraduate and M.Phil. programmes offered in colleges that are autonomous and those seeking autonomous status. The parent university will confer the status of autonomy upon a college that is permanently affiliated, with the concurrence of the state government and the University Grants Commission. The Act and Statutes of the universities ought to be amended to provide for the grant of autonomy to affiliated colleges. Before granting autonomy, the university will ensure that the management structure of the applicant college is adequately participatory and provides ample opportunities for academicians to make a creative contribution.

Target Group and Eligibility Criteria

All Colleges under Section 2(f) & 12(B) of the UGC Act are eligible. The criteria for identification of institutions for grant of autonomy are as follows:

i) Academic reputation and previous performance in university examinations and its academic/co-curricular/ extension activities in the past.

ii) Academic/extension achievements of the faculty.

iii) Quality and merit in the selection of students and teachers, subject to statutory requirements in this regard.

iv) Adequacy of infrastructure, for example, library, equipment, accommodation for academic activities, etc.

v) Quality of institutional management.

vi) Financial resources provided by the management/state government for the development of the institution.

vii) Responsiveness of administrative structure.

viii) Motivation and involvement of faculty in the promotion of innovative reforms.

The Role of the State Government

i) Avoiding, as far as possible, transfer of teachers, especially in colleges where cademic innovation and reforms are in progress, except for need-based transfers.

ii) Conveying its concurrence for the extension of autonomy of any college to the Commission within the stipulated time of 90 days after receipt of the review committee report, failing which it will be construed that the state government has no objection to the college continuing to be autonomous.

iii) Deputing nominees on time to the governing body of government colleges and other bodies wherever their nominees are to be included.

Pattern of Financial Assistance and Other Enabling Provisions by the UGC

The UGC will provide assistance under this scheme to autonomous colleges to meet their additional and special needs.

i) Guest/visiting faculty

ii) Orientation and re-training of teachers.

iii) Re-designing courses and development of teaching/learning material

iv) Workshop and seminars

v) Examination reforms

vi) Office equipment, teaching aids and laboratory equipment

vii) Furniture for office, classrooms, library and laboratories

viii) Library equipment, books/journals

ix) Expenditure on meetings of the governing body and committees

x) Honorarium to Controller of Examinations (full-time).

xi) Accreditation (NAAC) fee.

UGC funds cannot, however, be used for creation of posts, payment of salary to any of the college staff, paying honorarium (except clause [x] above) to existing staff to meet normal college contingency requirement or to subsidies. Examination fee should be fixed so that income from fee can meet the expenditure on examinations and other staff appointed in examination branch. In government colleges the principal has to obtain administrative approval from the Director of Collegiate Education before apportioning the grant that causes undue delay. Hence, the principal of the college has to be authorised to spend the autonomy grant as soon as it is received from the UGC.

The ceiling of normal assistance (Eleventh Plan) has been as follows:

Undergraduate level only

i) Arts/science/commerce: One faculty only: Rs.9.00 lakh p.a.
ii) Arts/science/commerce More than one faculty: Rs.15.00 lakh p.a. Both Undergraduate and Postgraduate levels:
iii) Single faculty: Rs.10.00 lakh p.a.
iv) Multi-faculty: Rs. 20 lakh p.a.

Autonomous Colleges in India: The Present Scenario

Though autonomy seems to be closer at hand than before, the debate on the level of freedom that institutions enjoy is at its peak today. There are also apprehensions that autonomous institutions may follow arbitrary employment policies and charge high fees from students, thereby putting higher education out of reach of the poor. Everyone agrees that autonomy is a must; however this freedom cannot be without responsibility. It is felt strongly that autonomy has to be linked to accountability. There is also criticism today that, "In real terms, autonomy has been used to introduce programmes but not mechanisms by which the standard and quality of the programmes can be improved". It is also felt that "autonomy and a possible increase in fees as a result would especially affect students in rural areas".

In an attempt to bring about quality in higher education across the country, the Central Advisory Board on Education (CABE), Govt. of India, in June 2005, after extensive interactions across the country, has made the following recommendations:

i) Autonomy to higher education institutions is strongly recommended on the ground that it is a prerequisite for enabling them to achieve the higher education objectives of the country.

ii) Institutions should be given autonomy for designing curricula.

iii) Granting autonomy to HEIs to start self-financing courses.

iv) An Internal Quality Assurance Cell (IQAC) to be set up in institutes to assess their performance.

v) All institutions to adopt certain disclosure standards with a view to containing malpractice in relation to fee structure. Also the government could set the ceiling on fees.

vi) Higher Education Institutes should be given autonomy to establish links for academic collaboration with their counterpart academic and research institutions, industry and professional organizations both in India and abroad.

vii) Code of professional ethics to be developed for teachers and mechanism evolved for complete observance.

While it has always been the endeavour of educationists to suggest innovations in the educational policy of the nation, pragmatism and implementability are the areas of concern. These concerns are addressed by foreign universities in the Western world by setting in place a codified 'Ethics Policy' to each of their universities. Broadly the Code of Ethics is meant to serve as guide to assist the Governing Councils/ Board of Governors, administrators, faculty and staff collectively called as 'Members of the University Community' in making ethical decisions and engaging in appropriate, lawful conduct. It is the intent of the Governing Council that compliance with the Code of Ethics will foster a work-environment that stimulates and challenges the development of abilities and pursuit of personal and professional growth while maintaining the highest ethical standards and goals of the university. The Governing Council of the University encourages the members of the university community to develop moral and ethical commitments to themselves, work, society and the world.

The Ethical Standards of the Members of the University Community

i) *Selflessness:* Holders of public office should take decisions solely in terms of the public interest. They should not do so in order to gain financial or other material benefits for themselves, their family or their friends.

ii) *Integrity:* Holders of public office should not place themselves under any financial or other obligation to outside individuals or organizations that might influence them in the performance of their official duties.

iii) *Objectivity:* In carrying out university activities including making public appointments, awarding contracts, or recommending individuals for rewards and benefits, holders of public office should make choices on merit only.

iv) *Accountability:* Holders of public office are accountable for their decisions and actions to the public and must submit themselves to whatever scrutiny is appropriate to their office.

v) *Openness:* Holders of public office should be as open as possible about all the decisions and actions that they take. They should give reasons for their decisions and restrict information only when the wider public interest clearly demands.

vi) *Honesty:* Holders of public office have a duty to declare any private interests relating to their public duties and to take steps to resolve any conflicts arising in a way that protects the public interest.

vii) *Leadership:* Holders of public office should promote and support these principles by leadership and setting themselves as examples.

In view of the above international developments of far-reaching consequences and national level expectations in our Indian higher education system, the following quality-based roles are to be put in practice in our country in order to achieve the autonomous college system to its full dimensions.

Role of Government to bring about Autonomy with Accountability

i) The government shall improve the system of governance to bring legally proof quality standards and the 'academic audit system' to authenticate and monitor all HEIs especially self-financing colleges and deemed universities keeping the concept of developing higher education institutions of high quality.

ii) The governments should ensure quality standards achieved in all the existing government colleges by strengthening their manpower and infrastructure deficiencies to cater to the socially and financially deprived higher education seekers of the country.

iii) All state governments should make legal provisions to provide autonomy and accountability to colleges, deemed to be universities and universities in the respective states by bringing about changes in the Acts/Statutes of the respective State University Acts.

iv) A separate set of external monitoring norms to be framed to assess quality standards in self financing institutions.

Role of Teachers for Accountability:

i) The accountability of teachers in autonomous system can be ensured by adoption of student evaluation of teachers. This assessment should be made more comprehensive by including different constituents of the system including management, infrastructure, curricular aspects and other dimensions as well.

ii) The performance of teachers in autonomous system may be assessed in terms of some objective parameters such as their innovations in curriculum designing and updating, teaching and evaluation techniques(pedagogy), research and extension orientation, capacity building of students and contributions to managements of the institutions in which he or she is employed.

iii) Teachers are to be motivated and capacity built by periodic updated orientation and refresher programmes on every aspect of higher education including educational administration to be linked with their career advancement.

iv) Performance-linked incentive schemes should be implemented with well defined parameters and benchmarks by providing specific fund allocation by universities, managements and governments.

v) Vacancies in all HEIs shall have to be filled up at the earliest and the age of retirement for the teachers in all HEIs across the country should be uniform to retain talents, quality, experience and expertise.

Role of Administration in Autonomy and Accountability

i) Implementation of autonomy and accountability by managements should be absolute in both letter and spirit.

ii) Transparency of administration, utilization of finances and complete decentralisation must be voluntarily done along with subjecting themselves for feedback appraisal of administration by teachers, students and public with built-in review process.

iii) Autonomous institutions are to be performance evaluated through the IQAC mediated academic audit system using the NAAC defined performance indicators for providing annual financial assistance and continuity of autonomous status.

Role of the Public

i) Grievance Redressal Cells should be fully operational in each of the HEIs to address all aspects of higher education institutional functioning with a built-in documentation and periodic reporting system.

ii) Parent-Teacher–Administration Cells must be in place in all autonomous institutions with periodic joint meetings to assess, assimilate and implement the feedbacks received.

iii) Operational studies are to be encouraged by in-house and third party agency supported survey to evaluate demand-supply interface and quality standards in the HEIs.

Conclusion

It is important to understand that the most critical challenge facing most HEIs will be the capacity for adapting to the changes in higher education requirements. Universities and colleges must seek to remove the constraints that prevent them from responding to the needs of a rapidly changing knowledge-based society. They should strive to challenge, excite, and embolden all members of the academic communities to embark on what should be a great adventure for higher education. Only a concerted effort to understand the important traditions of the past, the challenges of the present.and the possibilities of the future can enable HEIs to contribute at this very important juncture of higher education in the globalised era.

7

Autonomous Colleges — Prospects and Challenges

— Mariamma A. Varghese

Introduction

Amidst the enormous quantitative expansion in higher education since independence, the growing number of colleges affiliated to a university has proved to be a major obstacle in making education innovative and relevant. The result is that universities lag behind in their functions of pursuing excellence, building theoretical models and scientific knowledge. They are burdened under their own weight of monitoring the large number of affiliated colleges with reference to the academic programmes and examination. The choice then remains to continue with the status quo or to initiate strategies to better the system by strengthening the sector of autonomous colleges as a partial solution to the problem.

The Concept of Autonomy

The concept of autonomy has always had a unique value and status for the higher education system. Autonomy can be defined as freedom, independence, non-interference from other external systems, self-governance and so on. The historical fact in our own country is that the Presidency Colleges are the forerunners of all universities. The Presidency College, Calcutta, functioned independently until the Calcutta University was established in the year 1857. The concept of academic independence of colleges found a renewed acceptability a hundred years later, when the provision of autonomous colleges came to be incorporated in Agra University statutes in 1954 by the untiring efforts of

Prof. V.V.John, the then principal of Government College, Ajmer, and Prof. R.K Singh, the then Principal of B.R. College, Agra.

We have always praised our ancient Gurukula system of education with its close relationship between Gurus and Shishyas. Today, the students in colleges are completely alienated from the educational system. Their main contact with the teachers is as passive listeners to the lectures of the teachers. If we want to bring greater contact between students and teachers, internal examination system is necessary and for that, college autonomy is a must. The proposal to provide autonomy to colleges was based on the principle that teachers should have academic freedom so that promotion and development of an intellectual climate can be created in an institution, which is conducive for the teachers and the learners.

The need for autonomy has been reiterated in the National Planning of Education (NPE 1986) document. It states "In view of mixed experiences with the system of affiliation, autonomous colleges need to be helped to develop in large numbers until the affiliating system is replaced by a free and more creative association of universities with colleges. Similarly, the creation of autonomous departments within universities on a selective basis should be encouraged. Autonomy and freedom will be accompanied by accountability".

The progress of implementation of the policy slowed down between 1989 and 1992 on account of political reasons and changing priorities. But the minor modifications in the policy made in 1992 have not diluted its emphasis on autonomy of colleges. The conservatives utilized these years in expressing misgivings about the scheme and doubts about its success.

The concept of autonomy of colleges has three dimensions: academic, administrative and financial.

a) Academic Autonomy

Coming to the most fundamental dimension of autonomy of a college, viz., academic autonomy, the very origin of the concept lies in the dissatisfaction with the prevailing system of affiliation. The three freedoms of deciding what to teach, how to teach and how to evaluate relate to the relationship with the universities and not with the government.

Each autonomous college has its own boards of studies, academic committee and governing council corresponding to, and on the pattern of, boards of studies, academic council and syndicate of a university. Each one of such bodies has on it, the university nominees and external experts. Through its nominees the university is in closer contact with an autonomous college than it is with an affiliated college. The curriculum, academic calendar and other norms prescribed by the university for all colleges is the base line for reference. An autonomous college would be encouraged and supported in excelling such norms in as many areas as it can. For example, it may make innovations in the syllabi and curriculum, achieve large number of teaching days with better regularity of classes and of students therein, conduct evaluations more objectively and expeditiously, undertake social service and extension projects and so on. There is provision for periodical review of autonomy to ensure they perform as per the objectives laid out for autonomous status. A college must earn autonomy continuously to stay autonomous.

b) Administrative Autonomy

Although the colleges which become autonomous get the financial grants from the State government, still they can have a separate registered society with the governing council as its apex decision-making body. Its composition is in accordance with the guidelines issued by the UGC. The council has on it, educationist members nominated by the University, the UGC, the government and members co-opted by the Council itself besides the teachers' representatives. However, according to the UGC guidelines, the management is authorized to nominate three members, one of them being the chairman. These members are nominated by the trust or society running a private college and by the government in case of government colleges. One of these three is the special secretary in the department of higher education or the director of college education. Another nominee is usually the collector of the district, whose involvement has been found useful in view of law and order problems and desired coordination with various departmental agencies. Some times an eminent educationist is one of the three persons who could be nominated as the chairman.

c) Financial Autonomy

Financial Autonomy is the most sensitive dimension of the autonomy. All the colleges if they are aided, get 90 per cent of the grants from the government. In such a situation, they are not in a position to incur any recurring financial liability without obtaining prior concurrence of the government. Until recently, their fees income and savings also used to be adjusted towards the grants–in-aid. Their autonomy is limited to utilizing the resources generated by them or received as gifts or endowments, or making some adjustments in reallocations within the amount of block grants received. The same applies to autonomous government colleges. They are given block grants these days to simplify the procedures. Each autonomous college has the identity of a separate unit and its financial requirements are given full consideration against the practice of a lump sum amount grant.

Organization

The organization and set-up of autonomous colleges represent a radical departure from the existing structure of the university system in India. An autonomous college will have the freedom to:

a) Determine its own courses of study and syllabi;

b) Prescribe rules of admission, subject to the reservation policy of the government;

c) Evolve methods of evaluation and conduct examination.

If implemented, these would provide ample scope for colleges for innovation in curriculum, evaluation and assessment.

UGC Policy

The UGC policy supports the Education Commission's stand, which had recommended "autonomy to an outstanding college or a small cluster of good colleges within a large University, which has the capacity to improve itself markedly". The role of the parent university will be limited to general supervision and the actual conferment of degree. It is envisaged that these autonomous colleges in course of time will be able to stand on their own. They will develop their own safeguards to maintain standards, provide credibility to the examinations conducted by them and award their own degrees. They are expected to perform and attain excellence and maintain it through self-regulation and self-discipline. Periodic reviews will be conducted by a special committee and appraise the college. In the event of malfunctioning or decline in standards, it will be the responsibility of the university to revoke the autonomous status.

Selection of Autonomous Colleges

The grant of autonomy is based on the academic reputation of the college, performance of the college in the university examinations, curricular achievement, demand ratio of admissions, physical facilities like classrooms, laboratories and libraries, management responsiveness, the extent of freedom enjoyed by the faculty for pursuit of advanced scholarship, research, experimentation and involvement in educational innovations and reforms, etc.

Functioning of Autonomous Colleges

To ensure proper governance of autonomous college, the governing body of the college will have representatives from state government, the parent university and the UGC besides the principal and the representatives of the staff and students. The Academic Council will have representations from the UGC, the state government, the principal of the college, heads of the departments, staff and student representatives.

In order to establish the credibility of autonomous colleges, it is important that norms of performance be laid out. It is essential that the institution should have minimum interference from the political system to be able to function effectively and introduce some innovation in the system.

A study conducted on autonomous colleges in Tamil Nadu (where the largest number of autonomous colleges are established) revealed that autonomous colleges by and large were successful. Most of them were convinced that the expected advantages of autonomy have been achieved or within the reach of attainment. Examinations were conducted systematically and with rigour. Faculty assumed responsibility and they felt accountable. The teachers of autonomous colleges have assumed the responsibility to see that:

a) All admissions are on merit.
b) All examinations are fair and objective.
c) Minimum time is spent in conducting the examinations and evaluations.
d) All appointments are fair and objective.
e) The university curriculum is modified in order to use the expertise of the faculty and the needs of the region.

In spite of the supportive policies, the scheme has not picked up momentum in the rest of the country. This is attributed to many reasons. In some cases, the teachers are themselves not fully willing to assume the full responsibilities of autonomy. There are apprehensions that college degrees may not have the same status as a university degree. In some states, the governments are not prepared to give up their powers over the government run colleges and the managements of the private colleges are apprehensive that they will lose their powers.

There are a few important points one has to safeguard. One is coping with the multiplicity of standards arising from the different syllabi offered by the institutions. Another point is the linkage between undergraduate education, postgraduation and research. At any point in time this should not be weakened. Autonomous colleges should equip themselves fully in terms of academic personnel to undertake the task and the targets they have set for themselves. Since there is emphasis on employability, growth of physical, liberal and social sciences and thus basic research may not get the importance it deserves. Some efforts have to be made to achieve a balanced approach to curriculum development in autonomous colleges.

Autonomous institutions across the globe function effectively be it a college, school or research institution. They are accountable to the community they serve. Therefore they are very successful. Of course success varies from institution to institution. Autonomous colleges offer a way out, but it needs courageous minds to accept the challenge. Every successful autonomous college will give a new face to our educational system. Heads of institutions and teachers alone cannot change the entire educational system in the country. But they can work hard and network with other teachers from other institutions, and make a difference in the system.

8

Institutional Autonomy for Quality Improvement of Higher Education

— A. Sukumaran Nair

In the fast changing world scenario of education, where the quality of higher education is accepted as an important determinant of a country's development, nations all over the world are experimenting with new instrumentalities for improving the quality of their higher education. An important instrumentality which needs urgent consideration is the management model which is used to control the functioning of colleges in the country which we describe as the affiliating system. Under this system, a number of colleges functioning in a region are controlled by a university located in the same region which has the authority to prescribe the details of the academic functioning of the institution. The affiliating university performs mostly the role of an examination-conducting and certifying body. The colleges under it are assigned the role of preparing students for the memory oriented examinations, prescribed by the university, on the basis of a stereotyped curriculum prescribed by it.

Freedom for Institutional Functioning and Quality

Any close study of the functioning of modern education would convince us of the fact that giving greater freedom to educational institutions and making them socially accountable for their performance is a better method of ensuring quality than exercising rigid controls over them and testing student learning at the end, using the conventional memory-oriented tests. A vast majority of higher education institutions all over the world function as autonomous institutions in respect of their instructional strategies, conduct examinations and declare students as qualified to receive their degrees. Our colleges unfortunately are denied the right to act independently. They are denied their legitimate right to be responsible for the learning of their students.

The Indian system of higher education, for historic reasons, took the wrong decision way back in 1857 when the first three universities were started in India. The three pioneering universities set up at Calcutta, Bombay and Madras were affiliating universities. The model was adopted from the model used by the London University of the time. The London University adopted this model purely for administrative convenience validating the courses conducted by colleges functioning in different parts of the British empire of mid-nineteenth century. The London University discontinued this model after a few decades of its creation, possibly because it found the system to be inadequate to control the quality of education provided by colleges in remote areas. But we in India blindly continued this system during the rest of the British rule and for nearly 60 years following independence.

The UGC attempted a reform of the affiliating model by suggesting the starting of autonomous colleges, where a few properly functioning institutions would be identified and given reasonable freedom for their academic functioning. The idea, unfortunately was not properly received by Indian academic community. It was introduced in a few colleges in a slipshod manner. Some states totally opposed the new reform and did not permit the introduction of the scheme in any of their colleges. Even in the few colleges which were granted autonomy, it cannot be said that the concept of autonomy has been properly implemented. Apart from several discussions and debates and a few evaluation studies of autonomous colleges, very little was done to give proper operational meaning to the new educational concept and implement it in a big way. It is surprising that some of the institutions of higher learning which had immense potential for growth were excluded from the operation of the scheme. A few institutions which came forward for autonomy were given the system after certain peripheral forms of assessment. The non-committal introduction of the scheme did considerable harm to the cause of autonomy. While some of the very superior institutions which were granted autonomy improved their tone of functioning, a few undeserving institutions which became autonomous only deteriorated further in quality. The failure of the second group of institutions is often quoted by the critics of autonomy 'for opposing autonomy'. They often make a blanket assumption that the affiliation system (which has become extinct in almost all parts of the world) is the last word in quality higher education. The definite advantages of making the college itself responsible for its functioning and maintaining world-class performance was cleverly overlooked by the opponents of the new scheme.

We conveniently turn our face away from the fact that world-famous institutions like the London School of Economics, Harvard School of Law, Johns Hopkins School of Medicine, Columbia Teachers' College, etc., which set world standards in education in their respective disciplines are able to do so because of the unlimited freedom they get in defining their functioning styles. We have also cleverly avoided facing the widely accepted fact that academic freedom is an important ingredient of all forms of higher education. It is this freedom which helped the great thinkers of the past like Isaac Newton, Karl Marx or Harold Laski to publish their revolutionary ideas often ignoring popular views or public criticisms about the path-breaking new ideas they propagated. We know that the freedom which was extended to present-day academics like Noam Chomsky or Paulo Friere helped them to project their revolutionary new ideas about language learning human intellect the new role to be performed by education. This aspect of the functioning of higher education also needs to be used for reconceiving our notions about higher education.

If we want to maintain international standards and compete with advanced nations and become a knowledge power within a short compass of time, we certainly have to redefine the paradigms used for running our colleges by giving them greater academic freedom to act. Ideally all colleges have to be granted full autonomy on the lines of the autonomy enjoyed by similar institutions in educationally advanced countries. We have to free our colleges from the dull uniformity which we have maintained for several decades at the cost of quality.

The Meaning of Real Autonomy

Real autonomy means full authority given to a higher education institution to take appropriate decisions about their academic functioning and enforce such decisions on the basis of informed discussion of all concerned. Decisionmaking is extended to all aspects of institutional functioning like defining the goals to be achieved by the institution, designing new courses and prescribing the modalities for curriculum transaction, delineating the procedures for student selection and student certification, use of funds for proper institutional functioning, defining methods for teacher selection and teacher assessment, assessing the quality of functioning of the system, defining time-limits for action, etc. This would mean empowering the system and its functionaries, especially the teachers. We know that all these powers are currently exercised by the affiliating university which tests the quality of performance of a college by 'remote sensing'. By even assuming that a highly efficient system of university administration is available, it is unthinkable how the university will be able to 'reach out' to the 200-400 affiliated colleges under it. No university can claim that it is able to perform even the minimal functions expected of it, when it has to deal with so many institutions at the same time. The affiliated system was introduced at a time when universities were expected to deal with around 10-12 colleges at a time.

The affiliating system has a negative effect on the functioning of not only the affiliated colleges, but also on the functioning of the universities which control them. Most of the top-heavy universities are never able to perform the real functions expected of them, viz., teaching, research and extension. They have little time left to perform these functions since they are for most of the time conducting examinations and declaring results. The fact that the non-affiliating universities in this country perform the higher roles better than the affiliating universities is proof of the fact that it is time to free universities from the local affiliated colleges. The recent NAAC assessment of different universities in India would bear testimony to the fact that the affiliating-type universities by and large, are not able to discharge their academic functions on par with non-affiliating universities. We are far behind such world-class institutions like Oxford, Cambridge or London in every aspect. In a system where even a small change in the curriculum needs about two-three years to be processed by the mammoth university bodies, real changes never happen, or happen in the system of higher education, much later than when they are needed.

The Scope of Autonomy

Although we started granting autonomy to a few select institutions in the country nearly three-four decades ago, we have done this without a full understanding of the real purposes of autonomy. This will be obvious once we make a survey of the criteria used for granting autonomy in different parts of the country. Even different universities within the same state have given different meanings to autonomy. While some colleges interpret autonomy as freedom given to colleges to conduct their external examination, other universities interpret this as the authority given to a college for evolving a parallel curriculum and conducting examinations, based on the new curriculum. None of the autonomous colleges in the country enjoy full autonomy as in advanced educational systems.

Ideally, an autonomous college should have full freedom to design and operate degree programmes on par with the powers enjoyed by universities. All colleges are expected to have the freedom to experiment with any new experiment which the institution deems necessary for delivering quality education, subject of course to certain broad constraints fixed by the society. This means the freedom to innovate, to experiment and still be answerable to society for its quality. A few such modalities are listed below:

a) Laying down new institutional goals and structure the programmes differently to achieve such goals (e.g. organizing new courses for achieving global standards; introducing an innovative management curriculum based on Indian ideas about system management; designing an optional paper on India for a postgraduate course in Psychology; implementing a degree programme in Waste Management at the degree level, etc.)
b) Introducing an enriched honors degree programme (with two additional papers) for superior degree students; starting an integrated B.Sc and M.Sc. or an M.Sc. and M.Phil. in one of the strong departments of the college for superior students; substituting one optional paper for a postgraduate degree with a dissertation, etc.

c) Introducing upgraded special degree programmes in select subjects to achieve global standards (e.g. starting an economic degree equivalent to the first degree offered by the London School of Economics or a degree in astrophysics on the lines of the same degree offered by the California Institute of Technology).

d) Introducing innovative degree programmes to meet local or regional specific system needs (e.g. a new degree of Master of Mathematics/ Master of Chemistry for upgrading the subject knowledge of college teachers in their teaching subjects; introducing a special degree programme in Oriental Hospitality Management, etc.).

e) Adding new requirements for completion of degree requirements to develop added works skills for gaining global employment. (e.g. spoken language as an add-on course to law degree/teacher training degree; adding additional non examination requirements for completing a regular degree like completion of a period of approved social service, completion of a research project, etc.).

f) Establishing contacts with reputed foreign universities/ research institutions and getting the service of foreign experts for teaching, research and other forms of educational services.

g) Organizing special courses for talented/ superior students (e.g. research methodology in specific subjects; arranging for special lecture programmes, extra help in conducting projects, etc.).

h) Using new management models for improving organizational efficiency (e.g. elected students and teachers in the college managing bodies; decentralizing the administration of colleges; teacher rating by students and parents, system evaluation by stakeholders/ consumers, use of student evaluation profiles for reporting work skills; use of formative evaluation for assessing student learning, etc.).

How to Correct Past Deficiencies

The above list is only indicative of the broad possibilities connected with autonomy which will help us to change the system and help it to catch up with advanced educational systems. Institutions willing to change will not have any difficulty in designing new procedures which would help to upgrade their mechanisms for delivering educational services. Educational systems in India look upon educational reform or innovation as the adoption of routine improvements or peripheral changes as and when directed by the affiliating university. The time for status-quo changes and cosmetic reforms is over. The rigid affiliating system permits only minor changes, because it expects institutions to be conformers and not innovators. Changes have to be effected in a big way where institutions decide to identify the areas for change and implement the changes on their own.

We have to seek the reason why a system of higher education which was close to the top British universities at the time of independence declined in quality during the post-independent period. During the pre-independent period, educational change was relatively slow and the affiliating universities in India with a small number of affiliating colleges under them were able to maintain reasonably high standards, even when they functioned within the constraints set by the affiliating system. But in a new society where educational changes occur at a fast pace, we failed to catch up with the levels achieved by advanced countries. A higher education system which produced academic luminaries like Dr. S. Radhakrishnan, Dr. J.C. Bose, Dr. P.C. Ray and Dr. Mehanad Saha, found itself inadequate to generate the scholars and researchers demanded by the new knowledge society. It is useful to remember that many of the eminent scholars of the post-independent period, like Dr. Chandrasekhar, Homi Bhabha and Amartya Sen, were mostly products of foreign education. Their numbers are few as compared to the number of equivalent scholars turned out by advanced educational systems like those of Britain, USA, Germany or France and even in terms of what we were able to produce in pre-independent India.

Our standing in the field of higher education, as per independent assessments, leaves much to be desired. We are far behind most of the advanced countries in providing quality higher education. The quality of our research output in critical areas is dismally low. The number of nobel laureates, fellows of royal society, etc., produced by the country is very small compared to the size of our higher education system. The number and quality of international publications by scholars from the country is negligible. Against this dismal picture of higher education, we have to take into account the fact that the higher education system in India is dealing with very superior students who possess all the needed intellectual potential to deal with higher level abstractions taught in higher education, and can stand on their own in the competitive knowledge society of the twenty-first century, provided they are given the right type of education. What we need is a system which can train the youth to play the new roles expected of them in the knowledge society of the twenty-first century.

What Ails the System?

The reason why our higher education institutions lag behind similar institutions in the advanced countries can be attributed to a great extent to our failure to give greater autonomy for our colleges. This would make the institutions themselves responsible for their quality. Corrections should start with scientific changes in the unrealistic curriculum used, the archaic course structures and subject groupings adopted, the unimaginative verbal modalities and content-based methods used for instruction, and the non-accountable system of management we follow. The memory-based examinations and the irrational resistance to change further complicate the situation. The system has developed a mindset to resist all kinds of changes, especially when changes to be introduced reduce the privileges already enjoyed by the teaching community. Not many institutions are prepared to go beyond the set boundaries of conventional functioning and experiment with new ideas in a global scenario where even the lesser nations of Asia have overtaken us in accommodating new instrumentalities for achieving quality.

The total insulation of the system from contemporary developments needs urgent correction. We have to develop an empowered new system of higher education by granting the system greater autonomy. It will be useful to remember that the main mandate of today's society is to reorder it to accommodate the vast changes needed for containing the educational demands of twenty-first century.

What Next?

We have to confer autonomy on all our colleges within as short a time as possible, in three phases, spread over about 15 years or less. The operational aspect of autonomy has to be spelt out by the apex national bodies like the UGC and the NAAC. Autonomy should not be interpreted as freedom of an institution to do anything in the name of higher education, or to experiment with a few innocuous academic reforms, but as the freedom to exercise academic discretion in evolving all academic policies and run the system as per the accepted policies, in a transparent and accountable manner.

It will be ideal, if the UGC appoints a committee of experts to frame a common code of conduct and operational procedures for granting autonomy together with adequate safeguards against the misuse of autonomy. The minimum requirements can be laid down as an acceptable rating by the NAAC. An intensive programme to prepare colleges for autonomy can be organized by the UGC to all college heads, in the form of a certificate course given on-line by national apex bodies like the IGNOU and prepare all the key functionaries in colleges for playing the new roles expected of them once they are granted full autonomy.

References

1. John Hariss, "The Onward March of the New Great Indian Middle Class", "Independent India at 60", *The Hindu*, p.18.
2. University Grants Commission, *Guidelines for Autonomous Colleges during the Eleventh Plan Period (2007-2012)*, Introduction, p.1.
3. Ibid., p.10.
4. Ibid., pp.1-2.
5. Ibid., p.1
6. University of Virginia, *Assessment Guide*, Office of Institutional Assessment and Studies, p.7.
7. Ibid., p.23.
8. Indiana University Kokoma, *Indiana University Kokomo Assessment Policy*, Center for Teaching, Learning and Assessment, 9 *Principles of Good Practice for Assessing Student Learning*, p.2.

9

College Autonomy

— D. Peter Jayapandian

Why Give Autonomy to Colleges?

In this introductory remark, we raise the question "Why give autonomy to colleges?" We try to answer this question by briefly looking at the history of the affiliating system and some of its serious drawbacks. Colleges existed long before universities were set up and the colleges were autonomous and independent. Naturally differences existed in the curriculum based on the objectives of the different colleges. At that time, Great Britain was establishing a government in India. To bring about some uniformity between the different colleges, especially with the motive of recruiting personnel for the government, to train English speaking "ladies and gentlemen", for the white collared administrative jobs of the then British Raj in India, three universities were set up in the year 1857—those of Calcutta, Bombay and Madras. They were based on the London University model, which had two colleges affiliated to it at that time. India had more colleges in these areas and each of these universities had a number of colleges affiliated to them. Thus, the affiliating system came into being in India.

Just as India adopted the affiliating system, the London University gave it up, because it was found to be detrimental for innovation and progress. But, we clung on to it as though it was the best thing we had received and the affiliating system flourished even after hundred years have passed. Colleges were created in good numbers by religious bodies and philanthropic agencies with their own objectives, but all of them were affiliated to these universities. As universities grew in size, more and more rules and regulations were framed to regulate the ever increasing colleges and common syllabi were set centrally by the universities and the universities conducted one final examination for all colleges affiliated to them.

Rapid expansion of universities and colleges took place after independence in 1947. Up to 1947, there were only 20 universities in India. In the 50 years that followed, there has been a very rapid growth of colleges and universities and therefore each university became very "large" because they had fifty or more colleges affiliated to them. There were a large number of teachers and still larger number of students in these universities and colleges. Universities set the syllabi; conducted annual examinations, evaluated the scripts, collected the marks and announced the results, and finally awarded the degrees. These tasks were so huge, that these became the foremost jobs of any university. Universities set the Boards of Studies, comprising very senior persons, and these persons were far removed from current studies and therefore the syllabi created were not relevant, and often old and repetitive. Conducting examinations for the very large number of affiliated colleges and publishing the examination results became the primary function of a university. If a university published the examination results within two months after the conduct of the last examination, then, it was considered a good university. Therefore, research and extension took a backseat. Even the efforts of good Vice-Chancellors did not bring about any significant change. The situation was succinctly expressed by Dr. D. S. Kothari, who was the chairman of the Universities Grants Commission at that time. He used Newton's II Law of Motion to describe the situation, which says that, Force=Mass times Acceleration (F=MA). And he said that the universities has so massive (i.e. the M is so large) that there is very little acceleration, even when large forces were applied.

Large public exams were conducted either annually or every semester. What the students did in-between exams did not matter, as the final exams were all in all. This kind of system, promoted extensive roaming of students throughout the year, and intensive cramming just before the exam. The questions were stereotyped, long or essay type, inaccurate and with no clear objectivity in testing. Guessing what would come in the exam was a hectic pastime of many students including teachers who wanted good pass percentages for their classes. This resulted in selective studying to somehow get through the examination. Systematic study and learning and hence good education became the casualty of the system. Colleges lost their initiative and were reduced to mere 'teaching shops' (with notable exceptions of course). Private tuitions were the order of the day. Many teachers had a taste of this unaccounted money and soon got addicted to it.

Exam papers were evaluated by a set of different teachers. Here also persons, who may not be teaching that particular subject, were asked to evaluate them. There was a lot of time required in valuing all the papers and hence results were often published after a great deal of delay. In the mean time some students undertook 'educational tours' chasing the papers. There was corruption by 'clerks' at entry point in the records. Anonymity bred carelessness and finally the student suffered. There was no accountability of individual institutions as every college came under the broad umbrella of a university. Least common standards were set, which allowed mediocrity to thrive. Examination-oriented teaching and studying only for examinations were even considered all right. Innovation and creativity were the casualties. Colleges became teaching outlets instead of being centres of learning. For many teaching meant dictating notes and students had to just memorize the same and reproduce it verbatim in the examination. Research was not encouraged. Universities became mostly 'Exam conducting centres', and not a place where new knowledge is created and its boundaries extended. Industries were least bothered about the universities, as there was no exciting research findings, related to what was happening in the country.

Thus teachers came to play a very secondary role in the whole process of teaching, learning and evaluation. The profession was not exciting and many looked for 'side jobs'. Some looked for retirement and quite few even 'retired' while still on their jobs! Thus the affiliating system, instead of being affable, became an afflicting system. Universities were too bureaucratic and too big and massive for any quick change. Dr. D.S. Kothari said that the huge mass must be broken down into smaller pieces in order to get some acceleration with the kind of forces that are available to us, so that we can move ahead. And he proposed that the colleges should be made autonomous, responsible and accountable. Thus, a small beginning was made in 1978 when 12 colleges in Tamil Nadu were made autonomous.

WHAT IS ACADEMIC AUTONOMY?

And, now, we turn to the next question "What is academic autonomy?" and try to answer it briefly. Under academic autonomy, the main functions of the college are the following:

a) The college decides the curriculum.
b) The college sets the syllabi and plans the teaching.
c) The college plans and conducts the evaluation.
d) The college publishes the marks, declares the results, and issues the mark certificates.

Teaching, Learning and Evaluation: this trinity of functions should belong to the teachers and it is given back to the teachers under autonomy. The person, who teaches, also, sets the syllabus, along with other experts. The person, who teaches, also, evaluates. Thus the primary role of teachers is restored under autonomy. This is a very responsible work and cannot be done without commitment, scholarship and zeal from the teacher. The teachers ought to keep learning, in order to keep abreast of new knowledge and to know what is happening elsewhere. It is common parlance to hear people say after their post-graduation, "I have finished my studies". We ought to say "Do not finish, please begin". Institutions ought to become centers of learning, as the teachers begin to learn new material, some get involved in research, some are grasped by new teaching methods and others in meaningful community service, as planned by themselves.

Students learn with the teachers, what has been planned by them. Students want to learn from teachers who know and not from those who simply 'dictate' from a book. The days of 'learned professors' have gone, giving way to 'learning professors.' Students want to drink from clear running water, and not from muddy stagnant pools. He who is not learning is unfit to teach. This means constant updating of knowledge through in-service training and summer and winter workshops and these should become integral parts of colleges and universities. Remember, teachers are the backbone of an institution and if it is not properly maintained, the institution cannot stand erect! The principals along with the heads of departments should be constantly planning conduct of workshops on examinations, objective tests, new learning and teaching methodologies, etc., for the sake of educating the teachers. This kind of updated knowledge base and understanding are essential for any teacher to willingly and fearlessly face any class. Those who are not motivated enough for this teaching job should be encouraged to find other jobs. Student feedback and student evaluation of teachers should become integral parts in the teaching, learning, and evaluation process.

Examination reform and training all teachers in these will go a long way in not only proper evaluation, but in meaningful changes in the way teaching is done. Setting of clear objectives, for each subject and the sub-topics, aims at not just 'filling' students with new knowledge but more usefully as to how to get and understand necessary knowledge, how to apply the knowledge gained to solve real problems, analyze, synthesize and make judgement.

If the objectives are precisely given and explained, then, exams are no nightmares and there are no surprises. There is no such thing as 'out of portion' questions. Good learning calls for continuous study and continuous evaluation, as the study progresses through the semester. The threats of a single final examination with huge portions are never more there. Papers have to be shown back to the students for scrutiny. The results are published immediately. Each test is also a learning point. There will be differences in the way things are done but still innovation and creativity have to be encouraged. The present 'strait-jacket' system of fields of study, must give way to a 'choice based credit system' in which a student may choose what he/she wants to study or change course of study midway. There are students who are slow learners and may take more time to complete their course of study. Greater flexibility is the need of the hour and it can be done only by giving autonomy to institutions. There will be greater participation by all concerned that of the administration, the teachers and the students. People sometimes say that doing all that is described above will be more work for every teacher. It is not more work, but more responsible work. Colleges have to be prepared to meet the challenge of establishing autonomous colleges, and therefore workshops on college autonomy must be conducted to prepare each college to take up this challenging task and run it well.

The first step of the government is to make appropriate changes in the Universities Acts to include creation of autonomous colleges and pass it in the legislative assembly.

Let colleges bé made autonomous.

Where is the knowledge that is lost in information,

where is the wisdom that is lost in knowledge,

where is the life that is lost in living,

twenty cycles of living has brought us further from God and closer to the dust.

10

Teaching, Research and Extension in Autonomous Colleges

— S. John Britto S. J.

Introduction

Autonomous colleges are said to be pioneering, innovative, pace setting and ensuring quality improvement. Teaching, research and extension are the most valued aspects in fulfilling the college/ university's mission and purpose. The contribution which an autonomous college can make in the above domains is significant. Research and teaching are synergistically to advance knowledge in a discipline, which in turn influences the nature of teaching process. In an autonomous college, the academic strength and quality lay on relevant curricular design and appropriate pedagogical patterns.

The Global Era

The global era has transformed education as web-based, involving the use of internet in learning and research, international visits, immersion programmes, international exchange programmes, international partnership in teaching and learning of the group, class and individual levels, interactions and sharing through video conferencing across countries, communities, institutions and individuals.

Curricular and Pedagogic Reforms

Curricular reforms in India often concentrate on innovation and vocationalisation. New subjects to match recent technological development and incorporation of the vocational stream are major features. There is urgent need to reorganize curriculum to make our youth confident enough to speak, write, think and perform. Curricula must be made essentially functional. We need to have subjects and syllabi enabling in the art of speaking and writing, to sharpen the mind to think independently and to develop a socio-ethical sensibility. Curricular reform should tie up with curricular restructuring, so that all the subjects included in the curriculum have a scale of academic value integrated into the total goal of the programme.

The Role of Teachers in Curricular Design

The responsibility of the teachers in autonomous college includes designing and implementing new academic programmes and improving existing ones continually both in content and structure so as to make them up to date and relevant to the diverse and changing needs of the society and the individuals. This involves improving quality and effectiveness through evolving better curricular strategies, methods of instruction and of evaluation. It is essential that all participate in all aspects of the total education process.

Staff members need to have a clear awareness of the goals and objectives as well as the possibilities and potentials of autonomy. Autonomous working requires a willingness and keenness to innovate and experiment. Subject matter competence should be matched by an allround teaching ability, curriculum framing, curriculum renewal and teaching and evaluation methods.

In the light of growth in knowledge and number of specialties and new emphasis in the subject content, the teachers should be able to modify and update the curricula. The curriculum should be so organized to provide flexibility with regard to student aptitudes and interests. Curricular strategies should be so devised to stress self learning, problem solving and trans-disciplinary perceptions among the students. Analytical and practical skills should be imparted by means of project work, field training, community service, role play, case analysis and such other diverse teaching and learning methodologies.

The teachers should inculcate in the students an attitude of mind which regards the critical assessments of facts and values as more important than dogmas; a grasp of underlying principles more valuable than accumulation of information and acquision of skills and techniques. The students should be encouraged to be receptive to new ideas, eager to explore and cope with it and fortify their ability to think for themselves. Close linkages with probable employers such as banks, industrial houses, commercial establishments and civil service organisations should be established and they should be involved in curriculum development of relevant courses and solicited to provide practical training and placement.

The teachers of autonomous colleges should be conversant with the latest model of student centered curriculum designing process. This process includes the following: initial need analysis, goal and objective setting, selecting/grading content, ongoing needs analysis grouping learners, devising learning activities, instructing learners, monitoring/assessing progress and course evaluation

A climate which demands accountability and relevance in educational programmes requires 'needs analysis' as the initial step. Need analysis serves three main purposes; it provides a means of obtaining wider input into the content, design and implementation of a programme; it can be used in developing goals, objectives and content; and it can provide data for reviewing and evaluation of an existent programme. The more teachers and students are involved in developing the curriculum, the more successful it is likely to be. One important outcome of involving learners in the ongoing curriculum development is that they will develop skill in 'learning how to learn'.

Teaching

It is unfortunate that higher education in India has thus far been perceived as a process of pumping knowledge from full vessels (our ivory-tower scholars) into empty vessels (our learners). Firstly, knowledge is not just out there encapsulated in books and manuals, waiting for experts to uncover it and push it down the throat of learners. It is not a product — total information gathered or received or uncovered — but a process, a process of growth, of maturation triggered by a network of interactions between a particular, biologically given, complex system — the human mind—and the physical and socio-cultural world. Secondly, teaching should not be viewed as a teacher-controlled unidirectional activity; it is a multi-directional, interactional activities. Thirdly, the learners are never passive recipients of 'ready-to-use' packages of 'information'. They are alive, active participants in teaching-learning activities. The teacher must be a realist that he has more than one role to play. He has to play the role of a facilitator, of a leader of a cooperative enterprise in which development occurs through reciprocal give and take, the teacher 'giving' but not shying away from 'receiving'.

Teaching–Learning Techniques

Every teacher has to be most resourceful in ensuring the optimum implementation of teaching-learning. With fast development in modern techniques and use of electronic and technological devices in teaching–learning process, the teacher is the pivot of everything, however advanced infrastructural aids be. The teacher gauges the entry level behaviour, efficiency and need of each stakeholder and plans the methodology of teaching accordingly. In the present scenario, the target group remaining heterogeneous invariably, the teacher plans her teaching in such a way that the late bloomers are not at a disadvantage.

Gone are the days when the academic mentors present lectures in class room; there is a paradigmal shift from teacher–centred activity to learner–centred tasks, from lecture mode to interaction mode. The more participatory the learners are, more learning with correlated soft skills are acquired. The teachers have to break the hard shell of rigidity and tradition, accept and implement what is most suited and needed for the hour. Hence teaching is not a mechanical oft–repeated activity; every teacher has to make each class innovative and unique.

Technology-Mediated Learning

The phrase 'technology–mediated learning' represent a broad range of activities from the use of audio-graphic conferencing to three-dimensional simulated worlds. This definition includes those instances where computers are used to enhance face-to-face learning or to deliver a course completely on line—and everything in between. The delivery of TML through consortia is identified as a recent innovation in distance education.

Web-Supported Collaboration in Higher Education

The integration of web technology into higher education instruction is receiving growing attention within the university community. According to the partners' (students, teachers) needs and goals while performing learning assignments, interactions may fulfil varied functions, e.g. cooperations, collaboration, competition, distribution (of knowledge), or sharing (of knowledge resources).

ICTS in Higher Education

The development and implementation of information and communication technology (ICT) forces today's universities and colleges to respond to societal trends that point to a transformation of our society into a so-called 'Knowledge Economy'.

Globalisation and ICT applications place new demands on higher education establishments and hold important implications for their teaching and research functions, especially in the light of growing importance placed upon lifelong learning and upon more flexible forms of higher education delivery.

Innovative Educational Approaches

There is more emphasis today on critical thinking, creativity, parallel thinking and lateral thinking. Generally there is very little scope in higher education for lateral thinking. It is necessary to give students the independence to chart their own study schedules, perhaps after one year of lecture classes. This would in many ways help the overall development of student. Such a paradigm shift clearly entails drastic changes in the institutional make-up. Facilities conducive to self-learning will have to be made available. Well-stocked libraries and other spaces for students to hang out, discuss and learn are absolute necessities. At the same time, alternative programmes such as thematic lectures, technical festivals, seminars and symposia will have to be promoted. Research activities can be conducted in parallel, as students can participate by assisting during their off hours.

Besides, co-curricular activities that are so essential for all round development can be encouraged. Autonomous colleges can experiment in promotion of learning of exploring, which is often uncared for.

Research, Consultancy and Extension

One of the weakest areas in majority of the affiliated colleges in India is research and consultancy. There may not be many teachers qualified and interested in research for self-improvement or for guiding students and taking up research projects. Research and consultancy are not mandatory like teaching and evaluation. Being voluntary, a lot of motivation is needed to usher in a research and consultancy culture particularly in an undergraduate college. The management can play a pivotal role here either by making it a condition of employment in the institution or by providing incentives. It can seek recognition for senior teachers and major departments as research guide or research centre. The management could provide financial support and the additional infrastructure facilities and equipments needed for research and consultancy. It can also encourage teachers to submit proposals for research project grants from government, semi-government, NGOs, national and international organizations, industry, etc.

The management may appoint experienced and reputed teachers and researchers including those who have retired from universities, research establishments or industry as adjunct professor under the UGC scheme for taking up research and consultancy in areas where the college has substantial strength. They can also be requested to guide students for doctoral and post-doctoral research.

Forward and backward linkages could be established for augmenting for research and mobilizing fund. Joint patenting may be another way of promoting research and consultancy. Professionally qualified and experienced teachers could be encouraged to take up consultancy in the areas of their specialization. The management can make norms for sharing the revenue earned from research and consultancy between institution and the individuals for nurturing healthy relationship. Since there is hardly any fund available from government, it is worthwhile for the management to motivate the faculty and students with funding and participating in social and community extension activities.

The affiliating system has fragmented research and teaching under the assumption that they are mutually exclusive. What is more, ideal research *per se* has been pedestalised as an ivory-tower monopoly and wrongly accorded a status above that of teaching. The NAAC for example is quick to discern the integral connection between research and teaching on the one hand, and between research and extension as well as consultancy on the other. Teaching, extension and consultancy by themselves can be the launching pads of research, as it has been proved the world over in good universities, where research-industry nexus, research-service integration and research education technology inter-dependence are increasingly realized. This synergy is also justified by needs of development in developing countries.

The first and foremost criterion for the development of the best practices in research is the appropriate recruitment of the most qualified faculty. A brilliant teacher researcher alone can provide the best guided tours to the most modern knowledge. Quality of original research has a direct relation with the number and variety of available inter-disciplinary areas of pursuit. Teamwork is now required more and more to bring out real breakthroughs in research especially on the cutting edge. Although nobody can deny that the most important instrument of research is the human brain itself, output of the best of research also depends on the availability of modern infrastructure. An excellent library having the best of built-in practices for an accelerated flow of modern information and knowledge forms the strongest base for promotion of the research culture.

For seeding, sustaining, monitoring and promoting excellent levels of research, development of able, capable and sensitive administration is also extremely important. Encouragement and motivation of good research is possible by suitable incentives, awards, rewards and public recognition by the administration. Provision of seed money for research, especially for the younger teachers, puts them on the research-highways before it is too late. Administrative support and necessary expertise may also be required by young teachers while submitting good projects to different funding agencies. The best of publications, holding the highest impact factors / citation indices, need also be rewarded suitably.

Availability of faculty improvement programmes and provision for study leave or sabbatical leave are very valuable. Participation and organization of national and international seminars / workshops also rejuvenate the faculty with fresh inputs of global knowledge. Interactions with industries provide new avenues for applied research, so essential for every country. Securing MoU with other excellent institutions in India and abroad and development of twinning programmes brings in a quantum change in the ethos, tone and tenor for research.

Establishment of a cell for quality control of research, including periodic peer-reviews, can form a solid criterion as a regular and long-term best practice for excellent research.

Concept of Extension in University Education

Empowerment of weaker sections of society through extension activities is an important concern of several universities in India. The significance of the varied empowerment programmes have been highlighted in several policy documents of the University Grants Commission especially after the formulation of Policy Framework of Higher Education (1977) which recognized extension as the third dimension of higher education in addition to teaching and research. Although the role of university extension has been widely accepted, the operational strategies all along have not been well defined. Accordingly, to the ninth Plan UGC Guidelines was added Adult Continuing Education, Extension as the 'third dimension' of higher education. It is an umbrella term which includes adult education, continuing education, population education and community education – all of which aims at promoting a meaningful and sustained rapport between the universities or colleges and community. While on the one hand, extension programmes seek to transfer the resources, knowledge and wisdom of the universities and colleges for the benefit of community, the university or college also gains form the insights and interactions with the community and the socio-cultural realities. As a two way process, extension benefits both academics and community. The main purpose of university extension through adult education, population education, continuing education is the empowerment of weaker sections of society.

The objectives of Extension Programme as laid down by UGC are as follows:

a) To enable the universities to establish the necessary linkage with the community with a view to fostering social change through meaningful relationship and interactions, which are mutually beneficial by offering need based and relevant educational programmes that may ultimately facilitate self-reliance.

b) To provide opportunities for disseminating knowledge in all walks of life in different segments of population and to enable individuals and groups.

c) To encourage faculty and student participation in Extension Research and Action-Research in selected areas in relation to major problems of development in co-operation with government.

Although the UGC Guidelines have given equal weightage to teaching, research and extension, in terms of funding support, there is considerable disparity. One of the reasons for the ineffectiveness of extension programme may be traced to the lack of professional expertise in the area of extension among the existing staff members of the Departments of Adult Education and teachers in affiliated colleges.

It has been observed that in spite of UGC funding for adult, continuing education and extension during the last two decades, there are not many scholarly publications on extension work carried out for the empowerment of weaker sections by the Departments of Adult Education.

There is hardly any information on the impact of the extension programmes on the local community. The reports on extension work are generally silent on the extent to which the empowerment programmes have succeeded in improving the quality of life of weaker sections or raising their income.

The Key Role of Autonomous Colleges

Social reconstruction through HE is mandatory task for colleges and specially autonomous colleges and because of the academic freedom enjoined on them, they cannot afford to be indifferent to social dimension in their curriculum and course design. It is in this spirit that NAAC in its evaluative module for autonomous colleges has attached significant importance to extension dimension. It is worth recalling at this juncture the memorable words of our former President Dr. A.P.J. Abdul Kalam: "Ignited minds of the youth are the greatest resource compared to any resource on the earth, under the earth and above the earth, when ignited minds work and perform with indomitable spirit, a prosperous, happy and safe India is assured". He formulated a plan which has much bearing on HE. The plan is Providing Urban amenities in Rural Areas (PURA). This plan of action envisages enhancement of prosperity and development in rural neighbourhood by implementing four connectivities: Physical connectivity (providing road, electricity, health care), Electronic connectivity (Communication network); Knowledge connectivity (institutes of knowledge); Economic connectivity (linkage between farmer societies). This approach implies that the type of education we impart as autonomous colleges should include the following: practical component, exposure to field work and entrepreneurship training.

The upliftment of the socio-economically weaker section is the need of the hour and in this context, for the HE sector it is through the use of technology. This becomes all the more essential and needs to be emphasized and highlighted. To quote Dr. M.S. Swaminathan, "Technology helps to achieve a paradigm shift from unskilled work and thereby move larger numbers of the rural poor from the primary to the secondary and tertiary sectors of economic activity" (*The Hindu*, July 9, 2005). Technology is a powerful tool to change the mindset of individuals as well as the community. In this context, the purpose of the university can be formulated as: (i) creation of knowledge, (ii) dissemination of knowledge and (iii) transfer of knowledge and skill to society for its empowerment.

The third dimension of universities' activities, namely, extension that presently includes adult and continuing education is an important element, which needs to be further widened by reorienting it as link between business and society. The scope of extension education needs to be widened by reorienting it as a link between business and society. Indeed in the changed economic environment, outreach activities in lifelong education in aspects related to skills, health, environment, physical fitness, values, good citizenship, and other factors that leads to a good life, gain special importance. In addition, supporting disadvantaged groups (SC / ST, minority, women, physically handicapped) is a task in itself.

Conclusion

The Government of India has announced the national goal to become a developed nation by the year 2020. India aspires to be free from poverty, and to sit in line with G-8 nations. Our former President, Dr. A.P.J. Abdul Kalam wrote, "A developed India by 2020, or even earlier, is not a dream. It need not even be a mere vision in the mind of many Indians. It is a mission we can all take up". By 2020, the people of India will be more numerous, better educated, healthier and more prosperous than at any time in our long history. Goldman and Sachs' predictions for 2050 say that India, along with China and USA, will be the three top economies of the world. Going further, one can confidently predict that if India plays its cards right, by 2020, it can become the number one "knowledge production" centre of the world. Such is the prowess of Indian science and technology. It is in this direction that autonomous colleges have to redesign their academic strategies.

11

Autonomous Colleges in India — A Step Towards Quality Assurance

— B. S. Ponmudiraj

Introduction

The concept of autonomous colleges was crystallized on the recommendations of the Education Commission of 1964-66 with a view to providing academic freedom for potential colleges, specially in designing their curricula, evolving new methods of teaching, research and learning, framing own rules for admission, prescribe own courses of study and conduct of examinations. The intention was to provide greater opportunities to the teachers to play crucial role in the promotion and development of an intellectual climate, which is conducive to the pursuit of schoiarship and excellence.

In spite of the best efforts made so far and the incentives being given, the number of autonomous colleges is still very less as compared to total number of colleges in India. In this context, the University Grants Commission (UGC) has decided to play a proactive role in identifying well reputed colleges, which could be considered for granting autonomous status which would provide a greater academic autonomy in the country paving the way for better standard and more positive innovations in higher education. It is proposed to increase the number of autonomous colleges to spread the culture of autonomy, and the target is to make 10 per cent of eligible colleges autonomous by the end of the Eleventh Plan (i.e., 31 March 2012).

As per the procedure, interested colleges should send the proposal in the prescribed format duly recommended by the affiliating university along with 'No Objection', as well as concurrence from respective state government for grant of conferment of autonomous status by the UGC. The question here is whether there is provision in the parent Universities Act, statutes and ordinances; if not what measures have been taken by these universities for their amendment? Secondly the motivation and encouragement by the State Governments towards quality higher education by paving way for autonomy to reputed colleges in their States.

Retrospect and Prospect

George Haddad, a former president of the Sorbonne said, "There is no absolute model for higher education." Worldwide, postsecondary enrolment grew from 13 million in 1960 to 82 million in 1995. The figure is expected to increase to 200 million by 2025. Government financing of higher education has not kept pace with that growth.

In the present status of over 330 universities of different nature, viz., central universities, state universities, institutes of national importance (IITs, IIMs, IIIT, including the 109 universities (deemed to be universities) under section 3 of the UGC Act, the Indian higher education system is one of the largest and highly complex in nature. Amidst this the Indian higher education sector has unitary universities and affiliating universities. The country also has central open universities and state open universities, in addition to the universities offering programmes through Open and Distance Learning (ODL) mode.

There are 18064 affiliated colleges as on 31 March 2006 and around 330 universities across the country. In 2004-2005, an estimated of 104.81 lakhs students were enrolled in the institutions of higher education and the faculty strength was 4.71 lakhs. As per the National Knowledge Commission (NKC) report, the country's relevant age group attending higher learning institutions is approximately 7 per cent and to attain 15 per cent by 2015 the country may require 1,000 universities. In other words, country needs double the number of universities and colleges to attain 15 per cent of our young generation in the relevant age group. And there are 5661 colleges under section 2(f) & 12(B) and 691 colleges only under section 2(f) and not included under section 12(B) of the UGC Act, 1956 as on 31 March 2007 bringing the total number of UGC recognized colleges to 6352. Now there is a question of equity, accessibility and availability of higher education to all the strata of society. The country needs more relevant and qualitatively superior higher education institutions to become a developed nation. Autonomy is given by the UGC only to the colleges, which are recognized under the section 2(f), and 12(B) of the UGC Act. There are priority areas for the country, especially poverty eradication, health, basic amenities, primary education, employment, etc., which need immediate attention.

The quality of higher education is a concern due to the lack of adequate number of teaching staff and, non-teaching staff in colleges and universities. The following table gives the number and distribution of teaching staff-by-designation-in university departments and university colleges[2] and the number and distribution of teaching staff by designation in affiliated colleges[2] for the year 2005-2006.

Table 1. Cadre-wise Number of Teaching Staff

Teaching Staff by Designation in	Professors[1]	Readers/ Lecturer Selection Grade	Senior Lecturers	Lecturers	Tutor/ Demonstrators	Total
University Departments and University Colleges	16,591 (21.05)	24,986 (31.70)	12,059 (15.30)	23,260 (29.51)	1,923 (2.44)	78,819 (100.00)
Affiliated Colleges	23,951 (5.8)	100,520 (24.6)	61,232 (14.9)	210,202 (51.4)	13,279 (3.2)	409,184 (100.00)

[1] Includes principals and senior teachers who are equivalent to professors

Note: a) Figures in parenthesis indicate the percentage of the cadres to the total staff.

b) Part-time teachers / physical training instructors are included in lecturers.

The number of autonomous colleges in India as on 4 October 2006 is 234 covering 14 States (Andhra Pradesh, Chhattisgarh, Gujarat, Himachal Pradesh, Jharkhand, Karnataka, Madhya Pradesh,

Maharashtra, Nagaland, Orissa, Tamil Nadu, Pondicherry, Uttar Pradesh and West Bengal) and 48 affiliating universities. The success behind the autonomous colleges in India is quality consciousness in all their endeavours. Academics very rarely try to fully understand the concept of autonomy. Innovations in curriculum and new experiments can be done only in autonomous colleges. Despite the restrictions of the concerned state government and limitations of the parent university, these autonomous colleges have excelled over a period of time and also stood the test of time.

The experience of autonomous colleges especially in the states of Andhra Pradesh and Tamil Nadu over 30 years has proved that autonomy has a lot of scope and potential for revamping our higher education system, particularly in the area of curriculum, teaching-learning processes, and examinations system.

Since the teachers are not given sufficient role in evaluation in the affiliating system, the motivation of teachers to innovate in their teaching pedagogy is very low. Hence, it is absolutely necessary that the teacher be given the responsibility of teaching as well as evaluating. If adequate measures are taken to train teachers in the pedagogy of teaching and objective evaluation, our educational system will prove far more successful than it does now. Use of question banks and adopting latest technology in testing would make evaluation more objective and reliable and it is hoped that at least autonomous colleges would lead other institutions in such innovations.

Autonomous colleges are also affiliated to the parent university as a college and even for individual programmes of study for award of degrees. Freedom is given to the autonomous colleges to experiment and to award their own degrees under the banner of the parent university with their own name and emblem. The question here is about the recognition of the college and its programme of study within the country and abroad. Earlier the UGC has been trying to float the concept of 'Empowered Institutions'. In fact, all Higher Education Institutions (HEIs) may be allowed to award their own degrees, diplomas, certificates with checks and balances from the state government, statutory bodies and the parent university. Then, comes the question of recognition, mutual recognition, reputation, equivalence, etc. Here quality assurance plays a vital role.

Quality Assurance

The NAAC, an autonomous institution of the UGC, with its prime agenda to assess and accredit institutions of higher learning in India, has so far assessed 140 universities and 3,492 colleges as on 31 March 2007 bringing the total to 3,632. NAAC has accredited around 100 autonomous colleges across India including re-assessment and re-accreditation. The quality consciousness of HEIs is high among the autonomous colleges as may be revealed by the establishment of Internal Quality Assurance Cells (IQACs) in these colleges and its effective functioning – by regularly sending their Annual Quality Assurance Reports (AQARs) as per the NAAC guidelines. This act by these institutions clearly can be seen as one step ahead of other institutions regarding quality sustenance and quality enhancement activities.

NAAC has been promoting three major concepts for quality sustenance and quality enhancement systems in the accredited institutions as post accreditation initiatives in the recent years:

i) Student Participation in Quality Assurance (SPQA).
ii) Best Practices for Quality Improvement (BPQI).
iii) Internal Quality Assurance Cell (IQAC).

Regarding IQAC, NAAC has been insisting right from its existence that all universities and colleges may establish a system/cell/mechanism/structure that can take care of the Internal Quality Assurance (IQA) of the respective institutions. NAAC has declared the Year 2006 as 'Student Participation in Quality Assurance' and the Year 2007 as 'Promotion of Internal Quality Assurance Cell' and the Dissemination of Best Practices in the HEIs has been done through five major publications of NAAC, viz.,

i) *Best Practices Series: Internal Quality Assurance Cell Activities*
ii) *Best Practices Series: Community Engagement – Case Presentations*
iii) *Best Practices Series: Library and Information Services – Case Presentations*
iv) *Best Practices Series: Student Feedback and Participation – Case Presentations*

v) *Best Practices Series: Evaluation of Students - Case Presentations*

By and large autonomous colleges are convinced that these quality initiatives are a great success in their endeavours. Though most of these quality initiatives are regularly and systematically practised in most of the institutions of good reputation, it is in the autonomous colleges that these practices more effectively adhered to.

Curriculum

Introduction of new and innovative courses and changes in the existing courses is easy and quick in the autonomous mode compared to the affiliating mode in which it is very difficult and time consuming. Another advantage is that a variety of diverse courses that could be offered to suit local needs and context, whereas there is uniformity and stereotyping for all the affiliated colleges belonging to the parent university immaterial of the locale. The feedback mechanism on the curriculum by the students, teaching staff, employers and alumni is effectively utilized by the respective Boards of Studies of the autonomous colleges to redesign and do mid-course correction. The balance of the curriculum with theory and practical component in each paper and aligning with the entire programme for application is meticulously done in autonomous colleges. The testing procedures also takes into account various components of the curriculum, viz., subject knowledge, skills, application of knowledge, theory, practicals, core competencies, analysis, synthesis, etc.

Teaching-Learning

The efficiency of the teaching-learning process largely depends upon the active involvement of the teacher in the entire process. Motivation and the performance level is much higher for the whole autonomous college and the teaching staff in particular. This is rarely seen in the affiliated colleges pattern. Attending seminars, workshops, paper presentation, etc have always been on the increase in autonomous institutions since there is provision for them under autonomy. There is always a scope for the course teacher to assess the students' performance by way of teaching, setting the question paper, invigilation and evaluating the answer scripts including the external examinations.

Differential weightages have been assigned to the Continuous Internal Assessment (CIA) examinations, which is formative, and term end (semester, trimester, annual, etc.) examinations, which is summative. The CIA includes test, quiz, assignments, seminars, field study report, mini projects, term papers, attendance in class, religious studies, communication skills, sports activities, cultural activities (music, dance, drama, theatre), etc. This type of testing pattern helps the qualitative assessment of the students' performance. In the formative evaluation, the teacher designs appropriate testing procedures, e.g., number of tests, different type of tests, viz., announced tests, unannounced tests, snap tests, online testing, objective type, essay or subjective type of questions in testing, etc.

More importantly, the transparency in the assessment procedures of the autonomous colleges reflects the nighest form of quality endeavour. Test papers are corrected and returned within a specific period of time. The answer scripts of individual students, including the marks obtained in oral tests are discussed by the class teachers in the class. The scheme of valuation and answers provided by each student for all the questions are elaborately reviewed in the class on a one-to-one basis. There is always a provision for students to appeal, first to the course teacher, while returning the test notebooks, assignments, etc., after perusal. In case the student is not satisfied, he / she can appeal to the head of the department (HOD) regarding the status of the grades/marks/credits obtained. At the third stage, there is a Grievance Redressal Committee (GRC) at the institution level by the controller of examinations, which looks into the matter. This three-tier approach gives a lot of transparency and accountability on the part of the teacher as well as the taught and brings in high level of quality in the functioning of the autonomous colleges in India.

Students are normally encouraged and not penalised for appealing for marks if they feel they deserve more. Usually the students are asked to sign and return the test note books if they accept the evaluation. There is a place for student's signature in the statement of marks as well as in the consolidated/cumulative mark statement. Most of the college records (answer scripts, assignments, mini reports, etc.) are maintained and preserved only for a specified period of time – maybe three to seven years.

Evaluation Systems

Some of the departments of the autonomous colleges have fully internal examinations including the term end examinations. Most of the autonomous colleges have developed setting up a highly exhaustive question bank for each course or a paper. The course teacher teaches, sets the question paper and the same teacher evaluates the answer scripts perhaps combined with one more teacher of the same department. Autonomous colleges follow different evaluation methods. The following table tries to give a consolidated form:

Table 2. Different Models of Evaluation System

Models	Question Paper Setting	Moderation of Question Paper	Answer Scripts Valuation	Moderation of Results
I	Internal examiners	At the college level	Internal examiners	At the college level
II	Internal examiners	At the college level	Internal and external examiners	At the college level
III	Internal examiners	At the college level	Internal examiners	At the college level
IV	Internal examiners	At the college level	Internal examiners	At the college level
V	Internal examiners	At the college level	Internal and external examiners	At the college level
VI	Internal examiners	At the college level	External examiners	At the college level

Two well-known models are model I and model II. Model II and model V involve basically double evaluation of the answer scripts with an allowance for a specified marginal difference and they also have the provision for a third evaluation with an average of the top two scores. In most of the autonomous colleges, the highest marks given by the internal/external examiners or average of the marks given by the internal and external examiners are taken into consideration.

Models III, V and VI are rarely practised among the autonomous colleges in India. This clearly gives the message that there is transparency and accountability in the autonomous colleges and that they are quality conscious in their examination system. Such a system in which the teacher who designs the curriculum does the evaluation also, gives more motivation and encouragement for the teacher to be up-to-date in his/ her subject syllabi of teaching. It is indeed a challenge to teach in an autonomous college.

The success of the autonomous colleges in India is the declaration of the results announced within the stipulated time, usually between 10 days and 30 days from the date of the last examination. Most of the autonomous colleges issues photocopy of the valued answer scripts to the students. This practice has helped autonomous colleges to build their image and it has called for a lot of transparency and accountability among the teacher, taught and the institution.

Leadership and Governance

Autonomous colleges reflect quality in all the aspects of higher education. An autonomous college functions like a mini university in all respects - the organization structure include Governing Council, Executive Committee, Finance Committee, Planning Board, Academic Council, Boards of Studies, Office of the Controller of Examinations(CoE), etc. The effective and efficient functioning of the institution in its totality reflects quality of the higher education institution. The checks and balances for the organization structure and the officers / people of the college—principal and secretary, deans / directors, vice-principals, CoE, etc., take care of the quality.

Conclusion

The futuristic concerns of global education has seen the light of day by the autonomous colleges in India. The autonomous colleges provide human resource not only for government jobs but also for national and international industries and other services. The hue and cry for foreign degrees for affordable Indian students is mainly due to want of good curriculum, high standards, type of skills taught, needs of the market, quality assurance, etc. All these autonomous colleges in India were able to achieve to a good extent. Therefore, it helps the talented younger generation to get retained in our country. The assessment report and the grade of the institutions assessed and accredited by NAAC is available in NAAC website. This helps foreign universities and colleges to have twinning arrangements and collaborations for teaching and research. Hope by the end of the XI plan UGC may be able to achieve the ten percent of the eligible colleges to be autonomous in nature, thus making a step forward towards more quality higher educational institutions in India.

12

College Autonomy — A Privilege to Practise

—Annamma Philip and Ordetta Mendoza

The concept of college autonomy was mooted by the education ministry over four decades ago and came into effect in about 50 colleges from 1978. Many colleges later opted for autonomous status in the nineteen eighties and the succeeding years. Today, there are only about 300 autonomous colleges even after 30 years of this concept entering the realms of higher education.

There are several factors that need to be taken into consideration when opting for autonomous status. The pros and cons of autonomy has been discussed and elucidated by stalwarts in the field of higher education.

Autonomy as envisaged by the Education Commission was: "Where there is an outstanding college (or a small cluster of very good colleges) within a large university, which has shown the capacity to improve itself markedly, consideration should be given to granting it an autonomous status. This would involve the power to frame its own rules of admissions, to prescribe its courses of study, to conduct examinations and so on. The parent university's role will be one of general supervision and the actual conferment of the degree. The privilege cannot be conferred once and for all – it will have to be continually earned and deserved and it should be open to the university, after careful scrutiny of the position to revoke the autonomous status, if the college begins to deteriorate in its standards".

The foregoing criterion is clear in its objective of giving autonomy to a college at various levels. But several governments being non-committal towards higher education have neither given institutions the financial freedom nor the liberty to become institutions of excellence.

The other salient features like 'power to frame its own rules of admissions and to prescribe its course of studies', have been watered down due to lack of political will.

Reservations and merit play a major role in determining who is admitted into an institution of higher learning. While facilitating access to higher education to the poor and the marginalized should remain the mission of higher education institutions, the institutions need not dilute standards in the name of making the 'degree available to all with no accountability'. This is happening across the country and students seem to make hay while the sun shines!

The criterion of 'prescribe its course of studies' in an autonomous college is limited to introducing new and relevant courses within a particular degree programme. An autonomous institution cannot begin a new Bachelors or Masters level programme without the concurrence of the parent university because the university confers the degree. Also, the college has to follow a cumbersome procedure from start to finish when its needs to begin a degree programme with the involvement of a financial burden.

Self-financing courses especially in newer areas of study are hardly given any encouragement and support from the UGC and the state government. The only plus point in such cases is that the university confers the degree.

The only area where autonomy is evidenced is the academic freedom expressed through curriculum revision, updated syllabi and examination reforms that have been carried out every few years.

While it is not the aim of this paper to point out the flaws in the implementation of a system that would have revolutionized the face of higher education in the country had it been implemented in the spirit in which it was perceived, I would like to highlight the role of the teacher, especially in an autonomous institution around whom all learning revolves. Henry Brookes Adam once said: "A teacher affects eternity, he does not know where his influence begins or stops". In an autonomous college a teacher is the one who determines the whole teaching, learning and testing process.

Autonomy granted to a college gives teachers the limitless freedom to be innovative in designing a degree programme within the framework set out by the university. The quality of students is also ensured through introduction of innovative programmes.

A challenging curriculum which suits student needs, hones the intellect and caters to meeting the demands of market forces can be offered in an autonomous college. Faculty members enjoy this privilege to develop or modify the curriculum by integrating various aspects for the all-round development of the student. Co-curricular and extra-curricular courses can become a requirement for the degree programme. Vocationalisation of education enables students to gain hands-on experience and acquire valuable skills. Internships can be included as a major component of such courses. This exposes the students to the realities of the corporate world and gives them a competitive edge once they themselves enter the job market. It also develops in them entrepreneurial skills thus becoming job makers and not job seekers.

Content development is of prime importance since the relevance of a course is a direct consequence of its content. Autonomy enables the teacher to draw up syllabi depending on the scope of application of the subject and emerging trends. It also helps the teacher gauge the learner's needs and update the syllabi accordingly from time to time. Thus academic freedom can be exploited to a great extent and courses made more learner-centred / need-based.

Today, technology-based teaching can be used extensively if designed and implemented professionally. Teachers can use various technology-based techniques to deliver course material sometimes more effectively than using a blackboard. Financial assistance granted for the implementation of autonomy ensures that classroom teaching can be made more vibrant and interesting. Autonomous colleges can make use of distance education in the near future to deliver at least a part of a course or even offer courses online during the summer vacation with the objective of maximizing the learner's potential. Thus faculty members need to become familiar and technology 'savvy' with advanced teaching aids and methods that would substantially enhance the quality of education.

Examinations reform is another area where teachers can be creative and ensure that there is free and fair assessment of their students. In the affiliating system, someone develops the courseware, another teaches it and a third assesses the student's knowledge level of that particular subject. Very often students feel that they are denied the actual marks they ought to have obtained because of the vagaries of the system including evaluation methods.

All of these can be removed to a large extent in an autonomous institution. Once again, technology based assessment and evaluation can be adopted to make the teaching-learning -testing process challenging and fulfilling for the student. The methods that can be adopted range from online submission of assignments and take home tests to computer-based testing and evaluation. These methods can be used for both continuous assessment tests as well as the end-of-semester or end-of-year examinations. The benefits of using technology based testing methods (if the programme is well developed) are that it ensures objectivity, enhanced confidentiality and a quick return of the marks. Students may be able to view their marks at the end of the examination itself!

Another aspect is a question bank, which will have to be developed with the levels of difficulty defined. Students can choose a particular level of difficulty that can be indicated on the marks statement reflecting the students' intellectual capability.

Several other innovations are possible for a teacher whose ultimate aim is to make teaching–learning–testing an enjoyable experience for both the teacher and the taught.

Since the number of students in an autonomous institution is far below the number in an affiliating university, it is very easy for the college to publish its results quickly thus enabling students to seek jobs or admission into other institutions on time.

The exercise of autonomy in its present form is directed towards the teacher and hence it is imperative that persons hired for this job are willing to invest time and reap the benefits of a satisfying career as a teacher whose influence on students knows no bounds. Autonomy is mainly for the teacher and gives teachers the powers to assess not just the students and their knowledge level but review their own professionalism and integrity. Feedback from students and other stakeholders allows a teacher to develop capabilities and competencies for the profession of teaching. Participation in professional development programmes at the national and international level adds vitality to the foresight and vision of a teacher.

Financial assistance from the UGC is a boon to the teacher since a major portion of the grant pertains to developing infrastructure for the teaching-learning–testing process including development of the library resources, question banks, faculty training programmes, and examination reforms including computerizing evaluation.

Thus autonomy can become a useful tool through which the higher education system in our country can be made more relevant with such institutions actually becoming centres of higher learning.

13

College Autonomy—Gains and Constraints

— Nirmala Jeyaraj

India's vision is to become a super power and a developed nation by 2020 through a knowledge-based economy, producing high quality professionals who would create, share, use and manage knowledge effectively. Institutions of higher learning have a major role to play in nurturing and producing such competent professionals. To make this possible, our educational system has to be thoroughly revamped. It is imperative that the afflicting, affiliating system be replaced with 'academic autonomy' in colleges across the country. Dr. M.A. Thangaraj rightly stated: "Autonomy is the one beacon light that can steer the ship of higher education through shoals and rocks of stagnation, irrelevance and mediocrity".

Although college autonomy was introduced in our higher education system some 30 years ago, it has not taken off well due to many impediments. Out of more than 16,000 colleges, it is estimated, only 314 colleges have been conferred the status of autonomy until this day, in spite of UGC and NAAC promoting and encouraging colleges to become autonomous. Unfortunately, a few state governments have resisted totally until this day, so also many teachers' union and the teachers themselves, fearing increased workload. Tamil Nadu tops the list of states having the highest number (116) of autonomous colleges. Recently, there has been renewed interest in college autonomy particularly driven by the global competition and demand for quality and relevance.

Lady Doak College has the privilege of being one among the first nine colleges which became autonomous in the year 1978. Having been a student and a teacher prior to autonomy in the affiliated set up, and having experienced its successful functioning and benefits for the past 30 years, I feel confident, to share my views on college autonomy.

Autonomy: Definition, Objectives and Teachers' Role

Autonomy in essence, as I understand, means academic freedom coupled with responsibility, as the two sides of the same coin. A certain amount of self-regulation has to be practised, coupled with responsible decision making. The whole process of education namely learning, teaching, research, evaluation and extension is aimed at nurturing and developing persons and institutions. It is necessary to mention a word of caution here that autonomy should neither be mistaken for freedom to misuse power and authority nor to be considered as a status of prestige or elitism. It is only a privilege for the educators and the educated, making the teaching–learning process more participatory and a fulfilling experience.

Academic freedom for the teacher / educator encompasses three main areas, namely:

a) to design relevant, need-based and innovative *curriculum.*
b) to plan and devise appropriate *instructional* methods, materials and education technology.
c) to develop and evolve suitable *evaluation* procedures and tools.

In an autonomous set-up, the three important functions namely the curriculum framing, teaching and evaluation are rightly entrusted to the hands of the teacher who is expected to use the freedom innovatively and responsibly showing utmost integrity and accountability and keeping the student as the focus and effective learning as the goal. In the affiliated system, on the other hand, the teacher mainly performs the role of teaching where as framing the syllabi and evaluation are under the control of the university. This is comparable to a worker labouring in a garden for wages. One has to just perform one's duty under specific instructions and get paid for the job. The ownership and decision-making lies elsewhere and there is no freedom to change anything. A teacher in an autonomous set-up, on the other hand, is like a worker who owns the garden. She / he decides, executes and enjoys the benefits. There is freedom, flexibility and satisfaction provided one functions with responsibility and commitment and is willing to take risks.

The objectives of autonomy are:

a) to promote excellence in an atmosphere of true freedom.

b) to fulfil the mission of higher education and the mission of the particular institution.

c) to promote holistic development through education of the head, heart and hand.

The challenges for a teacher in an autonomous set up are many. The teacher is required to be highly motivated and aspiring to achieve the set goals and objectives. He or she has to be a continuous learner keeping oneself updated and well informed of the current trends in the regional, national and global level. The teacher needs to be dynamic in order to make the curriculum dynamic, relevant and need-based. This requires a lot of hard work and commitment on the part of the teacher.

It is not enough for the teacher to have the expertise in the subject. One should acquire the know-how of the teaching methodology and the fast developing technology. Autonomy challenges the teacher and provides opportunities to innovate and adopt appropriate teaching methods. The latest gadgets such as OHP, direct projector, multimedia power point presentations could be used for classroom teaching to capture the attention of students and make learning more interesting. The task of evaluation also could be meaningfully performed integrating it well with day-to-day teaching (continuous assessment) and following the pedagogical approach of Bloom's taxonomy. The teacher is required to show high objectivity and integrity to ensure credibility of the system. It would be ideal to have 100 per cent internal evaluation. Thus autonomy makes teaching and learning a fulfilling and meaningful exercise.

Preparing for Autonomy

Proper planning and adequate preparation is highly essential to venture into autonomy. It would be worthwhile to make a study of the structure and functioning of autonomy visiting a few reputed autonomous colleges and interacting with their faculty members and other educational experts. Seminars and workshops on curriculum development, effective teaching and evaluation methods equip teachers to play the desired role in autonomy. Brainstorming sessions and discussions at different levels involving students, teachers, parents and support staff, management and external experts ensure their active involvement and support in implementing autonomy. Augmenting the existing infra-structure (laboratory, library and audio-visual facilities, etc.) provides an atmosphere conducive for learning.

Benefits of Autonomy

Advantages of autonomy are many and everyone involved in the learning process, the system and the society benefit from it. The UGC provides adequate funds as autonomy grants which is a boon to the autonomous colleges. College autonomy, when successfully implemented, makes higher education meaningful and useful, promoting academic excellence, all-round personality development and employability. Teaching and learning becomes a satisfying and fulfilling experience both for the teacher and the taught. The teachers experience personal and professional growth through the various opportunities provided for academic interaction and enrichment. The many challenges they face make them grow as persons. Autonomy fosters a favourable academic climate promoting research and extension activities which help them relate to local communities and contribute to societal growth. All these aspects help the overall development of the institution, making it unique with its own identity in the academic arena.

Autonomy provides ample scope in curriculum design for matching the current trends, societal demands and teacher expertise to the course offerings which make higher education more meaningful. Procedures become less cumbersome and changes are implemented with much ease and quickness. On the part of the students, they are able to have more choices and enjoy flexibility of curriculum. The evaluation is continuous and the students could possibly earn credits for every academic activity that he or she engages in. Endless waiting for the publication of results no more hamper the students' progress. In fact, the students are given additional chances to clear a few arrear papers if they have, so as to qualify for the degree without losing a year (e.g., June repeat exams).

Constraints and Limitations

There are a few constraints and limitations in the present autonomous system. Some of them are listed below. Thanks to UGC for revising the guidelines on the scheme for autonomous colleges under the Eleventh Plan with welcoming provisions and easing out some of the constraints. UGC has been very liberal in providing grants under the autonomy scheme. But there are restricting clauses in utilizing the grants according to the need of the institution, specifically, there is no grant for salary or building infra-structure.

Some of the state governments are not implementing scheme of autonomy to any of the colleges in their states. A few other state governments who adopted autonomy have restricted the academic freedom to a great extent so that true autonomy is difficult to be achieved. Similarly, a few universities also restrict the freedom of autonomous colleges in starting new courses or giving autonomy to PG and self–financed courses. Some universities have a fear that they will lose good colleges, if become autonomous, from their control. This mind set has to change and the UGC and the Ministry of Education need to take appropriate steps in this regard.

Another area of concern is the work load of the teachers. A differential norm of work load has to be set for the teachers of autonomous colleges so that they have time to upgrade themselves and keep abreast with the latest development in their field of study. Provision of sabbatical leave may be extended to teachers of autonomous colleges for their research and publication. If this could be recommended by UGC and adopted by state governments, more colleges would opt for autonomy with the support of their teachers and management.

Further More Suggestions

A few tips for the success of autonomy are suggested. Setting up a good control and monitory system in curriculum design, teaching and evaluation will ensure proper use of the freedom by both administrators as well as the teachers. The motivational level of both the teachers and the students has to be kept high and the administration has to consciously take steps in this regard. Involving students, parents, alumni and the public at various levels is necessary for a participatory approach which is one of the keys for success. Such participatory style of management has been found to promote their whole hearted involvement and co-operation. They identify with the institutional goal and feel as part of the whole system. The academic reform and administrative reform should go hand in hand.

Finally, to conclude, autonomy has proved a worthwhile and rewarding educational experience at Lady Doak College. We have developed new courses, centres and programmes for exposure and involvement, innovative methods of teaching and evaluation, infrastructure, periodical training of teachers, support staff members and students and the academic freedom provided by the autonomy system to relate our teaching and learning process for transforming the teachers and the learners, local communities and building the nation. Our college has undergone tremendous growth enjoying the autonomous status for three decades so much so it seems impossible to progress otherwise. Autonomy is the only way to keep Indian higher education relevant and viable. Otherwise the traditional system of higher education will die a 'dinosaur's death' as some educationists fear and predict. Let us promote and strengthen the autonomy for the progress and excellence of higher education.

14

Academic Autonomy

— A. Albert Muthumalai S.J.

Introduction

The novel and innovative idea of autonomy was conferred on Loyola College in 1978, and functioning of autonomy was reviewed every five years. Based on the experiences of the assessment and accreditation in 1999, the major breakthrough was the trendsetting of the restructuring of the curricula implemented in 2000. This path-breaking spirit was recognized by UGC and Loyola College became one of the colleges with potential for excellence in 2004. The restructuring Phase–II in 2005 attempted to reengineer education to suit the needs of tomorrow and to join our relentless search for relevance making the academic programme student-oriented, relevant, interdisciplinary and flexible. The College was re-accredited at A+ level by NAAC in 2006. Loyola has completed 30 years of autonomy. Change is inevitable in an educational system that has to meet the present day needs and prepare the future citizens of our nation.

General Objectives

The academic programmes have the following objectives:

i) To develop language skills in students.

ii) To open the students to the social realities with a view to making him/her a responsible citizen and other-centred.

iii) To develop the personality of the student to be able to realize full potential.

iv) To develop an indepth knowledge in a selected area of study.

v) To train a student in a specific skill, in case he/she enters the job market.

vi) To broaden the outlook of the student through interdisciplinary approach, to be able to access knowledge and use the same meaningfully.

vii) To make higher education a cutting edge of development and to measure its contribution in enhancing the economic social, political, cultural development of the country.

Circumstances Leading to Academic Autonomy

a) To achieve the national goal of sustainable development with social justice in a pluralistic and democratic social order.

b) To make higher education relevant to knowledge-age and to keep pace with global standards.

c) Widening the base of higher education to include the excluded.

d) To establish linkages with economy, with backward sectors, with rural areas and the so-called mismatch between education and employment.

e) Mainstreaming of social sciences in the science courses.

f) Countering the evils such as pauperization of the poor, globalization, communalization, etc.

Outstanding Features of Autonomy

a) Semester pattern is introduced requiring six semesters of study for a Bachelor's degree and four semesters of study for a Master's degree. The duration for a semester is 15 weeks of six working days per week.

b) Choice-based credit system is very much appreciated. The boards of studies of the departments and the academic council of the college have given a face shift to the standard of the syllabi compared to university.

c) Each course offered in a semester is assigned a certain number of credits depending upon the quantity of work required of a student. Credit consists of listening to lectures and active participation in tutorials, seminars, laboratory work and directed library work. Credits represent the proper weightage to each course according to the amount of work desired by the respective department. Only when a student passes a course he/she will earn the credits assigned to that course. An aggregate of 130 credits is required to qualify for a Bachelor's Degree and 78 credits for a Master's Degree averaging 20 credits per semester.

d) The need to include extension activities, the third dimension of education into the curriculum is innovative.

e) The introduction of academic autonomy has made the teachers innovative, creative and professionally competent.

f) Students are to learn computer course related to the Major subject. However those who have previous knowledge of computers may be exempted from attending the classes after presenting proper evidences to the teacher concerned. But, they will have to take the required tests for continuous assessment of the course.

g) The final year students are given an in-service training in an industry related to the skill for four weeks during the vacation.

h) Evaluation of students is based on both continuous assessment and semester examinations held at the end of each semester. Equal weightage of 50 per cent each is given to continuous assessment (CA) and end semester examination. The first CA test is conducted in the middle of the semester and the second is on the last week of the semester. A student is assessed for 40 marks each for two tests and 20 marks are left to the student's creativity in terms of an assignment, term paper, project, group discussion and laboratory work. The end semester examination is for three hours and for 100 marks. Double valuation in UG level and supplementary examinations for outgoing students are welcoming signs.

Some Drawbacks

a) As per the guidelines of the UGC, the skill development and employment orientation is lacking.

b) An interdisciplinary approach is needed to facilitate the development of new courses. The collaboration of experts from university, IIT, industry and business is useful in this respect.

c) In its attempt to restructure the courses or to introduce new ones, the college is handicapped by the reluctance of the state government to approve grant-in-aid for additional teachers.

d) The attitude of the university towards autonomous colleges in general does not seem to be as encouraging as it should be.

e) The need for socially relevant courses needs to be fully realized.

f) The guidelines on restructuring of courses given by UGC also recommend starting one year diploma courses in areas of application leading to better employment opportunities so that the prevailing deficiency of our degree programmes could be remedied.

g) A specific quantum in each course should be allotted for field-work, projects, paper presentation on curriculum material, documentation, self expression, problem solving, case-studies, etc. All these must be part of the learning process attracting credit points.

A Response

a) The Loyola Institute of Vocational Education (LIVE) is allowed to offer as many job oriented courses as it could, and credit transfer is made possible to enter in the overall grade sheet.

b) Interdisciplinary courses such as Medical lab Technology, Biomedical Instrumentation Science and Media Arts are introduced.

c) Mentoring sessions are enhanced. Academic advancement, spiritual growth and personal guidance by the mentor are absolutely vital for the success of the students. Every student will be entrusted with one of the teachers of the department for the entire period of three years to guide him/her in the choice of the subjects and monitor his/her progress.

d) The Department of Foundation Courses is created. Integral formation helps a student to become alive to himself and to his emotional processes. This alone will help him to be a useful citizen in society. Therefore, the formation of the personality development becomes one of the most important components of the Foundation Courses. Since we are living in a pluralistic society, in a pluri-cultural and multi religious context, it is important that every citizen knows, understands and appreciates not only his own religion but also other religions. This will definitely foster communal harmony, tolerance, acceptance and the basic trust in one another. The Foundation Courses include a course on environmental studies which seek to inculcate the importance of ecology in the minds of the students.

e) The Department of Outreach is systematized. Loyola Empowerment and Reach out Network (LEARN) aims to transform the neighboring communities to change themselves through programmes like literacy, health promotion, women empowerment, youth clubs and reduction of dropouts in schools.

f) Industry Institution Interaction is strengthened. Loyola Career Expo draws a large number of industries. Interaction between academia and the industry has become an essential requirement to train and develop the manpower necessary to sustain and promote industrial and economic growth in terms of employability skills and entrepreneurship.

The Future Directions – An Ongoing Process

The following would be the steps to be initiated in order to make the entire teaching and learning process more meaningful and purposeful.

i) The system should be monitored continuously to plug the loopholes.

ii) The focus of higher education should include suitable job related courses with training/skill learnt in industry.

iii) The parallel diploma courses are to be planned for the benefit of students to take these courses in their leisure time.

The curriculum should be planned in the following way:

i) A 'Certificate' at the end of first year during which period, he/she should have learnt the proficiency in languages and communication with some basic and human relations.

ii) A 'Diploma' at the end of the second year during which period a student should be given a training pertaining to the core and the allied courses.

iii) A 'Degree' at the end of the third year.

iv) A 'PG Diploma' at the end of the fourth year based on a project work.

v) A 'PG Degree' at the end of the fifth year.

The above system will give freedom to a student to discontinue the course at any point of time and facilitate him/her to get a suitable job, based on the certificate, diploma, degree, PG diploma. Such students can re-enter the portals of education without any difficulties and complete the five-year course at their pace.

To introduce the concept of 'The Cafeteria' system which extends a complete freedom to the students to choose subjects as offered by the departments. It should provide:

i) The Choice-Based Curriculum

ii) The broad-based 'Interdisciplinary' courses

iii) The Flexi time so as to accommodate the choice of the subjects chosen by the students.

To introduce 'Centres of Excellence' which could be identified as

i) School of Languages

ii) School of Humanities

iii) School of Commerce

iv) School of Management

v) School of Media

vi) School of Sciences

vii) School of Basic Medical Sciences

To look into a possibility of:

i) Sharing and Networking of Resources

ii) Community Colleges
iii) Cluster Colleges
iv) Degree Awarding College
v) Deemed-to-be University

To continuously monitor the environment so that the curriculum and structures could be suitably modified. This could meet the challenges of globalization. A 'Think-Tank' in the college is the need of the hour.

CONCLUSION

Keeping in mind the needs of the country, an attempt has been made to modify the curriculum at the UG, PG and M.Phil level using academic autonomy. It is a Loyola experience and it is expected that it will answer the needs of the UGC guidelines, which state that the university curriculum should have three components, namely, subject knowledge, outreach programme and character and value formation. It is hoped that the academic autonomy will help the students to have broad-based knowledge, knowledge of the society in which he/she lives and a commitment to the growth of the country. It is further hoped that he/she would have at least one skill which will help him to get a job and make him/her a useful citizen.

15

Challenges and Problems of Higher Education in India — The Role of Self-Financing Autonomous Colleges

— K. Nirmala Prasad

The National Knowledge Commission, Government of India, in its report (2006) has said that "the most obvious solution to the problems of higher education is to provide Autonomy to colleges either as individual colleges or clusters of colleges". Yet if we go down in time, we can see that autonomy is not new to the Indian education scenario. The first autonomous college in India was the Hindu College of Calcutta which came into existence as early as 1817. However, the conferment of autonomous status to colleges by the UGC was recognized only from the year 1978.

An autonomous institution is an organization that has the ability to act by its own choice in pursuit of a mission that it has chosen for itself. It is a dynamic model of educational governance based on freedom and evaluation of performance. Autonomy does mean freedom but freedom implies greater accountability and responsibility. Autonomy means debates, discussions and continuous improvement for the cause of education. Autonomous institutions by virtue of this freedom become more innovative, rich in knowledge and are known to use available resources in the best possible manner. These institutes also put in place inbuilt mechanisms for continuous improvement.

Autonomous institutions have the following freedoms:

a) They have freedom to modernize curricula;
b) They can bring in industry and outside experts for framing or changing the learning content;

c) Students get more electives to select from across disciplines;

d) Methods of assessing students' performance, conduct of examinations and notification of results are qualitatively enhanced;

e) All content gets more relevant for industry and job requirements; and

f) College catalyzes the role of the students in community services, extension activities and neighbourhood programmes.

Before we look at the role that an autonomous institution can play in the educational scenario of a developing country like ours, it is important that we take stock of the reality of higher education as it exists today. Some interesting facts to ponder upon:

"There has been a huge growth in the size of the education sector—from a mere 27 universities in 1947; the figure was 365 in 2007.

"Yet for over 60 years the country has mourned of a problem of unemployment. Of the 400 million work force 333 million are under employed and 40 million are registered unemployed. Out of the 0.35 million professional graduates coming out of Indian universities only 40% are considered employable by Indian industry.

"The reasons for the poor quality of graduates are plenty and have been debated widely and the educational institutions have been held responsible for this state of affairs.

So how then can this quantity-quality mismatch of demand and supply of human capital be resolved? What are the initiatives that educational institutions especially autonomous colleges, given the fact that they enjoy greater freedom, can take to better the quality of higher education in the country today? Some of the initiatives that can be taken are:

a) Reforms in the teaching, learning evaluation mechanism
b) Thrust on skills training
c) Increased industry institution interface
d) Entrepreneurship as a job option
e) Optimum use of information technology

f) Innovation in all aspects
g) Lateralism.

Reforms in the Teaching, Learning, Evaluation Mechanism

The Central Board of Secondary Education has been on the path of academic reform for some time now, and most of these result-oriented reforms are worthy of emulation.

Some of the reforms that must be made in academic programmes are:

a) *Introduction of new areas*. You will be surprised to know that the high school curriculum of most western education systems include job oriented subjects like Disaster Management, Fashion Studies, Ecological Studies, etc. The Madras University has already introduced a subject on Environment Education and also proposes to introduce a paper on Human Rights shortly. These areas though not directly related to employment enable graduates to become good corporate citizens.
b) *Revision in existing curriculum*. For instance even the high school syllabus for computer science now includes topics such as Multimedia and Web Technology. Similarly, subjects like Accountancy must include the use of accounting software, statistics must contain the application of SPSS package, etc.
c) *Thrust on practical application*. The teaching learning process must focus on the practical applications of the theory learnt. Project work, laboratory practicals, etc. though have always been a part of the syllabus must be made a compulsory component in all papers accounting for a large percentage of the assessment.
d) *Assessment mechanism based on conceptual knowledge testing*. Most employment tests include objective questions and test only the conceptual knowledge. Unfortunately the traditional assessment mechanism being followed by most Indian educational institutions place more emphasis on the ability to write essays rather than define concepts and understand their applications. It is this aspect that is most sought after in the job market.

e) Thrust on self-learning. American historian Henry Brooks Adams (1838-1918) once said, "They know enough who know how to learn". Industry wants their employees to be knowledge centres that assimilate new concepts and unlearn old ones. The educational system must focus on tutorial components like assignment, book reading, article review, classroom seminars wherein students are taught to learn basic studies skills which enable them to become life long learners. The time spent on mastering the art of learning is a worthy investment to generate long-term profits.

Thrust on Skills Training

The recruiters of IT and other industries who approach colleges for campus recruitment claim that they find the students unemployable as they lack the skills required by them. The problem in college-based education is that the students are trained in the superfluous aspects of the theory and are not fully equipped with the practical aspects of the study required for employment. The students do not satisfy the standards prescribed by the companies and thereby become unemployable. Many company recruiters claim that the recruitment costs increase since they have to approach many colleges to find suitable students for employment. In addition their training costs swell as the already recruited students are not immediately usable and their skills required to be honed.

The skill requirements of graduates are twofold:

a) *Soft Skills*: In today's highly competitive job market, the expectations of the recruiters are high. A good number of candidates who otherwise possess required technical skills are not recruited, as they do not possess the soft skills required. A soft skill encompasses a cluster of personality traits. A person's ability to communicate, social grace, personal habits, friendliness, attitude, negotiating ability, leadership qualities, initiative, conflict management, innovation, creativity, lateral thinking, decision making, interpersonal skills, self-control or emotional maturity, time management, assertiveness, team spirit, capacity to work under pressure and stress – all these and more comprise soft skills. Soft skills are imperative for employment as they are portable skills that affect every aspect of an employee's performance on and off the job. All employment processes today include a competency interview to assess the soft skills quotient.

b) *Hard Skills*: A widespread training programme that teaches job skills to people all over India can transform the economy of the nation within the next 10 years, said the Principal Advisor, Confederation of Indian Industry (CII), Y. S. Rajan. With the right job skills in place, the nation can be lifted out of poverty in the next 10 years. The placement record of community colleges that impart only skill-based education is proof of the fact that technical and job oriented skills are most relevant for employment.

Increased Industry-Institution Interface

Educational instituitions should have a holistic policy to hold hands with industry, and work together for producing knowledgeable and competent graduates who could be absorbed fully for productive employment.

Some of the areas for a potential industry-institute partnership:

a) *Internships*: Chinese philosopher Confucius (551-479 BC) said: "I hear, I forget; I see, I remember; I do, I understand." Students must be required to train in industry during weekends, annual and semi-annual holidays or during specific intervals.

b) *Industry institution tie-ups*: Though universities provide an excellent learning environment, they cannot be expected to provide students real-time input and support.

This paradigm has given birth to the IBM Academic Initiative. The innovative programme partners with colleges and universities worldwide to educate millions of students for a more competitive information technology (IT) workforce. The programme aims at three key objectives: training an IT workforce to fill the new kind of jobs that emerge at IBM and across the industry; mapping education to provide the right skills to IT workers and ensure they are qualified for the jobs of tomorrow; ensuring that universities have the relevant curricula. IBM is currently working worldwide with 245 new target institutions having more than 281,000 students worldwide, the target being 400 institutions to reach 350,000 students overall. In India, IBM will reach out to over 200 institutes training over 50,000 students in IBM and open standards-based technologies.

Effective partnership between industry and educational institutions is a potential win-win situation for both parties; the industry is involved in training the potential employees while educational institutions can provide need-based training.

Promotion of Entrepreneurship

The former President, Dr. Kalam, was once in his inimitable style chatting with some school children. One of them asked if there would be enough jobs in India for all of them when they were grown up. Dr. Kalam's answer was simple, yet brilliant: "There would be no dearth of jobs if many of you grow up to become job providers, instead of becoming job seekers!" Only by multiplying the number of job providers within the country can we hope to take all the Indians on the economic climb up.

Trade and industry earned the bad name, during the licence-quota-permit-raj when a whole lot of hurdles existed in the way of doing business. All that is now almost history. Today, thanks to the sweeping changes in the functioning of the government, starting and running one's own concern is a far more straightforward venture. Unfortunately this is a reality that has not yet penetrated public awareness. There is a strong perception that being in business is like being on a roller coaster. It could take you very high in a short span of time but overnight it could also throw you crashing to the ground! Risk is undoubtedly an inherent and inseparable factor in any business, be it a purely commercial activity or an industrial establishment. But it is certainly not a luck dependant gamble, as many fear it to be. A certain degree of intuition is required for success but that, fortunately for us Indians, is not at all a rare trait.

Very often one hears parents' remark that their wards 'do not belong to business family'. It is here that educationists must recognize that entrepreneurs are made not born. Entrepreneurship can and must be taught in colleges. For when a thousand business ventures bloom, ten times as many would benefit. Team India would then be economically unbeatable!

Optimum Use of Information & Communication Technology

Lakhs of schools across the country are single-teacher establishments and lakhs of teachers in the country are untrained in pedagogical methods. These concerns have remained unsolved for decades. Information-communication-technology is an answer when it is used as a force multiplier.

What difference can ICT make? It can take hours for a science teacher to explain various aspects of a solar or lunar eclipse using chalk and blackboard. With some graphics and animation, every child can understand an eclipse in minutes and this experience lasts longer. Even if a teacher is absent from class, the children can still learn via the video.

Fortunately there have been several initiatives in this regard:

a) The National Project for technology enhanced learning, spearheaded by the IITs and IIMs, brings the best of lectures by subject experts to countrywide interactive classrooms via the DD network. There is also scope for digitally capturing classroom lectures in IITs or NITs and send them as CDs to the colleges to improve technical or general science education.

b) Sometime ago, a task force comprising chiefs of all-India bodies such as the AICTE, the Distance Education Council (DEC), UGC, and the NCTE proposed setting up a network of satellite interactive terminals (SITs) to address both these concerns. The IGNOU has pioneered the SIT network initiative and has plans to put in place over 100 SITs. Now, its regional centres have the facility and the two-way (point-to-point) video and audio interaction

c) The September 2004 launch of EDUSAT, a dedicated satellite for education, science and technology information dissemination, came in handy.

d) UGC INFONET, a library networking initiative that has provided the connectivity to online paid-content journals to more than 100 universities in the country. The networking programme for the library dates back to 1991.

The UGC had launched Information and Library Network (INFLIBNET) then, with a mission to facilitate resource sharing at different levels and promote scholarly communication among academicians and researchers. The UGC was thus able to reach out to automate and network over 142 universities across the country. In recent years, INFLIBNET expanded its role to cover e-learning due to increased bandwidth availability.

Thrust on Innovation

In the fifteenth century, China reigned supreme in innovations. And hence was a global power. It produced a variety of arms and ammunition. Tea, porcelain and its silk were sought all over the world. It had the largest fleet of dhows. In 1421, Emperor Zhudi died. Immediately afterwards, the Mandarians feared losing their primacy to explorers. China shut its doors to the rest of the world.

Another great innovator of the 1970s, Xerox was on the verge of taking over a new world of digital electronics. But after its innovative champions died, Xerox lost its primacy in the world of computers. Others took over with their bigger and more sustained innovations.

Both stories have a similar lesson—if you do not innovate, you will decay.

Does India have an academic culture that encourages innovation? We have so many departments in universities, but not one for innovation. India does not have many global branded innovations to display. Not that there is dearth of talent. Indians abroad do innovations and do it successfully to make successful enterprises.

Though it may be difficult to exclusively have a course on innovation the concept can be weaved into the existing curriculum Only then would the systems be able to foster and spawn innovation or think of creating an Indian brand acknowledged globally for an innovative application, rather for a cheaper alternative.

Lateralism

The dilemma in designing education systems across the world has been: should it be "top-down" or "bottom-up"? But a more important issue is: has it ever been side ways? i.e, if you are a teacher, and I am a teacher and you say you have got something wonderful going on in your school, that you have discovered something in your classroom, I want to know what it is. I ask, "Can I do it too?" This is literalism - a culture of sharing of best practices.

Further more autonomous institutions can use their status most optimally by introducing several initiatives that affiliated colleges might find curtailed from doing, like:

a) *Introduction of career-oriented graduate and post-graduate courses*: For instance, a self-financing automous college can capitalize on the growing power of the media industry and the obvious lacunae in talented media manpower by introducing latest and market-driven media education courses.
b) *Making the existing courses more job-oriented through specializations*: Autonomous colleges can introduce major and minor specializations in traditional courses to make them more job-oriented like corporate specialization in the sociology programme, marketing specialization in the B.Com. programme, B.Sc. Mathematics with IT specialization, etc.
c) *Introduction of inter-disciplinary courses*: Students can be given an opportunity to sample areas of other disciplines so that they may take up a multi-disciplinary career. For instance, a student of Business can be offered a course in Journalism to pursue a career in Business Journalism, etc.
d) *Provision for soft skills training in tune with requirements of job market*: Autonomous colleges can offer certificate programmes in soft skills such as:
   i) Communication skills
   ii) Personality effectiveness skills
   iii) Leadership and general management skills
   iv) Presentation skills
   v) Career management skills, etc.
e) *Introduction of certificate courses to develop professional skills in students*: While it might take universities and affiliated

colleges a longer time to introduce updated technical and hard skills into the core curriculum due to several operational difficulties, it becomes easy for self financing autonomous colleges to adopt these programmes as a part of their curriculum. The students from these colleges can benefit through courses in areas like:

i) Project Management
ii) Software Testing
iii) Accounting Software
iv) Statistical Package
v) Logic Building
vi) Culinary Course
vii) Cake Architecture
viii) Software Based Diet Counselling
ix) Insurance
x) Banking
xi) E-commerce
xii) Networking
xiii) Software Engineering
xiv) Data base Administration
xv) Web Designing
xvi) Computer Graphic Design
xvii) Food Preservation
xviii) Social Entrepreneurship

e) *Provision of real time work experience through internships*: At least two stints of four-six weeks of on-the-job training can be provided to every undergraduate student for her or him to have a feel of the corporate world.

g) *Introduction of projects to develop application skills*: Projects and research can easily be introduced as credited components of an autonomous curriculum in order that students be given hand on the feel of theory.

h) *Promotion of self-employment as a career option*: This can be done by introducing Entrepreneurship Development as a separate course in the curriculum. This will help create job givers rather than job seekers.

i) Introduction of Community Service Projects to promote social consciousness.

The twentieth century being an era of globalisation has required the redefinition of higher education. Education must not confine itself to mere academic excellence, but should open wider horizons, create new opportunities and empower the youth.

M.O.P. Vaishnav College for Women, Chennai, is a 16-year-old institution, affiliated to Madras University. Thanks to the University Grants Commission and the University of Madras, the college was given autonomous status in the year 2004. This has helped to introduce all these value additions as credited programs under the Choice Based Credit System. The structure of every degree programme includes besides:

a) Foundation Courses
b) Core and Allied Papers
c) Elective Courses

Value additions like:

a) Two inter-disciplinary elective courses
b) Two internships / Practice schools
c) Three soft skill training programmes
d) Three technical skill certificate programmes
e) Compulsory projects and research work
f) Entrepreneurship education and training
g) Community service and extension projects

This has resulted in the college producing not merely graduates but empowered women with enriched personalities who are motivated, creative, analytical, culturally rich, self sustained, humane and socially conscious individuals. The 90 per cent placement record with average salaries of Rs.2–2.5 lakh for undergraduate students stands ample testimony to the fact that self financing autonomous colleges can contribute valuably to improving the quality of higher education in this country – this being the greatest need of the hour.

16

Autonomy—An Analysis

— M. Thavamani

The roots of reform in higher education can be traced back to the late 1970s when the University Grants Commission decided to make constructive and fundamental changes within its colleges and universities to prepare to meet the demands of the twenty-first century. In a short persuasive and thought-provoking statement which remains relevant till today, the UGC expressed its desire to unleash the potential of higher education centres and learners to face the economic needs of the society. Higher education began its experiment with autonomy and diversity. Educational enterprises became overnight interesting and innovative. The few institutions which favoured UGC's new venture have today garnered for themselves an enviable status in not only the national scenario but also the international. The state governments which set up councils for higher education urged the institutions of premier status to try to be innovative keeping in mind the guidelines spelt out by the UGC. Autonomy ensured unprecedented human resource management. The University Grants Commission did not hesitate to extend its help, in the area of the capital outlay needed by these institutions which could manage their affairs efficiently and effectively.

Optimism regarding autonomy and its suitability did wane a little, during the 1980s but the end of the 80s and the beginning of the 90s witnessed a whipping up of spirits with a budget for higher education given the utmost importance. Since the Eighth Five Year Plan, UGC has been implementing directly and indirectly financial assistance towards strengthening infrastructural facilities and research needs. The challenges described by the Commission for the higher education system of the twenty-first century were upon us even as early as the 90s. The time was ripe for isolated institutions to explore more options for governance.

The ninth Five Year Plan found many institutions coming forward to check the many benefits of autonomy. Dozens of meetings with the agencies, academic councils of the universities and the University Grants Commission itself gave significant strength for implementing autonomy. A challenging time indeed, for colleges and universities which continued to face larger enrollments and higher expectations from the stakeholders. Autonomy focused on the four pillars, namely, capacity building, research, economic development and an employable human resource. Higher education stepped up its infrastructure facilities and governance by laying the foundation for measurable accountability in these four areas.

It is common knowledge that all institutions are eroded by the passage of time. Improvements in technology, economic realignments, and changes in societal values render most organizations obsolete within a generation or two. Institutions of higher education are among the most permanent, but they too become irrelevant if they fail to adapt to changing conditions. The challenge all colleges had to face during the last phase of the ninth Five Year Plan was providing values under conditions of constant change, since education offered by the colleges no longer seemed to add values or meaning to people's lives. There was a steep fall in enrollments and the institutions started realizing that a good organization structure and a strong leadership were essential to meet the challenges. The advisory committees set up by the UGC and the various schemes introduced by it for financial assistance helped the higher education centres to be discerning in their appointment of team leaders. The Academia started believing in proper organization structure and independent decision making capacities. They also instinctively understood that the time for agile institutions with competitive spirit had at last arrived. The following facts made the backdrop:

i) Global economic changes and increased competition.

ii) Increasing awareness regarding the importance of higher education to our social and civic life.
iii) Profound changes in our population and economy.
iv) Regional and socio-economic disparities in achievement.
v) Scarcity of resources versus increased awareness regarding global innovations.

With the above-mentioned facts forming the backdrop, the Tenth Five Year Plan insisted that the higher education centres define and redefine their missions to enhance productive work in times of such challenging environments. The evolution of institutions, it was observed, "like individual development, requires a balancing of continuity and change" (Berg,Gary A. 2003) in response to it. In fact these facts had to be integrated with the institution's internal vision of a better reality. Good work in a profession often depends, first and foremost, on the criteria for and standards of excellence that the domain imparts to its members. It also depends on the intended impact of the work on those to whom the profession holds itself responsible and how it aims to contribute to a larger good. These criteria and aims in turn determine in large part the degree to which an individual professional's work provides personal enjoyment and meaning. Autonomy, it was felt unanimously, would provide all the above mentioned. Hence institutions came forward to attain autonomous status.

Why Autonomy?

In contrast to our sister professions, law and medicine, the professoriate tends not to study its own ethics. Legal ethics, medical ethics, and even business ethics are offered as courses but academic ethics has never been taken seriously. Data is not available on faculty understanding of the social needs, academic freedom, and professionalism. The academic profession needs the help of all those who have a deep stake in its survival. Faculty, therefore need to internalize a higher degree of professionalism and autonomy aims at creating this awareness by having accountability as one of its hidden agendas.

The concept of ethics derives from the Greek term ethos, denoting the customs of a community. According to Aristotle, not only people but institutions too can be ethical. He uses the term ethos to describe the "characteristic spirit, prevalent tone of sentiment, of a people or community; the 'genius' of an institution or system" (OED). The complex domain of higher education consists of many kinds of institutions and each institution is distinguished by its own definition of excellence and of the social needs that it aspires to meet. However varied the missions may be, the contention is, that to survive and prosper, and to enable the good work of the people who work there, an institution must live up to a set of ethical guidelines embodied in a mission that expresses the spirit of a community and constitutes an implicit contract between the institution and the wider society. If an institution's mission is to express the spirit of the community – if individual good work is to merge into a larger collective good work – a college must find ways to bring into alignment, the strengths of its multiple internal stakeholders: administrators, faculty, staff, trustees, and the current student body. Autonomy helps in a large way to achieve this balancing tactics.

What is Expected of Institutions Which want to Become Autonomous?

To have a credible identity, an institution must identify its strengths and forge a mission around them. Firm bases for excellence should be there in the institution's programs and departments; in its culture, history and location; it's human and material resources; its student population; its capacity to make decisions tempered by the perception of the community; or its rich healthy practices. Such features are its sturdiest basis for doing outstanding work. Institutional identity is often both visible in the character of its daily life and embodied in special and distinctive events.

The institution's continued good work depends, first and last, on the commitment of its faculty, staff, administrators, and trustees. Having a clear, agreed upon, and relevant mission matters greatly since it focuses the energies of both the institution and the individual who works in it in at least three related ways. At first it means an established relationship between the immediate society and the institution. Secondly, it ensures the integration of the internal stakeholders in the realization of the mission and thirdly a clearly defined institutional mission establishes an overarching goal toward which any given individual worker can meaningfully direct his or her energies. In addition to these the institutions seeking autonomy should pay attention to the following:

i) Make higher education accessible, especially for the under privileged.

ii) Make it affordable, regardless of family income.

iii) A broad range of academic programmes to be envisaged.

iv) Maintain high academic standards.

v) Improve student retention and progress toward the timely award of degrees.

vi) Develop a uniform curriculum with other colleges.

vii) Stimulate economic development and aim at developing the backward areas.

viii) Increase externally funded research and improve technology transfer where appropriate.

ix) Work actively with the neighbouring colleges to improve student achievement.

x) Prepare a plan for the next few years with the economic growth of the individual and the nation in mind.

One of the effects of "knowledge expansion" on higher education has been a proliferation in the number of academic fields and curricula. The curricular choices that academics make are influenced by the institutional frameworks within which they work.

In the modern era of mass systems of higher education, the combined demand of new student clienteles and the international growth in the number and variety of disciplines, specialities and inter- or multi-disciplinary subjects, has led to a proliferation of academic curricula that on a world wide scale appears to be essentially uncontrollable (Clark, B.R,1983)

The growth and diversification of higher education system has given new prominence to questions of access and participation. The traditional faculty will resist these changes, and it is these who have to be convinced about maintaining academic quality despite changes. They will have to enhance their professional identity by adhering to accreditation of their faculty, self-evaluation, peer evaluation and student feedback. Autonomy helps to provide scope not only for these but also offers the necessary scaffolding needed for individual exploration along with instructional support to the learner. The traditional role of information dispenser / broadcaster is giving way to a more facilitative relationship with the learner (Brennan, John et.al, 1983).

Perhaps the most significant area in which autonomy works best is associated with the assessment and certification of skills and knowledge.

Accountability and Autonomy

"*Academic Integrity*: Ten Principles", published in the 1997 by well known educationists Donald L. McCabe and Gary Pavela in *AAHE Bulletin* insisted on the faculty practicing academic integrity by maintaining a high degree of accountability. The principles laid down by the duo were discussed on the American university campuses through the length and breadth of the country. The same pair updated the principles in their 2004 article "Ten Updated Principles of Academic Integrity", published in *Change,* an education quarterly, keeping in mind the changing challenges and the campuses of higher education centres. The pair through the article drew the attention of the academia to the fact that accountability of the professoriate lies in creating honest future citizens.

To achieve this, the academia themselves are told to maintain a high rate of academic honesty. The autonomous institutions may take the principles laid out in the article as model to frame their healthy practices within their campuses.

i) Institutions should recognize and affirm academic integrity as a core institutional value since there seems to be a loss of values all around with youngsters having no role model and moorings.
ii) Institutions should foster a lifelong commitment to learning and the faculty should deem it their first duty to

let the youth to know that "learning can be a captivating and joyful experience".

iii) Academicians, should affirm the role of teachers as guides and mentors, since the "time of Plato's Academy teaching has been seen as encompassing conscientious companionship, grounded in the shared pursuit of truth."

iv) Help students understand the potential of the e-sources and how that potential can be lost if online resources are used for fraudulent activities. The Internet which is a comparatively recent innovation has immense potential for quick human development. This has not been till date adequately and properly used since most of the youngsters and faculty do not have disciplined ways to use these sources. Faculty members should learn to use it discriminatingly and emphasize that "the culture of freedom and openness associated with it depends on virtues like self–restraint, civility, and proper respect for the work of others."

v) Encourage student responsibility for academic integrity. McCabe and Pavela opine that students who want to work in societies where competition is fair also know "that one of the greatest inducements to engaging in academic dishonesty is the perception that it is already widespread."

vii) Clarify expectations for students. Students and their needs must be given priority by the academia. The faculty members who design the educational environment and curricula should guide the students in their selection of the course and the syllabus.

vii) Develop fair and creative forms of assessment. The faculty members should continuously revise the forms of assessment that require active and creative thought which promotes good opportunities for learning.

viii) Reduce opportunities to engage in academic dishonesty . Care should be taken that students are not tempted or instigated to engage in academic dishonesty by "looking into ambiguous policies, undefined or unrealistic standards for collaboration, inadequate classroom management, or poor examination security."

ix) Response to academic dishonesty when it occurs. The faculty should take excessive care about their behaviour on and off the campus since students observe how they behave and what values they follow. "Faculty members who ignore or trivialize academic dishonesty, send the message that the core values of academic life aren't worth enforcing."

x) Help define and support campus-wide academic–integrity standards. The faculty should always be the primary role models for academic integrity and this in turn should "serve as a foundation for other efforts to enhance student ethical development."

Autonomy – A Healthy Way to Refining Higher Education

In conclusion it could be said without any fear of exaggeration, that autonomous status not only helps the academia to construct their own curricula, syllabi, choose the pedagogic tools, teaching methods, extend research activities and consultancy services to less privileged institutions, keep up the heritage of the institutions, and retain the primary aim of creating worthy citizens of the world, but also prepares the student to be a life long learner, who can transcend disciplines in the search for knowledge. Institutions of higher education, like other organizations and enterprises operate in an increasingly dynamic environment. Boards and academic leaders must respond to changes in society's needs or put their institutions at risk. Governments, as sources of funds and loans, also must take such changes into account. There are three possible arenas of "big change" in the colleges. First, what is to be taught and learned. Second, how is that curriculum to be taught and learned, or how will pedagogy or instructional production function in the future? Third, who is to be taught, and for how long and / or what public expense; or what is the future of accessibility?

Some changes, for example, technological advances that affect research, teaching and learning are inevitable. But faculty could deal with these changes in a way that would strengthen rather than erode the social contract and our professional autonomy (Hamilton, Neil W) With the larger arena of India 2020 in focus there may be profound changes, particularly those wrought by technology. General intellectual skills, critical thinking, ethical reasoning, lifelong learning and development and communication skills need to be strengthened. These changes do prognosticate great opportunities and autonomy is the most, healthy way to achieve them.

17

Autonomy for Colleges in The 21st Century—Relevance, Challenges and Suggestions

—Sr. Philomena Cardoza

Globalization, industrialization and information technology advancement have brought immensely changed consequences in higher education. This has created a need to serve a new generation to achieve the goals of higher education. To revitalize the very thinking and to put it on the right track there is a need to provide an inbuilt self-sustaining mechanism in universities and colleges. And this is made possible by conferring autonomy by the universities to the colleges.

In the realm of higher education in India, the concept and implementation of the scheme of autonomous colleges has come to stay for the last 30 years. The autonomous college has emerged as an alternative to the conventional system of affiliated colleges in terms of curriculum, continuous internal assessment (CIA), admissions and examination system.

The Origin of College Autonomy

Autonomy for colleges is not a new idea. The colleges were virtually autonomous universities since 1817 until the birth of the three affiliating Universities of Calcutta, Bombay and Madras in 1857. The universities were established for the purpose of holding common examinations and to ensure common standards. Philanthropic individuals and Christian missionaries established private colleges at different times. The Poona College, the Elphinstone College, Bombay and the Hooghly College, Madras

Christian College were all autonomous colleges enjoying full freedom in the admission of students, in designing syllabus and conducting final examinations and awarding degrees. The three universities mentioned above adopted the affiliating pattern from London University (1835), a unique legacy of the colonial regime. Twenty seven autonomous colleges were affiliated to these universities.

The issue of autonomous colleges was revived by the Principal of the Presidency College, Calcutta at the beginning of this century in the context of the postgraduate studies. But the attempt failed. After independence, the Principal of Balwant Rajput College, Agra, Dr. R. K Singh, revived the idea of autonomous colleges in 1950. The Committee on Standards of University Education (1965), under the Chairmanship of Prof. S.K. Sidhanta discussed for the first time the need for introducing the autonomous scheme along with the affiliated system. The idea of giving autonomous status to well-established colleges with a view to raising standards and encouraging the pursuit of excellence in higher education was proposed by Kothari Commission (1964-66) that made the first formal and specific recommendation to the nation that autonomous colleges should be established. In 1978, acting on the basis of the recommendations of the Kothari Commission, the UGC granted autonomous status to twelve colleges in Tamil Nadu.

Shortcomings of the Affiliating System

The system of affiliating the colleges to a university was designed at a time when the number of colleges and universities was small. There were only eighteen universities in the country at the time of its independence in 1947. Their number has risen to more than 230 today. A university, which has a number of colleges under its academic control (not administrative or financial control) distributed over a large area, the whole state, a region of the state or more than one state is an affiliating university. The affiliated colleges, today, have grown to 9,278 in number. The affiliated colleges constitute a major sector of the university education in India.

As stated above, the system of affiliation was designed more than a century ago at a time when the number of universities and colleges was small, and the functions of the universities were limited to conducting examinations and grading the products for purposes of general employment, mainly secretarial services. In the situation prevailing today, the number of colleges has multiplied at an enormous rate and the expectations of the public, authorities and the society at large have become far more complex. The existence of a large number of colleges with uneven standards of teaching and commitment to education has become a dead weight in their efforts towards modernization, reform and improvement of standards. The affiliating system became irrelevant and decadent for the following reasons:

a) The management of many affiliated colleges does not have sufficient funds to develop the institution, and the university too cannot do much in this regard.

b) The communication from the universities to the colleges does not always get similar interpretation and in the process of clarification, a lot of time is lost. Therefore there is a delay in the pace for making quick academic decisions.

c) The affiliating system does not have the necessary and required freedom to make the college an instrument of social change.

d) Close-knit relationship between the university and its colleges were designed for a small number of colleges. But over the past few decades, universities have grown in size with the proliferation of affiliated colleges giving rise to enormous social problems like academic dissatisfaction, student indiscipline, campus violence, closure of institutions, mass copying, leakage of question papers, intimidation of invigilators, legal disputes in filling up vacancies, conspicuous absence of academic freedom, etc.

e) Colleges in remote areas affiliated to the university have to approach the university for every major and minor activity. The level of understanding between the 'centre' and 'periphery' being low, chances of personal interactions are almost absent.

f) Repeating the old type of education for the new generation of students is not going to be helpful to them and therefore autonomy alone can bring hope.

g) The sudden expansion of higher education has led to a lowering of quality, especially in the remote areas of the university district. Many colleges do not have even adequate physical infrastructure, not to speak of innovative and community related, socially relevant courses.

h) The monitoring of the quality of teaching, research, physical facilities and lab and library equipment by the university is often nominal and sometimes politicized.

i) Though affiliated colleges in India are independent, self-governing units as far as their financial operations are concerned; the government pays the salaries of their teachers. The college management can affect no effective quality control as the government is the pay master.

j) The system of affiliation puts the responsibility of updating or revising the syllabus on the shoulders of the university. The colleges themselves must be made responsible for such revisions.

The First Phase of Evaluation of Autonomy

Just before the end of the first five-year term in 1983, all autonomous colleges in Tamil Nadu were subjected to a detailed review and evaluation by independent teams consisting of eminent experts mostly drawn from outside the state. These teams interacted with students, teachers, employers, managements and others concerned and assessed the performance of these institutions. Their observations were:

a) New and relevant courses were introduced

b) Innovative teaching methods and better evaluation techniques had been adopted.

c) Courses were revised and updated.

d) Semester system and internal assessment brought faculty and students closer together.

e) Efforts were made to achieve higher levels of performance.

f) Project work, seminars, home assignments, field surveys, book reviews etc. had been introduced.

g) Examinations were held and results announced well in time and there were clear efforts to achieve higher levels of academic performance.

Advantages of Autonomy

The autonomy is a challenge for each college to stand on its own and make a gallant effort to justify itself through tireless pursuit of excellence. Teaching, learning and evaluation are a trinity of academic functions, which to be effective should be carried out by the same persons. In the affiliating system, the teacher teaches a curriculum prescribed by some other body and prepares his/her students to be examined by yet another body. The teacher has the responsibility neither for the course he/she teaches nor for the evaluation of the students he/she trains. His/her involvement is understandably very low. The teacher should have greater freedom. Academic autonomy will be a challenge to the teacher to be at his best and also to give out his very best.

a) Autonomous colleges helps to overcome the feeling of helplessness in the affiliating system regarding the introduction of reforms.

b) The new ideas like education based on work experience, internal assessment, better use of libraries, etc. can be tried out in individual institutions.

c) It is possible for autonomous colleges to introduce internal assessment, continuous evaluation of the students, 50 hours work in a week on a regular basis and introduce projects work which make students work harder.

d) A great deal of time spent by the universities in conducting examination and in evaluating the scripts can be saved and devoted to provide meaningful education.

e) There is a great deal of decentralization under autonomy.

f) The autonomous college is an important concept, which can be implemented for raising standards and encouraging the pursuit of excellence in carefully selected institutions. The basic prerequisites include motivated students, dedicated and committed staff, infrastructure and visionary management.

g) The Board of Governors and other academic bodies in an autonomous college are constituted with university and industry representatives.

h) The UGC nominates its representative on the Governing Council for a period of six years.

i) Autonomous colleges are given autonomy to modify the syllabus in the light of relevance, promotion of research and development and market requirements for students for placement and prescribe their own admission policy complying with the reservation policy and devise their own assessment procedures.

j) The parent university will award the degree certificate in an autonomous college, but with the name of the college and its logo.

k) Development grants on a liberal basis are provided for the development of autonomous colleges.

l) The autonomous institution can break away from the deadweight of the traditional curriculum and the complex and time-consuming procedures surrounding the syllabus modification.

m) Opportunity for introducing the system of internal assessment by replacing the outdated system of examination of the university.

n) An autonomous college can switch over its academic work to the semester system and assess the progress and attainment of its students through the techniques of self evaluation as well as assessment by the teachers.

While these are some of the positive aspects of autonomy, there exist several apprehensions and arguments against autonomous colleges.

Some General Apprehensions

a) Students will have too many assignments and written tests coming in quick succession.

b) In spite of working hard, the students may score less marks than their counter parts in non-autonomous colleges.
c) Teachers and students may be victimized by the management.
d) Standards may fall if the teachers are not able to resist pressures and threats from the students.
e) Under autonomy the course teacher would wield enormous power and might misuse the power out of prejudice or favouritism.
f) An autonomous college may boost the marks of students either due to pressure from the parents or from a desire to show high percentage of pass in the examinations.

Some of these apprehensions are without any basis. As long as the college keeps in mind its steadfast goal of academic excellence, it will be able to overcome most of the negative arguments raised against autonomy. Although there are certain problems, there exist much larger advantages through autonomy. Without doubt, one can say that autonomy is one of the most significant innovations introduced in the higher education sector of India.

Suggestions

a) The colleges being the temples of learning, autonomous institutions should be able to promote human, ethical, social and spiritual values.
b) A committed and dedicated approach is needed by the Principal, teaching and non-teaching staff and students to work relentlessly as a team.
c) Autonomous colleges should strive for quality improvements in all the spheres of administration, academic work, teaching and learning processes, examination procedures and the employability of the students.

Preparing Jyoti Nivas College for Autonomy

Faculty preparation, departmental preparation, institutional preparation and preparation of students and the local community were the areas where proper care was taken initially before implementing autonomy.

Faculty Preparation

It was necessary that the staff get familiar with the concept, objectives and rationale of autonomy. Several seminars, workshops, discussions and consultations were organised to ensure the involvement of the staff in the planning process of autonomy. The principal, the vice-principal, deans and the heads of departments share the responsibilities of administration, continuous internal assessment, examinations and discipline of the college with the entire faculty of the college. This created a sense of participation among the faculty motivating them to be involved in the whole exercise of autonomy.

Departmental Preparation

The general objectives of autonomy and the specific objectives of the education agency are always kept in mind in designing regular courses and short term courses in various subjects and in renaming and restructuring irrelevant courses by changing their subject matter and updating the syllabus in each discipline.

Institutional Preparation

Since an autonomous college is a miniature university, adequate preparation is made to equip the institution to perform all the functions—academic, administrative/management and financial in an effective manner.

Curriculum Development

a) Units of courses which replaced the traditional syllabus in each discipline are allotted to faculty members.
b) Interdepartmental linkages and a coordinated orchestration of academic programmes/courses are made.
c) The impetus to bring changes in the curriculum was tempered by practical considerations and by certain prudence.

d) Teachers given support and encouragement by colleagues, especially by the concerned HOD and the BOS.

e) Internal and continuous assessment, well-designed tests, etc widen the scope of evaluation and assessment of students.

f) Project and field work are introduced.

Conclusion

After becoming an autonomous institution, the management of the college has positively responded to the increasing demands of quality education; the faculty members have generously given their expertise, time and talents; students have actively engaged themselves in various projects, research and enhancement of knowledge; parents have given their encouragement and support and the university has extended patronage.

Jyoti Nivas College has taken great care in framing the curriculum of different courses which give importance to fieldwork, project work, paper presentsation, documentation, self expression, problem solving, case studies, etc. New programmes like MCA, MBA and MA were introduced. An international tie up was established with Deakin University, Australia, and a centre of Indira Gandhi National Open University was started on the campus. The college has made considerable improvements in the infrastructure, upgraded the laboratories, built a modern auditorium, set up a PG centre, established a research cell, started publishing a national level academic journal and organized several training courses, conferences and seminars. The working of the autonomous programme was reviewed periodically, both at the department and institutional levels. Clubs like AICUF, NSS, etc. are involved in a number of extension activities. Several socially relevant courses were introduced. The value education and mentor-ward system help to promote the right human and social values among students. Ever since the college became autonomous, the placement level has increased and professional pursuit among the students has been rekindled.

The major goal of higher education is to develop to the fullest the physical and intellectual potential of the students and to inculcate social and human values, so that they can develop a strong character, live a better life and function as responsible members of the society. While focusing on academic excellence, the holistic growth of the students should not be neglected. Autonomy helps an institution to positively respond to desirable changes based on a noble value system.

18

Some Glimpses on the Style and Functioning of Autonomy in Colleges

—S. Sivasubramanium

A few random thoughts on the style and functioning of autonomous colleges in Tamil Nadu in general, and Madurai Kamaraj University and Bharathiar University areas in particular, are presented in this article. I had a long and close association with a number of autonomous colleges not only as a Vice Chancellor, but also as a member of the university Syndicate, as a member of the Governing Council / Board of Studies of a few autonomous colleges, as a member of the passing board / academic council, or as a member of the PG question paper setting and evaluation board, etc. The academic climate which prevailed in most of these autonomous institutions was indeed commendable. Some of the observations about the working of the autonomous colleges in the light of my longstanding association and experiences with these institutions are given below.

In general, women's colleges have an edge over men's colleges in the effective implementation of all aspects of autonomy. The reason for the female institutions doing well is that the women teachers and students are more than willing to take up the extra load of work due to autonomy. They are relatively more responsive, willing to participate in all spheres of activity and are more adaptable. Of course, there are exceptions to this observation.

Minority institutions are effectively implementing the concept of autonomy in colleges than the non-minority institutions. The reason may be that the teacher association activities are almost curbed or they are restricted to a minimum level in most of these colleges. In fact, there is a healthy competition among these institutions to excel in teaching-learning process, examination reforms, creativity, innovations, etc. The major problem with several non-minority institutions is that the teacher associations are very active in these colleges, but the managements are not willing to listen to their problems or understand them. Such a situation had led to the surrender of the status of autonomy by two colleges. However, in a few non-minority institutions which have a relatively more accommodative and understanding management, autonomy is found to be functioning effectively in spite of the presence of strong teacher associations.

Broadly speaking, urban institutions have an edge over rural institutions in effectively implementing academic autonomy. The main reason is that the urban institutions are generally better equipped and more technology- savvy than rural institutions. The urban student community and the faculty are quite often more progressive and innovative by virtue of their exposure. With regard to autonomous colleges situated in villages, the rural nature of these institutions has to a certain extent stood in their way to make innovations and to excel when compared with the autonomous colleges in urban areas. Even though the rural institutions are able to excel in a few aspects, they are unable to project their achievements like their urban counterparts.

A visionary head of the institution supported by a strong management and an efficient and committed team of teachers together are necessary for the success of an autonomous institution. In most of the prominent autonomous colleges, they have a 'core group'- a small number of committed and proactive teachers who are willing to help the management and the principal in the implementation of autonomy. It is this core group that builds and sustains the system effectively.

The innovations in the curriculum development, the participatory teaching-learning process, imaginative examination reforms and the academically congenial atmosphere created by the management, principal, teachers and the students are the most important factors for the successful implementation of the scheme in leading autonomous institutions. Successful autonomous colleges are the most sought after by the parents of the area in order to admit their wards.

Continuous innovations are responsible for the successful and effective implementation of autonomy in different institutions. Most of such colleges have shown willingness to adopt the latest technology available. Some of the autonomous colleges have given high priority to personality development and character building.

Several government autonomous colleges are functioning efficiently in Tamil Nadu. It is a core group belonging to an institution which takes care of the implementation of autonomy in spite of the fact that the head of the institution i.e., the principal is transferred quite often. The teachers of autonomous government colleges in Coimbatore area deserve special appreciation for their ability to implement and sustain autonomy in spite of the negative approach of the state government. Sri. Meenakshi Government College for Women, Madurai, also deserves special mention in this regard.

Yet another observation is that a committed male teacher working in an autonomous college is likely to be more innovative than a female teacher. This may be because the male teacher can effectively devote more time and energy for academic pursuits as he is relatively less confined to the mundane concerns and duties of home-making. At the same time, counselling, group study and tutorial system are found to be more successfully implemented in women's colleges.

While the University Grants Commission has been supporting the autonomous colleges in a very big way, the same kind of support is not available from the state government in terms of monetary support or in other aspects. Several autonomous colleges are unable to strictly adhere to the guidelines from the UGC for implementing autonomy due to the absence of timely and adequate support from the state government or the concerned universities.

Effective grievance-redressal mechanism is a prime requirement for the successful functioning of autonomous institutions. If the management and the principal are open minded and understanding, they can solve the grievances echoed by the teachers and students to a great extent. There are several institutions where autonomy has been successfully implemented in spite of the presence of active teacher associations.

There had been instances involving surrender of autonomy by two colleges. One autonomous college surrendered its autonomous status to the UGC due to the difference of opinion that erupted between the then management and the teacher association unit of that college. (Now, the college has been functioning well without the autonomous status under a different management). In another college, autonomy was surrendered because of the strike by the teachers' association. After their problems were addressed to a certain extent, autonomy was granted to the same institution. One sad aspect of these strikes was that both the management and teacher association used the students as a pawn in their hands to achieve their ends.

To encourage teachers employed in autonomous colleges, a system need to be evolved whereby either they are paid some remuneration for their extra work or provided a separate promotion scheme as the work load of these teachers cannot be equated to the work load of teachers in other colleges.

An academic study on the style and functioning of autonomy in colleges need to be carried out under the auspices of the UGC by eminent academicians who belong to the system. The problems of autonomous colleges are to be identified and appropriate recommendations are to be made by this team for improving the functioning of the autonomous colleges.

In conclusion, it may be stated that autonomy has been successful in those colleges where there is a strong leadership in the form of an able principal, an understanding management, an effective core group which build and sustain all aspects of autonomy, committed teachers, participating students and a watch-dog society. One cannot blame simply the management or the principal or the teachers for the improper implementations of autonomy. It is the total team work by all the stakeholders which will make academic autonomy in colleges a boon or a bane.

19

Autonomy: Prospects and Challenges

— R.B. Lal

Introduction

'Autonomy' is the freedom for a country or a nation/ organization/ institution to survive itself independently. Further it is the ability to make decisions without being controlled by anyone.

Historically, the University Education Commission was appointed on 4 November, 1948, with Dr. S. Radhakrishnan as its chairman and nine other renowned educationists as its members. The terms of reference, *inter alia,* included matters relating to means and object of university education and research in India and maintenance of higher standards of teaching and examination in universities and colleges under their control. In the report submitted by this Commission, in paras 29 and 31, it referred to autonomy in education which reads as follows:

'University Autonomy' : Freedom of individual development is the basis of democracy. Exclusive control of education by the state has been an important factor in facilitating the maintenance of totalitarian tyrannies. In such states, institutions of higher learning controlled and managed by governmental agencies act like mercenaries, promote the political purposes of the state, make them acceptable to an increasing number of their populations and supply them with the weapons they need. We must resist, in the interests of our own democracy, the trend towards the governmental domination of the educational process.

Higher education is, undoubtedly, an obligation of the state. But state aid is not to be confused with state control over academic policies and practices. Intellectual progress demands the maintenance of the spirit of free inquiry. The pursuit and practices of truth regardless of consequences has been the ambition of universities.

The respect in which the universities of Great Britain are held is due to the freedom from governmental interference, which they enjoy constitutionally and actually. Our universities should be released from the control of politics.

'Liberal Education': All education is expected to be liberal. It should free us from the shackles of ignorance, prejudice and unfounded belief. If we are incapable of achieving the good life, it is due to faults in our inward being, to the darkness in us. The process of education is the slow conquering of this darkness. To lead us from darkness to light, to free us from every kind of domination except that of reason, is the aim of education.

There cannot be a better exposition than what has been observed by these renowned educationists with regard to autonomy in education. The aforesaid passage clearly shows that the governmental domination of the educational process must be resisted. Another pithy observation of the Commission was that state aid was not to be confused with state control over academic policies and practices. The observations referred to hereinabove clearly contemplate educational institutions soaring to great heights in pursuit of intellectual excellence and being free from unnecessary governmental controls.

Prospects and Challenges

The autonomy includes both 'administrative' as well as 'academic freedom' to an institution for its self-governance without any interference from outside.

The 'administrative freedom' includes:

i) Right of appointment of staff and employees,

ii) Framing rules and regulations

iii) Service conditions

iv) Discipline and work atmosphere

v) Financial management.

'Academic freedom' means:

i) Instructional design, and development of need based curriculum for degree and diploma programmes

ii) Content selection, packaging of content, updating syllabi

iii) Identify the learning objectives

iv) Competencies student need to develop

v) Attendance requirements

vi) Innovation of technology-mediated learning (TML), use of Information Technology, availability and reliability of technology

vii) Teaching in a technology-mediated environment (TML) requires different skills and approaches than teaching in a traditional classroom

viii) Introduction of need-based new courses

ix) Examination and evaluation of students

x) Feedback of students about teaching and research of each and every course offered in the university

xi) Giving and receiving feedback to improve the system

xii) Faculty to develop skills in teaching with technology

xiii) Training of highly qualified teachers/ personnel.

THE SYSTEMATIC TRANSFER OF BEST PRACTICES

As organizations looked for ways to survive and remain profitable over the past decade, a simple but powerful strategy called 'benchmarking' evolved "the process of identifying learning, and adapting outstanding practices and processes from any organization, anywhere in the world, to help an organization improve its performance". The underlying rationale for the benchmarking process is that learning from the principles and specifics of best practice cases is the most effective means of developing successful practices.

Along with the freedom, it involves responsibility also, i.e., the teacher who teaches the course should have the right to evaluate his or her students, which truly gives academic freedom to an academician imparting education fairly and justifiably. A student should have the right to see his or her answer book at the end of every examination, to ensure fair evaluation in an open and transparent system. Autonomy gives 'academic freedom' both to the teacher and the taught and thus improving the quality of teaching environment.

The Western universities and educational institutions have a different kind of set up, in which universities enjoy greater autonomy and 'academic freedom'. Government also has least regulatory controls over the universities and all the colleges preparing students for degree are virtually autonomous. The Indian counterpart has more regulatory system which often, creates an environment of excuse. While in the Western educational system the teachers and employees do enjoy academic freedom, they are accountable for their productivity and there is no automatic promotion system in their universities. The promotion depends upon their efficiency and productivity in the area of their specialization.

The Western universities initially began on self-financing and private stakeholders basis while the government's share was kept minimum. The Indian universities are often initiated by the state government or the central government and the private stakeholders are kept minimal and thus, universities remain on much greater dependence on government grants. They prosper at the time of establishment and after a decade they suffer decay.

Western universities are presently experiencing a great shock due to global market economy as the demand of the stakeholders are very specific and highly market-oriented, and the government grants are also being reduced. It is due to the fact that the needs of the other factors in the society are much stronger and the government is trying to make universities behave like an enterprise. Researches undertaken in most of the universities are also very much market-oriented and demand driven.

Indian universities, on the other hand, initiated by the government and supported in the beginning, are now facing a severe financial crunch due to reduction of government grants, and at the same time private stakeholders are kept away for decades. Universities are trying to survive on self-finance programmes, which are often, grant oriented and demand driven, thus, reaching almost the same level of global education explosion where the only survivor will be the fittest. The quality aspect of the education has to be critically examined and continuous evaluation system of students, and teachers in the institutions shall be the means for quality assurance.

Conclusion

According to Jawaharlal Nehru, "A university stands for humanism, for tolerance, for reason, for adventure of ideas and for the search for truth. It stands for the onward march of the human race towards ever-higher objectives. If the universities discharge their duties adequately, then it is well with the nation and people".

Freedom of education includes the freedom of establishing and administering educational institutions. This includes the freedom in the matter of selection of students, staff and curriculum. All these rights have been encroached upon by various legislations and re-asserted by the courts. It has been declared that these rights cannot be lost by non-use or waived by surrender.

It is a matter of policy or of a fundamental principle, whether there should be or should not be a private initiative in the field of education, or for that matter in any fields, as industry, transportation, etc. India opted for a mixed economy, a balanced socialism. Greater freedom has been added in the recent past, without deleting the word 'socialism' added to the preamble of the Constitution in 1977. Monopoly of the state as well as of private agencies in any field is dangerous. It is healthy competition and complementing each other would lead to progress and prosperity, without destroying the personality and individuality of the human person.

Freedom of education is among the fundamental rights of each and every citizen. This freedom includes the right of each one to learn what he likes as well as to teach what he wishes. It is part of the freedom of opinion and expression.

20

College Autonomy: A Must for Higher Standards

— M.V. Pylee

The proposal to give autonomy to select colleges was first made by the Kothari Commission in its recommendations. But the recommendation was not implemented by the UGC or the Ministry of Education for over a decade. In the meantime the Planning Commission of India had in one of its reports supported the Kothari Commission and suggested autonomy might be given to 500 colleges to begin with and repeat the same every year. The Planning Commission hoped that in 10 years the evils of the affiliation system would be mitigated and the country would experience a better system of university administration. The affiliation system had outlived nearly a century and half its utility as an essential part of higher education in India. It had become irrelevant and counter-productive long ago. Yet no effort was made to bring the system to a halt. On the contrary, year after year, more and more affiliating colleges were established all over the country.

The idea of autonomy was a well tried one, although for a short period, in the country since 1937 with the implementation of Provincial Autonomy under the Government of India Act of 1935. Under the Act, provinces which had elected responsible governments were given almost complete independence to run those governments. The Provincial Autonomy scheme was implemented in all the provinces where the Indian National Congress had legislative majority and established a cabinet system of government. Although provincial governors had been given overriding powers by the Constitution to veto the decisions taken by the cabinet, there was an understanding that the Governors would not interfere unless there were extraordinary situations. From 1937 to 1939 the system of Provincial Autonomy functioned smoothly. Under the system the provincial government enjoyed three types of autonomy: legislative, administrative and financial. This model was available to the colleges to implement the system of college autonomy. It was Madras University which for the first time granted autonomy to six colleges in 1978 and Madurai University followed suit by granting autonomy to two colleges. The UGC enthusiastically welcomed the new initiative and promised special grants to autonomous colleges as and when they were established. Yet other states were reluctant to give autonomy to colleges and hence the progress of the scheme was very slow. Today the total number of autonomous colleges in the county as a whole was 314 of which 116 are in Tamil Nadu. There are states where there is not even a single autonomous college.

It was the University of London which provided the model for the British to establish the first three universities at Bombay, Calcutta and Madras in 1857. But the London University had discarded the affiliation system years ago; but we not only cling on to that system today but go on adding more and more of that type year after year! With the creation of teaching and research departments as integral parts of the affiliating universities, their original purpose and character have been largely lost. The affiliating-cum-teaching university of today is unable to perform well either as an affiliating university or as a teaching university. It is so preoccupied with its own internal problems that it has very little time to exercise the right control over the affiliated colleges and maintain proper academic standards in those institutions.

The colleges are left without proper and effective academic leadership, guidance and supervision. The situation has been further aggravated with the explosion of student population and proliferation of colleges. There has been a mushrooming of substandard and unviable colleges in all sorts of odd places in the most uncongenial environment bringing down academic standards as well as making it impossible for the university to exercise even a modicum of control and regulation. The impact of the affiliation system on the university itself and on its own teaching and research departments has been equally deleterious.

It is not able to do full justice either to the colleges or to its own teaching and research departments. Caught in the quagmire of examinations, degrees and diplomas and unshackled by routine roles, rules and regulations, the affiliating universities are not in a position to devote adequate time and resources to improve the quality of teaching or research in their departments, nor do they possess enough dynamism and resilience to lead the colleges along the path of progress and academic excellence. Since the affiliating-cum-teaching system has ceased to be academically creative and useful and has become administratively unwieldy and ineffective, the search for a suitable alternative system is urgently called for. It is in this context that the relevance and importance of autonomous colleges loom large. A systematic and sustained plan of implementing the scheme of autonomous colleges will, in a reasonable time pave the way for the disappearance of the affiliation system.

Changes in the Higher Education Scenario

The university-affiliated colleges and the higher education system are riddled with the vestiges of colonial education. The current system of uniform higher education is largely outmoded because of the widening gulf between the demands of real life and the existing course contents which are both rigid and static. The growing size of the educated unemployed are definite pointers to the incongruity of the present education system vis-à-vis the man-power needs of the country. The need for swift changes in the pattern of higher education are apparent because of the following factors.

i) The unprecedented knowledge explosion of global dimensions.
ii) The increased number of aspirants for higher education.
iii) The reduced budgetary subsidy for higher education calling for liberalization, privatisation and globalization of higher education.

Role of College Autonomy in the Changed Context

Today there is a rapid expansion and explosion of knowledge in all spheres of life. The spectrum of knowledge is highly technical, specialized and at the same time multidisciplinary in nature. The turnover of knowledge is also very rapid, resulting in knowledge becoming obsolete and redundant within a brief timespan. College autonomy assumes significance in this context because these colleges redesign and innovate curriculum without the red tape and delay associated with the affiliated university system. Further, under autonomy it is possible for different colleges to develop varied areas of specialization thus providing the much needed diversification of subject content in higher education. This in turn will help the students to have a wider and more flexible matrix of choice of subjects more in keeping with the current labour market requirements. It will also ensure that the end product of higher education is not homogeneous and stereotyped but heterogeneous and specialized within a multi-disciplinary context.

It is estimated that at the current annual rate of growth of 4.5 per cent student intake in higher education, in the next ten years there will be about a million students enrolled annually in undergraduate classes. The sheer size of this large student body is intimidating and despite the technological innovations made possible by computers the sheer task of programming the logistics of academic curriculum and examinations in a university affiliated system for such a large student body is well neigh riddled with delays and problems which can be avoided if more colleges become autonomous. College autonomy is thus a must if the concept of Total Quality Management needs to be applied to higher education in the country.

In the context of economic reforms and the need to restrict budgetary subsidies to which higher education is no exception, privatization has become a must in this context. College autonomy is significant because it is easier for autonomous colleges to make use of their existing infrastructure to start self-supported courses. The need to make these courses attractive will ensure that increased emphasis is given to job oriented courses with a definite vocational tint. The need to attract funds from industry will further bring autonomous colleges and industries closer, thus for the first time paving way for industry institution interaction. This will encourage vocationalisation of higher education and help in a big way in extending on the job training in industry for students in graduate classes. The R & D facilities of industries will also be accessible for colleges and vice versa thus helping students and teachers to be in the forefront of knowledge development. Industry could also benefit in the process by making use of accomplished academics for R & D and consultancy services. Thus higher education will for the first time become integrated to real life and hopefully the dimensions of the unemployment problem would be effectively solved.

Areas in which Autonomous Colleges Need to Focus Attention

In the current socio-economic milieu and keeping in mind the imminent objectives of higher education, autonomous colleges need to focus their attention on the following aspects:

i) Designing curriculum in such a manner that each autonomous college offers an area of specialization which will give it a competitive edge over other colleges.

ii) Special focus must be given to developing entrepreneurial skills among students so that a sizeable number of them can become job makers rather than job seekers.

iii) Develop self supported courses of diverse nature. Such courses can be: (a) full time degree programmes, (b) new subjects related to main discipline as a part of degree course, (c) additional job oriented part time courses. Opportunities must be given to students to study courses concurrently.

iv) Adopt the credit system and provide an atmosphere for net working among institutions so as to make it possible to have a flexible system offering maximum freedom of choice to students.

v) Develop a new set of institutional norms for working out MOU's with industry for closer institution–industry interface.

vi) Develop R & D cells and encourage a high degree of specialization for talented staff to become consultants and thereby augment institution earning through patenting and other entrepreneurial activity.

vii) Develop an effective system of performance appraisal both for the staff and the institution.

Conclusion

As the scheme of college autonomy makes steady progress there will be distinct global demand in favour of self-determination of people and transfer of power to grass roots. This demonstrates that the winds of change favour a decentralized approach which encourages better participation of people in decision making. In education, this indicates a change from a centralized university system to a decentralized net work of autonomous institutions catering to local needs of people and industry while still ensuring that qualitatively global standards are maintained. College autonomy in this context needs to be viewed as a democratic and participatory effort where students, parents, staff, industry, local people and managements sit together and have a say in the decisions that ultimately determine the system of higher education.

College autonomy is generally opposed by unionised college teachers as they fear that autonomy will give the managements too much of power and they will exercise undue authority over them. In Kerala all the college teachers' associations are generally opposed to college autonomy because of this misunderstanding of college autonomy. But if one were to study the working of college autonomy in Tamil Nadu which has the largest number of autonomous colleges, it will be clear that this is a mistaken notion.

Where autonomy works well, the teachers and managements cooperate and collaborate in a common endeavour raised standards and created a harmonious atmosphere. It is a pity that Kerala in spite of its claims that it is in the forefront of education in the country has not been in favour of college autonomy so far.

Kerala has some of the leading colleges in India. Several of them have been rated as top class by the NAAC and maintain high standards both academic and administrative. The Kerala government acknowledges this but they have not taken the initiative in favour of autonomous colleges. Unfortunately there is no political will in favour of autonomy. Consequently the state loses year after year huge grants from the UGC. All the talk of improving standards has no meaning so long as the colleges are not given autonomy which is essential to raise standards in higher education in the state. If we aim at world standards at least in a few of our colleges, autonomy is an essential prerequisite. For, that alone will release the colleges from the clutches of the university bureaucracy and the decadent rules and regulations. But who is interested in higher standards? Neither the state's politicians nor the unionised teachers. The managements have lost their interest which was there once upon a time, long ago.

21

Autonomous Colleges

— B. Ekbal

The relevance, feasibility, hurdles and problems related to granting of autonomous status to colleges affiliated to the universities need detailed discussion. An attempt is made in this paper to look at the various issues that need to be looked into while conferring autonomous status to higher educational institutions.

History of Autonomous Colleges

The colleges in India were virtually autonomous until the establishment of the three affiliating Universities of Calcutta, Bombay and Madras in 1857. The universities were formed chiefly for the purpose of holding common examination and to ensure common standards. The Indian universities adopted the affiliating pattern from the London University (1835), which was discarded in 1857. The affiliating system was designed at a time when both the number of colleges as well as those of the universities in the country was small. At the time of independence the number of universities were only 18. By 2006, there were 343 university level institutions and 16,885 affiliated colleges under them.

The universities in India are classified as Unitary, Federal and Affiliating. Unitary universities are campus universities. There will be constituent colleges under the federal universities. In affiliating universities there will be a number of affiliated colleges under their academic control. In India most of the universities are affiliating in nature and they also have a number of university departments under them.

CONCEPT OF AUTONOMOUS COLLEGES

Over the years the number of colleges affiliated the universities multiplied, consequently causing enormous hurdles in the smooth functioning of the very affiliating system. A steep decline in the academic standards, profiteering by the college management, low level of the quality of teaching, vulnerable examination systems, etc., were reported from a number of institutions from several states. There were also instances of frequent friction between universities and affiliated colleges on various academic and administrative issues. It was felt that the affiliating system stifles academic freedom and innovations in higher education. Nevertheless it was also felt that in the existing circumstances affiliating system is the only practical option before us.

It is in this context that ways to increase the academic standards in the affiliating colleges without radically altering the system itself was explored. A number of committees starting from sixties to the present day appointed for suggesting improvements in higher education recommended academic freedom to select colleges with the objective to encourage innovative changes so as to achieve academic improvement.

The first specific recommendation in this regard was made by Dr. K. S. Kothari Commission (1966). This was followed later by similar recommendation made by the Gajendragadkar Committee (1971) and the National Education Policy (1986) had also envisaged the establishment of autonomous colleges. The UGC meanwhile prepared concrete guidelines for setting up autonomous colleges in 1973 which was revised in 1998 and offered substantial financial assistance to newly formed autonomous colleges for activities related to improving the academic standards of the colleges.

Of late the National Assessment and Accreditation Council recommended conferring of autonomous status to well performing colleges. The recently published *Report on Autonomy of Higher Education Institutions* (2005) by the Central Advisory Board of Education (CABE) has also recommended the establishment of autonomous colleges.

Autonomy to Colleges in India

In 1978 autonomous status to 12 colleges in Tamil Nadu (8 Under Madras University and 4 under Madurai Kamaraj University) were granted. Later targets were fixed for the number of colleges to be granted autonomy during plan periods. The Tenth Plan target of granting autonomy to 10 per cent of the colleges (i.e. 500 colleges) could not achieved. By 2006 there were only 204 autonomous colleges in 11 states under 143 universities.

Kerala Experience

In Kerala the first serious initiative in the matter of autonomous colleges was made in 1987 when the government constituted an Expert Committee with Dr. K.Gopalan as chairperson to study the various aspects of the proposal to have autonomous college in the state. The Committee in effect recommended the establishment of autonomous colleges. No follow up action was taken on the recommendation of this committee.

The Inter-University Consultative Council (IUCC) appointed a committee in 1999 chaired by Dr. K.K.N Kurup, the then vice chancellor of Calicut University, and Dr. Cyriac Thomas, the pro-vice chancellor of Kerala University as convenor to study and report the feasibility of granting autonomous status to affiliated colleges. The committee submitted its report in 2000 and in this case also no further action was taken.

Meanwhile, Deemed University status was given to the Regional Engineering College (REC) in Calicut converting REC into the National Institute of Technology and initiative was taken to grant autonomous status to the Government Engineering College, Thiruvananthapuram under a World Bank-funded project. It may be mentioned here that the University of Kerala to which the college was affiliated was not consulted before the government order in this regard was issued.

The government made amendments in the University Acts in 2004 so as to empower them to grant autonomous status to the affiliated colleges.

Academic Autonomy in the Kerala University

It has gone largely unnoticed the academic autonomy given to the faculty and the departments in the University of Kerala from 1995 onwards as part of the introduction of the Choice Based Credit and Semester System (CSS) in the PG courses conducted by the university departments. As per the CSS system the faculty members of the various departments have the rights and responsibilities to design, review and revise the core and elective courses which will be examined by the department councils at the department level and the Academic Committee formed at the university level with the vice chancellor as chairperson and a senior professor as vice chairperson. Once approved by these committees the proposals will be submitted to the Academic Council for approval. In this system the academic programmes are initiated by the faculty of the university departments and the academic activities are not under the control of the Board of Studies and the Faculties of the University.

The CSS programme is based on continuous internal assessment and of the four semester examinations; the departments conduct the first three and the University will conduct only the end semester examination. The working of the CSS programme is coordinated and monitored by the Academic Committee regularly. All matters relating to the administration of the PG programme under CSS including registration for the course, examination, submission of semester performance reports, receipt of application for final examination, mark lists to each semester examination and the final consolidated mark list, issue of provisional certificates and degree certificates, etc are coordinated by the CSS office set up in the Kariavattom campus.

In India, the CSS was first introduced in the Pondicherry Central University. The other universities of Kerala have also taken steps to implement the CSS system for the PG programmes conducted by the university departments based on academic autonomy given to the faculty and the departments of the universities recently.

What is Autonomy?

All the reports suggested above and the UGC protocols take a fairly uniform approach with regards to the concept of autonomous colleges. The words of an eminent educationalist well sums up the essence of autonomy as the academic freedom given to teachers to decide "what to teach, how to teach, whom to teach and how to evaluate."

It should be understood very clearly that autonomous colleges does not come under the category of self-financing colleges. Autonomy means only academic autonomy and not administrative or financial autonomy.

As per the UGC guidelines an autonomous college will have the freedom to "determine and prescribe its own courses of study and syllabi, prescribe rules for admission in consonance with the reservation policy of the government, evolve methods of assessment of students, the conduct of examinations, notification of results and use modern tools of educational technology to achieve higher standards and greater creativity."

The initiative for grating autonomy status should be taken jointly by the university and the affiliated colleges. The university will have to appoint a committee with university and government representative to select the colleges applying for autonomous status. The list of the eligible colleges after getting the concurrence of the government will have to be forwarded to the UGC. After the UGC inspection and approval, the university can grant autonomous status to the selected colleges. The autonomous status is for five years initially and frequent monitoring by the university will have to be ensured. In the case of colleges that do not come up to the expected standards, the autonomous status can be revoked. UGC has suggested the formation of different set-ups like academic council, board of studies, etc at the institutional level for the conduct of various academic activities.

The Kerala IUCC report also recommends the establishment of a committee at the college level with student representation to monitor the functioning of the various activities related to autonomy. It further recommends that the existing staff patterns in the colleges should not be modified without the concurrence of the government and the universities. Also it is mentioned that the principle of communal rotation in the appointment of teachers and the enrolment of students should be maintained.

AUTONOMY EXPERIENCES

Several studies have been conducted by agencies like National Institute of Educational Planning and Administration (NIEPA) to assess the functioning of the autonomous colleges. The results are mixed in that there are a few colleges that have performed well but majority of the colleges could not achieve academic excellence as was expected. Instead new problems have come up in these colleges.

Francis Sundararaj, former principal, Kodaikanal Christian College, sums up the situation objectively, "The new experiment has brought about some good though it has fallen short of expectations. It is certain that autonomous colleges have not brought about the desired change during the past eighteen years, a period not too brief to expect results."

He also lists out the reasons for the failure of the autonomous colleges as follows:

a) Limited autonomy given to the colleges is woefully limited with the parent university still playing an arbiter for effecting major curricular changes.

b) The motivation triggered by the novelty of autonomy led to frantic pursuit of curricular innovation for its own sake. And it is on the wane when the gloss of novelty loses its luster.

c) The ethical commitment to maintain quality and standards is not exemplary in many colleges. Partialities, victimization, misuse of freedom and privileges and falsification as well as window-dressing are the woeful ethical lapses prevalent in some colleges.

d) Autonomy has fostered a pseudo-intellectual faculty ego, which has resulted in mediocrity.

His final comments are: "In short, the autonomous colleges in India are not different from their other counterparts within the affiliating system. The graduates who go out of these colleges share the same debilities suffered by other in affiliated colleges. They are poor thinkers, poor performers, and poor communicators, in addition poor in the awareness of their local and global environment".

He concludes by saying, "Autonomy emerged with much promise only to withdraw into the shell of ethical laxity, inertial and partial ignorance of the concept. The climb up the stair of impact making educational reform lies beyond autonomy." *(College Autonomy in India: Success and Failure: in Reforms and Innovations in Higher Education: Association of Indian Universities: New Delhi: 2001)*

Another major problem with autonomous colleges that was pointed out by other academicians is the tendency towards inbreeding of ideas and approaches since the course design, etc are done by the faculty members belonging to the same college.

Importance and Relevance of Autonomy

Even while we consider the limited success or failure of the autonomous college experiment, still a strong case can be made for the concept of academic autonomy to teachers and institutions for the following reasons.

1. The higher education scenario is fast changing with the world moving towards a knowledge society. Integration of academic disciplines is taking place at an amazing speed and application of information technology has radically altered the teaching learning process and pedagogical approaches. Tremendous possibilities and challenges are opened up by these changes. Newer concepts like multi-skilling, global skills, job shifting, lifelong learning, lifelong employability, anywhere anytime learning, etc. are emerging.
2. New knowledge providers like the corporate houses are emerging who have started marketing knowledge products and educational soft wares.
3. Corporate companies are bypassing universities and educational institutions by establishing set ups for imparting domain skills, skill testing and assessment and also starting various modern diploma courses.

4. Through the traditional academic approach and institutions these challenges cannot be over come with the result that the benefits of these developments are taken away by the students who can pay. From a public good education becomes a private property and commodity.

It is therefore necessary to initiate a bold and total reform process of higher education system to achieve academic excellence with social justice and in this context granting academic autonomy to teachers, institutions and departments with well defined responsibilities and under strict but viable guidelines should be considered seriously.

Financing of Autonomous Colleges

The whole issue related to the financing of autonomous colleges is not addressed so far. The UGC will be proving financial assistance to the newly formed autonomous colleges. However, UGC has made it clear that the funds cannot be used for creation of posts, payment of salary to the college staff or honorarium to existing staff (with a few exceptions) or to subsidise examination fee. The UGC guidelines in effect advocate a hike in examination fees to meet the additional expenditure. Introduction of new courses, etc., may require creation of posts and incur extra expenditure on conduct of examination and unless the government commits to provide funds for such expenditure college managements may meet these expenses through a self-financing mode. This can lead to student unrest and other problems in the campus. Also for sustaining the system government will have to continue funding on par with that of UGC grants once UGC funding period is over.

Kerala Situation

While implementing the autonomous concept the present educational scenario in Kerala should be taken into consideration: The following points need be looked into:

a) It is generally agreed that in Kerala there is an academic stagnation within the university system and the affiliated colleges with the result that the academic standards and employability of our graduates are coming down day by day.

b) It has to be conceded that the university governance system is not conducive enough for achieving academic excellence.

c) There is a general neglect of the arts and science colleges where the majority of students are still studying whereas there is an over-emphasis on professional education. There is a total anarchy in the courses run by the affiliated colleges that run into the following categories either with or without the concurrence of the universities:

   i) Traditional courses
   ii) UGC-sponsored courses
   iii) Self-financing courses
   iv) Off-campus courses
   v) Courses run by other universities.

d) Semesterisation was introduced in the PG courses but many undergraduate courses are still run on the old mode of terminal summative examinations. The Choice Based Credit and Semester System are introduced only in a few University departments.

e) The refresher and orientation courses conducted by the Academic Staff Colleges and the national seminars being organised by the departments in the colleges and universities have not resulted in the academic improvement of the teachers. Teachers also lack the knowledge about the modern teaching methodologies and technologies since there is no training programme to upgrade their pedagogical skill. The result is that the academic calibre of many teachers is so poor that they cannot enthuse the students.

f) In many colleges modern courses especially conducted under the self-financing mode are run by guest and contract lectures much to the erosion of academic standards.

g) The recent spurt of self-financing professional colleges, the attitude of the management of some these colleges, the court verdicts in effect denying educational opportunities to the poor have all contributed to a chaotic situation within the educational sector in Kerala. This has resulted in a feeling of suspicion and fear regarding any innovation that is brought in however well intentional and relevant they may be.

What to do Now

Before embarking on any new reform agenda the following steps need be taken urgently as regards the Arts and Science Colleges.

a) Mapping of all courses conducted by the colleges under the various universities.

b) Academic assessment of the courses and the calibre of teachers and the availability of infrastructure faculties.

c) Students assessment with regards to upward mobility, drop out rate, pass percentage, perception of the study, skill level and employability.

d) Semesterisation to be completed in the degree level also and move to Choice Based Credit and Semester System.

e) Government should take a final decision regarding excess and or the lack of teachers in various colleges. Redeployment and fresh appoints where necessary will have to be made.

f) To improve the academic caliber of teachers a massive teacher training programme on modern developments in various academic disciplines, modern teaching learning technologies based on IT will have to be initiated.

g) The academic possibilities opened up by Edusat, Inflibnet and granting of Add-on Courses by UGC should be exploited to upgrade the skill and academic caliber of students and teachers.

h) Formation of Cluster of Colleges to share resources and jointly plan modern skill based vocational courses.

i) Linking colleges with research institutes and sharing of faculty and infrastructure like library and laboratory, designing joint courses.

j) Initiate university, industry, college, government interaction.

What Universities should do

To implement these changes the universities should take the following steps:

a) Develop better organic linkages with affiliated colleges.

b) Design and show case new courses: Integrated inter-disciplinary courses and skill based and vocational courses.

c) Take steps to prepare educational softwares.

d) Massive teacher training programme in academic subjects and new teaching learning technologies.

What the State Government should do

a) Prepare an appropriate education policy taking into consideration the challenges and opportunities before the state.

b) Declare a policy on higher education financing so as to maintain social justice and equity in educational opportunities and access.

c) Initiate only consensus and transparent decision in educational reforms.

d) Establish Higher Education Council with the main objective to carry out Human Resource Development Planning for the state.

Conclusion

Autonomy to the departments and academic faculty in the universities and affiliated colleges is a desirable educational reform. However, this should be implemented only with the concurrence and consensus of all concerned like the teachers, students the management of the affiliated colleges. Definite norms and protocols should be laid out for giving autonomous status to affiliated colleges.

It should be understood that autonomy in the affiliated colleges works only in the presence of a well functioning university system and academic vibrancy in the affiliated colleges. In the absence of both these autonomy by itself will not bring in the desired changes as evidenced by the experiences of the autonomous colleges in other states. Autonomy should be a collective decision of the universities and the affiliated colleges. Within the colleges the demand for autonomy should come from the teachers and students.

The government should grant additional funds to the autonomous colleges for payment of salary of teachers and other supporting staff and extra expenditure required for conduct of examination and also supports the colleges after the termination of the funding by UGC.

The educational scenario in Kerala is totally chaotic presently with the advent of the self-financing institutions/courses. In this context a radical departure from the established practices should not be envisaged without taking everybody into confidence and also in a transparent and democratic manner. Granting autonomy to the affiliated colleges should be a consensus, conscious and transparent decision and should be implemented as part of an overall attempt to reform higher education.

Works Cited

Hand Book for Post Graduate Programmes (Credit and Semester System), University of Kerala (2004), Thiruvananthapuram.

Inter University Consultative Council: Kerala (2000), *Report of the Sub Committee on the Feasibility of Granting Autonomous Status to Colleges in Kerala,* Thiruvananthapuram.

Kuldip Kaur (2003), *Higher Education in India (1781-2003),* University Grants Commission. New Delhi.

Management of University Administration, Association of Indian Universities: (2004), New Delhi.

National Policy on Education Policy, Government of India (1986), Department of Education: New Delhi.

R.P Singh (Editor), *Indian Universities Towards Nation Building,* (1998), University Grants Commission, New Delhi.

Reforms and Innovations in Higher Education (2001), Association of Indian Universities, New Delhi

Report of the Central Advisory Board on Education (CABE) on Autonomy of Higher Education Institutions (2005), Ministry of Human Resource Development: New Delhi.

Report of the National Commission on Education (Kothari Commission), Government of India, 1966, New Delhi.

Revised Guidelines on the Scheme of Autonomous Colleges, University Grants Commission (1998), New Delhi.

Sharma, Kavita A, *Fifty Years of University Grants Commission*: (2003): University Grants Commission. New Delhi

Vision Statement, University of Kerala (2002), Thiruvananthapuram.

World Education Report: The Right to Education: Towards education for all throughout life: UNESCO (2000), UNESCO, Paris

22

The Autonomous College

—Ninan Abraham

The autonomous college is an educational and institutional idea worth implementing where a college has a convinced and committed teaching community and a management that is interested. So far the bulk of higher education in India has been imparted through the system of the 'affiliating' universities and 'affiliated' colleges. This is an arrangement found hardly anywhere else in the world except the Indian subcontinent. But here it is more than a hundred and 50 years old.

When in 1857 the affiliating university scheme was introduced, there were many considerations to recommend it. In the first place the government could provide modern higher education on Western lines without having to spend large amounts to set up teachinguniversities. The existing colleges were pressed into service and their work was guided and supervised from a central office with a vice-chancellor, a registrar and a small supporting staff. New colleges were also mostly started by private agencies or individuals without substantial expenditure on the part of the government.

There are some educational considerations also in favour of the affiliating system. It is possible to ensure uniformity of standards and objectivity in assessment as the courses and syllabi are fixed by the universities and the testing and evaluation are centrally controlled. But there are some limitations and deficiencies which became apparent as time passed and the numbers increased. The universities have become unwieldy, slow-moving and inefficient and unable to meet the needs of the times. They were not able to introduce new subjects and update the courses of study fast enough. The teaching methods were stereotyped and even good colleges had to follow the methods prescribed for all, good, bad and indifferent. The conduct of examinations for hundreds of thousands of students in hundreds of institutions was cumbersome, involving loss of study time for the students and inefficiency, delays and corruption.

In spite of the defects, the system continued and is likely to continue, for a number of reasons. One is the enormous expenditure involved in replacing the colleges by teaching universities. The number of universities required is very large. England with a population of 50 million has around one hundred universities and the number may increase. At that rate India should have at least two thousand universities. That is not a practical possibility at the present time. It is also not possible to close down the existing colleges. A possible alternative is to give to the colleges—to the better ones if not to all—some of the freedom and the opportunities for exercising creativity and initiative. The autonomous college scheme is meant for this. An autonomous college can decide what subjects it should teach, what the content of the courses should be and how the teaching and examining should be done.

Most of the existing autonomous colleges have started courses in applied subjects which are in demand in the employment market. They have also modernised and improved the course of studies in the traditional subjects. Further they have devised methods of teaching which stimulate the critical and creative powers of the students. The evaluation methods are also geared to test independent thinking. Good autonomous colleges have thus been doing significantly better work. An experienced educator wrote as follows after visiting some autonomous colleges:

"One has only to spend a couple of days on the campus of a good autonomous college and interact with the staff and students to find out for oneself the enormous changes that have taken place in the curriculum and the attitudes of students and staff to education as a change agent and a sub-server of society's needs".

If the scheme of autonomous colleges is educationally sound why are not colleges being made autonomous on a large scale? The idea was mooted more than half a century ago and statutory provision was made in one university as early as 1953 (ironically enough even to day there is not even a single autonomous college in that university). The idea of autonomous colleges was commended by the Education Commission in its Report of 1966. The University Grants Commission and various other bodies and committees have endorsed and recommended the scheme and even set targets for the spread of autonomy. But so far slightly more than three hundred out of a total of 19,000 colleges of the country have actually become autonomous. The reasons for the slow progress are manifold.

The central government is keen on the idea but most of the state governments are not in favour and the colleges are under state governance. The state governments fear that the authority that they have over education in the state will erode with college autonomy and they are not willing to shed any of their powers.

The authorities in the affiliating universities are also generally not in favour. The reaction of many a vice-chancellor has been that the university would 'lose' the best colleges. This is a misunderstanding. These colleges will be the colleges of the university and the degrees granted will be of the university, but they will be giving to the colleges the authority to hold the examinations. They may consider this as a 'loss' for them. Will not the university lose the privilege of holding the examinations for some of the best students of the university as it is the good colleges that will become autonomous?It may however be pointed out that the colleges of some of the world famous universities are all autonomous. For example, in the University of London all the colleges are autonomous. They hold their own examinations, but the degrees are of the University of London. This is true of even King's College and University College, both of which have more than twenty thousand students each and are larger than many of the Universities of England.

Another important factor is the attitude of the teachers and especially the teachers' associations. In Kerala, for example, most teachers are against college autonomy. Many of them tried to convince the committee appointed by the government under Dr. K. Gopalan (1987) that college autonomy was bad for education as well as for the society. The teachers' attitude is such an important factor in the whole matter of college autonomy that I take the liberty of giving below the summary of their arguments along with the comments of the Committee.

i) Autonomy for a college means and implies that the college and its teachers assume full responsibility and accountability for the academic programmes they provide, for the content and quality of their teaching and for the admission and assessment of their students. It means nothing more than that. The parent university will provide general guidelines, monitor programmes to ensure overall standards and confer degrees upon the successful candidates accepting the evaluation done by and mentioning the name of the autonomous college.

ii) India is perhaps the only country in the world where the major part of university education is imparted through colleges which are 'affiliated' to a parent university. The rigidity in the structure of the affiliating university has thwarted all attempts of reform in the higher education in the form of curriculum development, examination reforms, promotion of research, etc. The monolithic affiliating university with its centralised administrative structure has proved to be an obstacle to making education creative for the student and the teacher alike.

iii) Many arguments have been put forward in favour of autonomous colleges. In an autonomous college, the teacher is liberated. Autonomy will be a challenge to him to be at his very best. Autonomy will imply a spirit of adventure for the entire academic community, which will encourage innovation and experimentation. The whole process of education becomes dynamic, creative and efficient.

iv) Several arguments have been put forward against the establishment of autonomous colleges. While some of the problems presented are genuine, others are based on ignorance, prejudice, misunderstandings and misgivings. Some of the arguments against autonomous colleges are that they will give unbridled powers to the managements, foster elitism, promote corruption, bring down the standards and so on. It was obvious that while all the people who gave evidence for the committee had heard about autonomous colleges, most of them really did not know what exactly the concept meant. When the concept and philosophy of autonomous colleges was explained to them, even those who had come prepared to oppose the proposal said that they agreed with the concept 'in principle' but that they were highly sceptical about the proper implementation of the concept in the context of Kerala.

v) One of the main arguments raised against autonomous colleges was that the managements would have unlimited power under autonomy and that they would use them arbitrarily to victimise the staff. This is a baseless argument. The managements of autonomous colleges will not have any more powers conferred on them through autonomy than what they have at present.

vi) Some of the teachers feared that under autonomy they would be forced to do more work and that they would lose some of the privileges and service conditions they had acquired over the years through organised effort. This is more a propaganda than a fact. Under autonomy none of the existing privileges and service conditions will be taken away. If at all, the teachers will have some additional privileges and facilities. The work load of the teacher does not increase under autonomy. It will be the same 14 hours per week as for non- autonomous college teachers. It is not more work, but more responsible work that a teacher will have under autonomy.

vii) Another fear expressed was that under autonomy the course teacher would wield enormous power and that he might misuse the power out of prejudice or favoritism. There is some truth in this fear. But this can be taken care of effectively by making all assessment procedures open with provision for appeal. The teachers get completely 'exposed' in the process of showing any bias or prejudice towards any student because the whole system is an 'open secret'.

viii) It was also pointed out that the college as a whole might boost the marks of students either through pressure from the parents or from a desire to show high percentage of passes in examinations. Experience has shown that this sort of practice cannot be indulged in by any college since it would be suicidal in the long run. Moreover there are built-in mechanisms such as 'Results Passing Board' with nominees of the parent university on it to check such activities. The parent university has supervisory powers over autonomous colleges and would enquire into any kind of dishonest evaluation.

ix) There is opposition to college autonomy based on the fear that it would create an 'elitist' class of colleges enjoying special privileges thus creating a kind of 'superior-inferior' classification among colleges. The word 'elitism' is completely out of place here because autonomous colleges will not enjoy any special 'privileges' except the privilege of doing hard work, framing their own courses and curricula and conducting their own examinations. All laws/ rules/ regulations regarding reservation, concession in the matter of appointments, admission etc. will be equally applicable to autonomous colleges as in the case of non- autonomous colleges. It is not 'elitism' but 'excellence' that is being recognised and encouraged by college autonomy. The pejorative term 'elitism' is not applicable to the autonomous colleges since autonomy refers to quality or excellence of education and education is almost by definition the search for quality.

x) It has been argued that it would be impossible to take away autonomous status when once it is conferred. This argument is not acceptable. There are any number of instances in this country as well as elsewhere, when recognition/ accreditation given to academic institutions has been taken away for not maintaining the prescribed facilities and standards.

I am constrained to point out a small but significant contradiction in the report of the committee. In paragraph six there is a reference to the fear of the teachers that they will be required to do more work under autonomy. The committee tries to allay that fear by saying that this is not true and that teachers will have to work only 14 hours per week.

However in paragraph nine it is said that teachers will have "the privilege of doing hard work" Unfortunately it is a privilege that many teachers may not want. If autonomy is to provide a better and more creative education more work and more responsible work will be necessary.

This leads on to a crucial factor relating to the success of college autonomy. Autonomy involves greater responsibility in preparing the syllabi and in teaching and in examining. These will be done satisfactorily only if there is commitment, dedication and devotion and the willingness to do thoughtful and responsible hard work. Where a large majority of the teachers of an institution have these qualities autonomy can deliver a much better quality of education, otherwise not.

Provided the teachers have the sort of commitment indicated above, our colleges and the affiliating universities can develop into a condition comparable to that of London University. At present all the colleges of London are autonomous and the university describes itself as a federal university. The university provides some central facilities, has some sort of overall supervision and awards the degrees.

As a start we could go ahead with the scheme of clusters of colleges. Colleges which come within a radius of fifteen or twenty kilometers from a central point could be grouped into a cluster. The government should provide some facilities at the centre like a library, a workshop, a museum, etc. Cooperation among the colleges should be on a voluntary basis. To begin with the syllabi and the examinations will be the responsibility of the university. As the colleges qualify for autonomy they can have their own courses, syllabi and examinations.

23

Autonomy for Colleges in Kerala

— Cyriac Thomas

Introduction

In Kerala, the educational scenario always remain sensitive and touching issues are often viewed and debated more on religious, spiritual, political, commercial and sectarian orientations than on their genuine or real merits involving the quality enhancement. Vilifying campaign gains precedence over public debate on issues of merit. This fundamental character of the approach adopted by various factors in education, government, managements, teacher organizations, non-teaching unions, political parties and the respective student wings and so on and so forth—all have made quality and excellence the casualty in the educational sector. The very cause of education remains a victim in the sphere of education in Kerala. If we can believe the latest reports, the preeminent place hitherto enjoyed by Kerala in the sphere of literacy and education has now been taken by a smaller state than ours- the Meghalaya, proving the fact that while other states were striving for betterment in education, we preferred to bask in the glory of the past records than exploring the possibilities of further advancement in future, making use of our potential in full measure.

Often the Malayalee claims to be adventurous and daring, innovative and revolutionary. Yet the same Malayalee will prove himself or herself the celebrated conservative in resisting any change whatsoever if he or she entertains any fear about losing any of the prerogatives or privileges they enjoy as part of their career or profession. Many of us are very smart and even manipulative enough to preserve our privileges by labelling everyone else as conservative and reactionary as part of our attempt for anticipatory bail.

I am afraid, openness, academic and intellectual honesty, humility to admit facts and faults, forthrightness and transparency regarding one's stance and convictions - all seem more conspicuous by their absence rather than by their presence in the contemporary educational scenario of ours, more obviously in the sphere of higher education on all counts—in legislation, in policy formulation, in the running of universities and colleges, in teaching and research and even in the running of teacher organizations and employee's unions. The managements are no less guilty either. Fights and counter fights, campaigns and counter campaigns, hasty legislations and consequent battles in courts, criminal delays every year in admissions for professional courses, financial fortunes for lawyers—all seem to constitute the major agenda in the educational sector, paralyzing the possible growth and development in the field.

It is against this backdrop that we enter into a dialogue regarding 'autonomy', discussing and debating whether it will ever have a chance to be experimented in our state. In this connection I recall the stiff resistance raised earlier by many against accreditation of colleges refusing to be rated by anyone even on the basis of an evaluation and assessment methodology based on the self study report prepared and submitted by the colleges themselves. Now things seems to have changed a lot and even those highly critical academicians of the NAAC accreditation in the beginning concede at least half-heartedly that accreditation processes help to accelerate the development of those colleges which opt for accreditation.

In the matter of autonomous colleges too the present prejudices preserved by many might vanish in the days to come, once the academic community realizes that it is the academic autonomy which is mainly aimed at and the purpose of the same is for the all round quality enhancement of education and that of the educational institutions. But when the experiment of autonomous colleges is ever resorted to in Kerala, it is essential to take into account the educational ecology of the Kerala society too, so that any possible environment pollution in education is prevented. Let us try to avoid the extremes and it may be prudent to take every effort for a possible consensus before its introduction here in our state.

In the self-financing sector in professional education we already have made ourselves victims and casualties as a result of the arrogance and imprudence, infirmities and change of words with which we made the very sector, chaotic and confused. The government's contribution in making the confusion more confounded is also to be acknowledged. It is in the genuine interests of the cause of higher education that all those who subscribe to good intentions plead for a consensus on reasonable terms which will be convincing for the people. Such a consensus should protect the honour of the managements but of course without prejudice to the social justice principle enshrined in the constitution of our Republic.

The Readers Digest Great Encyclopedic Dictionary defines 'Autonomous' as that which is independent of the usual processes which regulate the growth of an organism. Autonomy is explained as freedom of the will. The fact is that almost all colleges in India were autonomous until the establishment of the three affiliating universities of Calcutta, Bombay and Madras in 1857. As everyone knows the universities were established chiefly for the limited purpose of holding common examinations and to ensure common standards. The Indian universities adopted the affiliating pattern from the London University (1837). However, the University of London discarded the affiliating pattern by 1857. No doubt that pattern may be considered part of the colonial legacy left by the British in India. In the long run it became the officially recognized system in the educational frame of the country and even today we find it difficult to revise or review that system as it has, for all practical purposes, become a very convenient one for everyone.

A Unitary University is usually a residential one and where the entire teaching work is organized within the campus. In a Federal University the teaching work is shared by the university with its constituent colleges. An Affiliating University is the one which has a number of colleges under its academic control. At present most of the universities in India have become teaching cum affiliating in character. The number of affiliated colleges in the country touches around 10,000 at present of which nearly 80 per cent are in the private sector. No doubt, the affiliated colleges constitute a major chunk of the university system in India.

Over the past hundred years or so universities have not only grown in size but their number also have multiplied, consequently causing enormous hurdles in the smooth functioning of the very affiliating system. A steep decline in academic standards, profiteering by the managements, dangerously low level in the quality of teaching, frightening dimensions of student indiscipline and campus violence, consequent closure of institutions, a very vulnerable examination system, occasional leakage of question papers, mass copying by candidates, intimidation of invigilators, legal disputes over appointments and promotions in the faculty, administrative and political interventions in decision making etc. are some of the very striking ills found in the current affiliating system. In addition to these, the frictions between the universities and their affiliated colleges on one issue or the other further vitiate the very sphere of higher education. Further, the absence of academic freedom for the affiliated colleges also affects the effective success of any attempt for a qualitative change in higher learning.

However, the affiliating system survives and has to do so as at present, in the given situation in India, the affiliating system seems to be the practical one, in spite of its ills and deformities as no other single system is equipped enough to cater to the needs and requirements of the sphere of higher education today. Hence the continuance of the affiliating system in India.

However, the Government, the University Grants Commission, the Association of Indian Universities, universities, educationalists etc., have been engaging themselves in probing the possibilities of appropriate reforms in the existing pattern as part of an effort in effecting possible qualitative change in higher education by identifying and experimenting alternative systems.

Evolution of Autonomous Colleges in India

The idea of autonomous colleges attracted the attention of educationalists as it was suggested as a probable solution for many problems in the affiliating system. A number of committees formed in the fifties and sixties for suggesting improvements in the area of higher learning hinted at the possibility of granting academic freedom to at least some select colleges as an attempt for a qualitative change in the educational scenario. The first formal and specific recommendation in this regard was made by the Dr. D.S. Kothari Commission Report (1966). The idea of giving autonomous status to well-established colleges with a view to raising standards and encouraging the pursuit of excellence in higher education was specifically proposed by the Commission. The Commission observed: "We should like to refer to the question of 'autonomous' colleges which has been under discussion for many years. Where there is an outstanding college (or a small cluster of very good colleges) within a large university which has shown the capacity to improve itself markedly, consideration should be given to granting it an autonomous status. This would involve the power to frame its own rules of admission, to prescribe its courses of study, to conduct examinations and, so on. The parent University's role will be one of the general supervision and the actual conferment of the degree. The privilege cannot be conferred once and for all. It will have to be continually earned and deserved, and it should be open to the University after careful scrutiny of the position, to revoke the autonomous status if the College begins to deteriorate in its standards. We recommend that provision for the recognition of such autonomous colleges be made in the Constitution of the Universities." (Education Commission, 1966, p.286).

A Committee of the UGC consisting of Dr. D.S. Kothari, Dr. P.B Gajendragadkar, Dr. A.C. Joshi, Shri. P. N. Kripal, Dr. B. Malik, Dr. A.L. Mudaliar, Dr. K.L. Sharimali, Dr. R.K. Singh, Shri. J.P. Naik and Shri. K.L. Joshi made further studies on the question of the feasibility and mechanism of implementing the recommendation of the Education Commission regarding Autonomous colleges and made a few stipulations in 1967 of which the major ones were the following.

i) The autonomous college is a very important concept which may be experimented only in carefully selected institutions. The purpose should only be raising standards and encouraging excellence.

ii) The basic prerequisites for selection are good students, good faculty, good facilities and good management. The Constitutions (Rules) of the colleges must be carefully considered.

iii) The proposal for the conferment of autonomy on any institution should originate from the university and the college concerned. Even if the UGC is associated with the process, the primary responsibility has to be undertaken by the university.

iv) Autonomous colleges may be permitted to restructure/ modify the syllabus and may prescribe their own admission policy and devise their own assessment and evaluation procedures.

v) The degree in an autonomous college should be awarded by the parent university but the name of the college should also be specifically mentioned in the Degree Certificate.

vi) Development grants on a liberal basis should be provided for the development of autonomous colleges.

The Dr. P.B. Gajendragadkar Committee (1969-71) also stressed the need of setting up autonomous colleges but the proposal remained yet to be materialized as there was no legislative enactment in that direction. The Gajendragadkar Committee in its anxiety to have autonomous colleges in the country even suggested as a model the relevant provisions of the Himachal Pradesh University Act, 1970, which read:

i) The University may grant, in the manner and after following the procedure prescribed in the relevant statutes, to a college, department or unit which satisfies the conditions laid down in the statutes in this behalf the privileges of modifying or changing for the students the course of study prescribed by the university and of holding examination in the course so modified and such college, department or unit shall be declared in the manner prescribed in the statutes to be an Autonomous College.

ii) The extent to which the courses may be varied and the manner of holding examinations conducted by such college or university department, as the case may be, shall be determined in each case by the university.

In this continuous chain of progressive support for the idea of autonomous colleges, the UGC sent a circular to all universities in 1973 recommending that they should set up autonomous colleges. The circular entitled 'Autonomous Colleges: Criteria,

Guidelines and pattern of Assistance' highlighted the objectives of autonomy, the distortions and consequences of affiliation system, the relationship of autonomous colleges with the parent universities, the procedure to be followed for the conferment of the autonomous status and the pattern of assistance given by the UGC to autonomous college. The circular also made it clear that it was essential to involve the university as well as the state government in the process of identification of colleges which are to be conferred autonomous status.

It was Tamil Nadu which took a bold initiative in introducing the autonomous system by granting some colleges the status of autonomy. The lead came from the Madurai American College (established in 1881). After much discussions and deliberations on the issue, the College submitted a detailed proposal to the university, the UGC and the state government in 1972. The University of Madurai approached the state government of Tamil Nadu to amend the University Act to provide for autonomous colleges under the university. The University of Madras also took the initiatives of asking several colleges to prepare and submit proposals for autonomy. More than a dozen colleges responded from which eight were identified as eligible for autonomous status. Subsequently, three more colleges in Madurai-Kamaraj University submitted their proposals for autonomy. The UGC sent an inspection team to visit all the colleges identified as eligible for autonomous status to satisfy itself with the facilities in this colleges and also to hold discussions with all concerned. In 1977, the Tamil Nadu government also gave its green signal for the autonomous experiment and subsequently the Tamil Nadu state legislature amended the University Act providing for autonomous colleges. Eight colleges in Madras University and four in Madurai Kamaraj University started functioning as autonomous colleges from June 1978.

The autonomous colleges are essentially and fundamentally different from self financing colleges. It is the academic autonomy that is granted and emphasized. Autonomy for a college implied that the college and its teachers assume full responsibility and accountability for the academic programmes they provide, for the content and quality of their teaching and for the admission and assessment of their students. It is the joint pursuit of truth and excellence.

However, it would be necessary to ensure that the terms and conditions of service for teachers prescribed by the government and the UGC should continue to apply to these institutions and the institutions continue to observe the needs of national integration and development.

The concept of autonomous colleges does not imply at all any permanent categorization of an institution under a separate label for any higher formal status. It necessarily requires an institution to be continuously subjected to scrutiny to justify its recognition as a centre of academic worth and excellence.

The National policy of education (1986) further suggested to make also statutory provisions, if possible, to enable autonomous colleges to award their own degrees or to confer Deemed University Status on them.

Initiatives for College Autonomy in Kerala

In Kerala, the first serious initiative in the matter of autonomous colleges was made in 1987 when the government constituted an Expert Committee with Dr. K. Gopalan as chairman to study the various aspects of the proposal to have autonomous colleges in the states and to make recommendations to the government.

The response to the concept of autonomous colleges has never been that much positive or enthusiastic in Kerala, given the political composition of the society and the ideological pretensions and prejudices carefully preserved by various shades in the state. The well-knit teacher organizations, student organizations, employees organizations, etc. have also generally refused to take kindly to the proposal as somehow there seems to be a strong feeling among these organized forces that the granting of autonomous status to colleges will ultimately affect the collective interests of these sectors in the field of higher education. One of the major apprehensions seems to be that the managements of colleges may acquire greater clout under the autonomous scheme. But the fact is, according to Dr. M.A. Thangaraj, an authority on the working of autonomous colleges, the managements would not get even an iota of additional authority as a result of autonomous status. It is nothing but academic autonomy that is granted to institutions.

In Kerala, education remains a delicate issue to be dealt with, as any attempt to reform or restructure it invariably invites stiff resistance from one section or the other in the sector on the plea that the scheme of reform will either harm one section's 'interests' or the other section's 'rights'. After an ongoing pubic debate in the media and on the platforms accompanied by some loud protests by various shades of interests—managers, teachers, students and employees unions and as a result of strong lobbying either in favour or against the proposed schemes by the concerned interest groups, finally the government also will agree to give a go by to the proposals by engaging itself in the art of pleasing everyone and the scheme will be placed conveniently in the cold storage. But in this process that gets often repeated here in Kerala, the tragedy is that enough and more harm is done to the very cause of education through this shameless on going drama.

While the government and the teachers generally seem to prefer to find fault with the management for anything and everything that happens in the sphere of higher education, the managements, on their part lament on the government's mala fide intentions in curbing the management's inherent and 'sacred' rights in the field. The teachers conveniently forgetting their own failings will put the blame of all ills on the wrong doings of the management, and the students. The students after abstaining from classes for the best part of the academic year usually tend to take the system to task for their poor show in the examinations. They will consistently clamour for structural changes in the system but at the same time will take enough caution and care to absolve them—and them alone—of all the sins in the existing order. The parents on their part, surprise everyone by remaining criminally indifferent in all matters concerning higher education. They are generally least bothered, it seems, about the happenings in the sphere of higher learning and even about the stakes they have in them.

The fact of the situation seems to be that almost all sections remain completely dissatisfied with the present scheme of things but at the same time surprisingly reluctant to support any serious effort or endeavour on the part of anyone to recast, remould or restructure the existing frame as almost everyone is afraid of getting his 'interest' harmed in the process.

It was, in fact, this ongoing 'hide and seek game' played by one and all in the sector of higher education for the last couple of decades that halted the possibilities and potential for improvement in the area of higher learning in this part of the country.

As part of any academic probe into the problems and possibilities of higher education in the state, it becomes obvious, that unless all sections in the sector concede, in all humility and forthrightness, that matters have gone somewhere fundamentally wrong and unless everyone agrees on the inevitability of a major surgery to remove the malignant growths affecting the normal functioning of the system, the area of higher education will still remain beyond the reach of any possible process of correction. It is in these premises that we have to probe into the problems affecting education and through that painful process of diagnosis, to arrive at a consensus in prescribing some urgent and effective remedial measures.

In one of the documents of the Kerala State Planning Board, prepared long ago, but which still very much hold the ground, Dr. V.R. Pillai, one of the doyens amongst our educationists of yester years rightly observed: "The state or condition of higher education in Kerala, in fact, presents a dismal picture. Colleges are over-crowded and without the needed physical infrastructure, laboratory equipment or library facilities. Higher standards of academic excellence have considerably deteriorated with the introduction of other criteria than merit for the selection of the staff in government colleges and the system of purchasing posts with donations in private colleges...non-teaching by teachers is countered by non-attendance by students. Frequent strikes make heavy loss of working days".

Dr.M.V. Pylee, former vice-chancellor of the University of Cochin, observed in one of his papers, "The higher education system has become a low level business proposition involving the students, parents, teachers, different categories of no-teaching employees and the management. Admissions are secured, degrees are bought and sold, and question papers are traded and answer books manipulated".

One of the possible answers to the present ills in the affiliating systems seems to be 'autonomous colleges'. Not that they are fully fool proof but it appears to be the best available experiment in the present context.

Under the affiliating system the quality of teaching and that of learning records a steep fall along with the very apparent decline in the standards of educational administration by the management, university and the government. Autonomous colleges also may prove defective in details, but that should not deter us from giving it a trial here. Many who oppose the introduction of the system of autonomous colleges seem to conveniently forget, that in the system, emphasis is on the academic and not on the administrative autonomy.

Major Problems of the Higher Education System in Kerala

If quality is to be assessed on the basis of quantity, Kerala's higher education excels than in other states of the Indian Union. On an average Kerala has 21 colleges for a district, having a total of nearly 300 colleges in the state. This is certainly a luxury which Kerala alone enjoys now because of the long tradition of higher education in the state. The very first college in Kerala was established in 1816 and the first university in 1937 – the University of Travancore which was renamed University of Kerala in 1957. However, one or perhaps the foremost problem of the higher education sector is the overload for the different universities in the state.

A positive side of Kerala's higher education is the sex ratio of students in colleges. For every male student in college, there are 1.15 female students. This means there are more women than men in colleges, in degree classes. Kerala seems to believe in the UNESCO dictum "if we educate a boy we educate a man, and if we educate a girl, we educate a family".

One of the prerequisites for any restructuring of our system of higher education should be a stipulation for a change of attitude towards the very concept of higher education. This can be possible only if a delinking of the degree and jobs is secured. If a delinking of degree and jobs can be effected, it will considerably reduce the present rush for admissions in colleges, and as a consequence the quality of the students admitted could also be enhanced.

To-day one of the major handicaps we confront is not only that the system produce poorly equipped graduates or post graduates who remain unemployed but most of those who pass out from our colleges and university departments are, indeed, unemployable also. Most of them neither have an expertise in their discipline, nor a talent for any communication skill whatsoever.

Whom should we blame for this disappointing state of affairs? Certainly not the students. The responsibility should be borne by the parents and the teachers who are supposed to guide and train them at home and in the centers of learning.

The collection of capitation fee for admissions and donations for appointments at least by a number of agencies, if not all in the field, also accelerate the pace of degeneration in the sphere of higher education. This widespread practice of capitation fee starts from the LKG, UKG level and continues up to the postgraduate and professional courses, polluting the very system all through.

The politically oriented students and their militant unions; the politically committed teachers and their equally politically bound associations also pull enough strings in the campuses as well as outside. Union elections are fought bitterly and expensively often marred with violence, rigging and manipulations.

In appointments to the teaching and non-teaching cadres, many of the managements are not free from accusations of diluting the criteria of selection and thus making their part of contribution in the over all decline of standards in our system of higher education.

Right students without right teachers will not produce the right results. Herein lies the importance of the selection of teachers. If the faculty proves of poor quality, rest of the efforts to improve the standards will be futile. The managements have to ensure that not only the best qualified is selected, but also the best motivated among the candidates top the list. The system of one year probation is also not enough and adequate to evaluate as it is too short a period to evaluate a person's quality and calibre. In the matter of quality and commitment of the members of the faculty, in most of the colleges things remain alarmingly inadequate. The duration of service alone should not be the criterion for confirmation or promotion of teachers to higher cadre or superior salary scale. Teachers need to be inspired, encouraged, prompted and compelled to take up and pursue further study and research in their own chosen areas of specialization to make them more equipped and competent to survive in a fast growing world of information and knowledge.

The cost of higher education in Kerala seems comparatively cheap (except for professional courses) and this may also perhaps make for the poor quality of students admitted in college classes. There should be a hike in the fee structure in proportion to the enormous increase in the cost of education. But, of course, provisions should be made to safeguard the interest of the intelligent amongst the poor by offering adequate number of scholarships and freeships to facilitate their studies.

As part of the efforts to improve the quality in the campus, we are constrained to search for the possibilities of depoliticizing the campuses to a certain extent. Educational ecology is as important as environmental ecology in preserving and sustaining the gifts of God and nature to the human society. Banishing politics from the campus is easily said than done. Yet it is the bounden duty of all concerned to make every effort at least to dilute the intensity of campus politics even if a total ban remain unattainable in the given circumstances in the state. A total ban on campus politics doesn't sound logical either.

Lack of accountability is another major defect in the existing system. It is for the principal to ensure this accountability on the part of everyone in the campus and for the vice-chancellor to see that it is ensured in the university.

If the sense of justice and fairness and the integrity and honesty of the vice-chancellors and the Principals are not called in question, things may prove wonderfully positive on this score. If the men at the top are fair and impartial, upright and bold, honest and truthful, clean and transparent, the situation will change for the better in the colleges and universities. Persons of such mould may be numerically less but not at all rare or impossible to be found if we have a mind for it. In most of the colleges and universities and other centers of higher learning in Kerala, it is the erosion of authority that has done maximum harm to the proper functioning of the system.

It is high time that in the sphere of education, the examination system is fundamentally altered to ensure better evaluation process. The details are to be worked out with enough vision, dare and insight.

Need for Granting Autonomy to Colleges in Kerala

The current educational scenario in Kerala certainly warrants some drastic reforms to effect a qualitative change in the sphere of higher education. But no reform can be made overnight as any reform in education requires the backing of a strong public opinion in its favour. The autonomous system is something that has already found a place in the frame of higher education in many of the states in India. And autonomy and accreditation are the two schemes strongly endorsed by the Association of Indian Universities and the Conference of Vice-Chancellors. The University Grants Commission also stands avowedly in favour of granting autonomous status to colleges and university departments. Assessment and accreditation also have found favour with the University Grants Commission.

Kerala had the unbeatable record of being in the frontline among the other states in India in the matter of literacy and education. Thanks to the benevolent policies pursued by the native rulers here and the initiative and selfless services rendered mainly by the Christian missionaries in the pre independence days and owning to the consistent consideration given by the democratic governments to the cause of education ever since independence, the educational development in Kerala has always remained encouraging and unique. But it has remained painfully static as any proposal for reform or change has invariably met with strong political resistance by one shade or the other. Now a time has come that we approach the issues connected with educational reforms on their merit, free from our political prejudices and blind resistance as far as possible. No one has ever questioned the intellectual potential of the Keralites, and now in the field of information technology also the Malayalee has proved his calibre and competency. It will be a criminal lapse on the part of us if we still remain totally blind to the speedy changes taking place around us and the daring experiments initiated and worked out in the field of higher education in other parts of India. It will only do more harm than good if Kerala remain out of reach for new ventures in education.

However, in the unique social situation prevailing in Kerala and also taking into account the sensitive nature of our society as far as educational reforms are concerned, we have to move very cautiously and carefully when we take any step or make any attempt to effect a change in the educational situation in Kerala. The social and political realities have to be considered before we take a step forward. But all the same we can no longer turn our face away from the changes that are taking place in the educational scenario in the country. Whether we like it or not, we are bound to remain realistic and positively responsive to the changes around us.

Conclusion

The idea of autonomous colleges as such cannot be ruled out even in Kerala where any freedom from the clutches of the government or the university is resisted by the academic community, particularly the organized teacher and employees groups. They often seem highly sensitive regarding any frame of supervising device emerging in the higher education sector except that of the government. Political parties or political fronts which enjoy power—maybe in alternate electoral turns—also are inclined to intervene in the sphere of higher education on one pretext or the other.

The teachers who consistently campaign for retaining their prerogative of evaluating or assessing their students vehemently resent their students being given the privilege of evaluating the performance of their teachers. 'Security' of tenure for teachers seem one of the main stakes for organized teachers unions without caring for the least for the quality maintenance of the teachers in colleges and universities.

It has to be conceded, by all concerned, that the quality and excellence in education can be achieved and preserved only by ensuring an academic ecology in the sphere of higher education. Any environmental pollution caused by any one of the factors in the sphere will prove detrimental to the environmental purity so essential for a positive and healthy educational ecology.

The experiment of autonomous colleges, even if it may face stiff resistance in the initial stages, may eventually prove a useful and effective system in the given situation without turning the affiliating system upside down. Any meaningful change in the educational set up of Kerala can be thought of only as part of an evolutionary process taking time as well as giving time for the experiment. The stakeholders in the sector have to make themselves receptive enough to new innovative ideas and enough daring to experiment them, of course with humility and good faith and with a vision for the future in view of the changing global scenario.

24

Why are We Still having the Burden of Affiliation in the 21st Century? Why not Autonomy?

—J. V. Vilanilam

It is baffling that the 150-year-old system of affiliation is religiously adhered to even after the British who introduced it here abandoned it in their own educational sector. And contrary to the popular impression, the British system was different as it never permitted affiliation of colleges far removed from the affiliating university both in geographic distance and central objectives.

Some reasons for the decline in the quality of university education in India are: an outmoded system of affiliation; a serious lack of autonomy; a top-heavy and highly politicized teaching community and even management; and a wasteful and unscientific system of evaluation of students. All these will have to go if quality is to improve and excellence is to be achieved. This article concentrates on affiliation which is not only anachronistic but also cumbersome. Other aspects are also briefly dealt with.

The fillip to modern education in India came from Macaulay's famous Minute of 1835 following which the attempt to educate the natives in English on a big scale was intensified through the establishment of English high schools in many major and minor towns. Port cities particularly needed English-knowing personnel and thus education of the local population was an imperial necessity.

The goal of education as enunciated by Macaulay is too well known for repetition here. Higher education for the masses was never an article of faith during the pre or post-independence period, although for various sociological reasons, the rush to colleges has become a major phenomenon now. The sad fact is that despite the very impressive increase in the number of universities, colleges, distance education institutes and open universities, India is still unable to meet the demand for higher education of the liberal variety.

Since the Indian economy cannot bear the burden of establishing more colleges and universities, the rising demand for higher education has to be met by private initiative. However, a thousand universities and fifty thousand colleges/institutes (as against the present 300 universities and 9,000 colleges) cannot meet the additional demand if the present trend for degree-oriented higher education continues.

Is the rising demand for the low quality college education aimed at some degree to be encouraged in the name of democracy? Is the creation of a system to grant degrees to all the burgeoning population of young men and women without any consideration for the essential needs of the country in various technical and scientific fields the real goal of post-matriculation education?

To improve the system of higher education, improvement of the system of lower education is a must. And provision of facilities for technical education at the high school level for all students is a must so that those who want to take up a technical job after high school education may do so and avoid the practice of earning some degree of no value for them in the future. This is a matter very much connected with higher education. Students must be given the choice at the school level itself after eight years of schooling to choose those courses of study that will equip them to take up some useful occupation after high school. Again, all high school education must be for 12 years. Let there be a 12+3 system throughout India and let the last four years of schooling include technical courses, some of them specially formulated for girls.

When the whole world is following the 12+4 system, why should we in India follow the 12+2 plus 3 system? A student who finishes 12 years of schooling will have gained enough general education plus proficiency in the basics of something technical/

scientific so that he or she can opt for a job and after a few years of working go back to school/college depending on the requirements of the job and earn a degree. This will reduce the pressure on colleges and universities.

I believe this system is preferable to the one we follow in Kerala and other states today where a very large number of unemployable graduates are turned out from our institutions of higher education, leading to immense waste.

Let us look deeper at the affiliation system. It is still true that the largest number of educated youth come out of the affiliated colleges, and those colleges cannot introduce new courses without a long waiting period for the sanction from universities and the government. The question of affiliation, autonomy and the government's role in all this has to be re-examined.

The present system of affiliation is quite rigid; the financial, administrative and even academic procedures the universities and their affiliated colleges follow are stunningly retrograde and straitjacketed. Therefore the system of affiliation needs a radical change for the following reasons:

The system was introduced when there were just a few colleges in and around the university city. And their number of students was also small. Communication between the university and the affiliated colleges in the same area was easy and smooth in the beginning. Today many universities have between 100 and 300 colleges affiliated to them. Thanks to the de-linking of pre-degree from colleges, the number of students is dwindling, but many of the facilities and buildings that had been provided before remain unutilized.

The affiliated colleges have to start new courses so that their unutilized facilities could be utilized to some extent.

a) Colleges in remote areas affiliated to the university have to approach the university for every major and minor activity. The level of understanding between the 'centre' and the 'periphery' is usually low. Personal interactions are necessary, but chances for them are almost absent.

b) Catering to the educational needs of students in remote corners of the country was not a major concern during the nineteenth and twentieth centuries because the number of students going for higher education was small. Repeating the old type of education for the new generation in the twenty-first century is not going to be helpful to them.

c) The sudden expansion of higher education has led to a lowering of quality, especially in remote areas of the university district. Many colleges do not have even adequate physical infrastructure, not to speak of innovative and community related, socially relevant courses.

d) The university's monitoring of the quality of teaching, research, physical facilities and lab and library equipments is often nominal and sometimes politicized. Although the university sets standards, there is no proper mechanism to monitor the observance of those standards.

e) The university has become a huge examination mechanism. Conducting examinations (thousands of them every year for regular, private and repeater candidates), evaluating answer books and declaring results are the major activities.

f) Although the practice of affiliation started in the London University (est. 1836), neither London nor other established universities such as Oxford and Cambridge had colleges other than their constituent colleges on the same campus affiliated to them.

e) Though the affiliated colleges here are theoretically independent, self-governing units as far as their financial operations are concerned, their salaries are paid by the government. No effective quality control can be effected by the college management; nor does the government succeed in curbing tuition and other private activities of teachers who receive their salary for public service.

g) The system of affiliation puts the responsibility of updating or revising the syllabus on the shoulders of the university. The colleges themselves must be made responsible for such revision. Autonomy in academic matters is to be exercised by the colleges, depending on the need of the people living in the college area.

h) The autonomous colleges should also do the continuous and end-term evaluation after conducting class exams at the appropriate time, according to a pre-designed calendar of teaching, evaluation and declaration of results.

i) Teachers in autonomous colleges must respect the pedagogic principle that the teacher who teaches must do the evaluation. Precious time is wasted by getting the questions set by people outside the university area and students are harmed by inordinate delays.

The most important objective of de-affiliation is the attainment of autonomy in all spheres- academic, financial and administrative.

Colleges and even some universities do not have any real autonomy now because of politicization, although in Kerala and some other states, we have already got many self-financing colleges which are again trying to obtain the status of affiliated colleges instead of taking up the challenge of reaching autonomy.

In democratizing education, autonomous colleges have an important role to play. They can fulfill their obligations only when they take upon themselves the responsibility of serving their catchment area primarily and other areas also taking into consideration the real priorities of development facing the nation. Merely clamouring for autonomous status for financial and prestige needs is not a worthy endeavour.

De-affiliation, autonomy, decentralization and democratization will solve many of the problems in higher education today. Along with these basic steps, we must have an Academic Council for each autonomous college that will strive constantly to review the syllabus for each discipline in view of the developments taking place nationally and globally. If autonomy is utilized for meeting the challenges of the twenty-first century, it will have meaning and relevance; otherwise, it will serve only for lowering the quality of our education further.

Every teacher in a college should have the freedom to innovate the contents of each course. For this the teacher has to be a hardworking student, a regular visitor to the library and user of his own Internet facilities at home or at college. Besides, the teaching methods have to be improved. Let there be discussions and let the students be encouraged to participate in them.

Similarly, let assignments be given to students every weekend based on library and general reading on topics connected with the topic discussed in class. The teacher in the college is a facilitator and not a lecturer. Let students bring to class new ideas and openly discuss without fear or favour.

Autonomous colleges should thus become the hub of intellectual activity under the distant supervision by teachers. Let local, national and international issues be the concern of science, social science and humanities students of autonomous colleges. But to reach this stage, teachers have to renew their mode of gathering information, storing them and retrieving them and finally sharing them through brief lectures and well-organised discussions in class, supplemented by audio-visual aids.

25

Academic Autonomy for Colleges in Kerala — Proactive Initiatives and Planning Need of the Hour

— Abraham George

Among the states of India, Kerala is well-known for its achievements in the spheres of education and social development. However, the state's performance at the higher education level leaves much to be desired. In spite of the advantages of academic autonomy, no higher education institution in Kerala has so far been granted autonomy. The potential of autonomy for academic excellence and as an agent of change has already been proven by the performance of a good number of autonomous colleges belonging to different states in India. The main focus of this article is to highlight the need for implementing the scheme in Kerala so that it will pave way for the emergence of several centres of excellence in the state in the field of higher education.

Autonomy and Kerala

Kerala is one of the few states in India without any autonomous colleges. Although the concept of autonomy was discussed at different levels on a number of occasions in the state, no concrete step has so far been taken for the implementation of the scheme. Ideological hang ups and opposition from the teachers unions had been earlier cited as the main reasons for the non-implementation of the scheme. In 1987, an Expert Committee was constituted by the Government of Kerala to study the various aspects of the proposal to grant autonomous status to colleges. Though the Committee had recommended granting autonomy to colleges, no action was taken on its recommendation. Later, in 1999, the Inter-

University Consultative Council comprising representatives of various universities in Kerala constituted a Sub-Committee to look into the possibilities of granting autonomy to colleges in Kerala. The Committee which submitted its report in 2000 also recommended to the state government to consider giving academic autonomy to arts and science colleges having 50 years and medical and engineering colleges with 25 years of existence. Though some hesitant moves were subsequently made in this direction by the government of Kerala, nothing came out of it. Frustrated by the attitude of the state government and the universities, a few colleges in Kerala directly applied to the UGC for autonomy. The UGC provisionally granted them autonomy subject to the concurrence of the state government and approval of the concerned university. However, as the state government and the universities were not supportive in this regard and since necessary changes in the university statutes had not been made, their efforts were in vain. In 2008, acting on a court order, the Mahatma Gandhi University, Kottayam, took a decision to grant autonomy to colleges which satisfied certain criteria (*The Hindu*,18 January 2009). Hardly any college under the university would be able to fulfil these criteria. So it was evident that the university was not too keen to grant autonomy for the time being. College autonomy is yet to receive serious consideration from the Kerala State Higher Education Council either.

Need for Introducing Autonomy in Kerala

a) Though Kerala has made remarkable achievements in the field of education in general, it has not reflected in the higher education sector of the state. It does not have any higher education institution which stands out at the national level as a centre of academic excellence. Even the better known colleges of Kerala lag behind prominent institutions of the country. Granting autonomy to colleges in this state with relatively greater potential for academic innovations will empower them to become top rated institutions in the country.

b) At present Kerala has the largest proportion of educated unemployed in the country. In spite of the growth in the number of professional colleges in recent times, majority of the younger generation of Kerala are still pursuing their higher education at different arts and science colleges in the state. Under the rigid framework of affiliation, arts and science colleges are unable to offer courses according to the requirements of the job market. A high proportion of the degree holders coming out of these institutions are unemployable. What Kerala urgently needs is a higher education system which is capable of providing courses with greater employment potential. Autonomous colleges will be able to improve the employability of the students by restructuring and designing courses in accordance with the new trends in the different sectors of the economy at the national and global levels.

c) As most of the brilliant students are not interested in the traditional courses offered by the affiliated aided colleges which still dominate Kerala's higher education sector, they go for job-oriented new generation courses offered by self-financing institutions within the state or outside, paying hefty fees. Granting autonomy will give the colleges in the aided sector the freedom to offer courses that are attractive to the present generation students at affordable rates.

d) The quality of education imparted through a wide network of affiliated colleges in the state has been gradually declining over the years. Since human resource is the greatest asset of Kerala, its quality is a matter of prime concern to all. In order to offer courses with high standard to the bright students at affordable costs, granting academic autonomy to colleges will be a step in the right direction.

e) As per the WTO agreement, even foreign universities are allowed to provide their programmes in India. Several private universities, both domestic and foreign, have already started providing their courses here charging very high fees. Autonomous colleges will be able to offer courses with comparable standard at affordable rates to the bright students of the state.

A major challenge in connection with the implementation of autonomy would be the introduction of semester system and Choice Based Credit System (CBCS) in all the colleges as UGC guidelines require every autonomous college in the country to implement them. Now the UGC has made it mandatory for all the universities in the country to introduce semester system and the CBCS. Accordingly, all the universities in Kerala have implemented the semester and CBCS schemes in all the affiliated colleges at the undergraduate level. Such a development has created a more conducive atmosphere in the state for the smooth transition from affiliation to autonomy.

Major Apprehensions and the Reality

The concept of autonomy has generated heated discussions and some kind of opposition wherever it has been implemented or proposed to be implemented. Over the last three decades most of the autonomous colleges have made remarkable progress and have performed much better than they would have otherwise. However, a great deal of apprehensions, prejudices and misconceptions regarding the scheme still exist even among the academic community of Kerala. Though some of the concerns raised against the scheme have been genuine, most of the arguments against it are found to be baseless. An attempt has been made in this part of the article to clear the most frequently raised objections against granting autonomy.

a) An argument against autonomous colleges is that academic standards will fall if control of the government / university is taken away. In reality, academic standards are found to improve much under autonomy. It is evident from the past experience that just being under the direct control of the university will not ensure quality. In spite of all the controls and regulations of the university and the state, the quality of education under the affiliating system has only deteriorated over the years. As the degree certificates issued by the universities are not held in high esteem, separate tests / examinations are held for admissions to professional colleges or for appointments. At the same time many reputed firms recruit directly from different autonomous colleges. Due to the healthy competition among autonomous colleges, these institutions are compelled to strive for quality improvement all the time. Under autonomy, only those colleges which maintain good standards will be able to survive. A recent study by the UGC has also found that the employability of students from autonomous colleges is more than double compared to that of their counterparts from affiliated colleges (*The Hindu*, Feb.7, 2006).

b) It is also argued that there will be considerable disparity in the attainment of students belonging to various autonomous colleges or between students of affiliated colleges and autonomous institutions where they exist side by side. The university will be awarding degree to students from different colleges with dissimilar syllabi, grading and evaluation patterns. Although such an argument appears to be true, even under the affiliating system, the quality of teaching- learning as well as the level of attainment of students coming out of different colleges are not always uniform. The quality of the products of different colleges does vary. In fact it is one of the reasons why there exist marked differences in the demand for the same course offered by different affiliated colleges belonging to the same university. However, such differences could be reduced to a great extent if the academic standards of different institutions are monitored carefully by the parent university.

c) Autonomous colleges are often criticized as elitist institutions which breed elitism in the domain of higher education by creating a small group of colleges with special privileges. Under the affiliating system also, some colleges are considered by the society to be better than certain others regarding the quality of education imparted. The differences found in the grades of various colleges in the accreditation process by the National Assessment and Accreditation Council (NAAC) also confirm the fact that the overall performance and the quality of education offered by various colleges are indeed different even under the affiliating system. One need not expect all the higher education institutions under any system to show uniformity in the matter of quality or attainment of students. While autonomous colleges are qualified to receive grants from the UGC for carrying out autonomy related responsibilities like framing of syllabus, conducting examinations, etc, all the rules and regulations related to admission, reservation, appointments, service conditions of the staff, etc. remain the same for both autonomous and non-autonomous colleges.

d) Internalization of the examination system under autonomy is often viewed with suspicion. One of the major apprehensions raised against autonomy is that there will be lapses and malpractices when examinations are conducted by autonomous colleges themselves. There is no denying the fact that the possibilities for malpractice are more under autonomy. However, it is also true that the examination system of almost all the universities in the state is in shambles with all kinds of malpractices quite rampant. Autonomous colleges which resort to unethical practices to boost examination results will not be able to survive long as it will adversely affect their reputation. In order to ensure the credibility of the examination system, most autonomous colleges have taken conscious steps like entrusting the question paper setting partially or wholly to external hands, valuation by external examiners, double valuation, etc. Moreover, the parent university has the power to take action if any such case of malpractice is found out.

e) An important concern of the student community is regarding the possibility for bias and victimization by the teacher, particularly in the internal assessment. Though the apprehension seems to be genuine, through better transparency and openness in the whole evaluation procedure and with provisions for appeal and revaluation, such fears can be allayed to a great extent. It has been observed that the majority of the teachers perform their evaluation work fairly and impartially when they are entrusted with such a responsibility. Instances of teachers misusing their power out of prejudice or favouritism are relatively low even under the already prevailing internal evaluation system of the affiliated colleges in Kerala. Autonomy hardly gives any more power to the teacher than under the semester and choice based credit system which has already been introduced in the state under the affiliating system.

f) There is widespread apprehension that if autonomy is granted, autonomous colleges will dilute the reservation policy of the state government. The truth is that every autonomous institution will have to strictly adhere to the reservation policy of the government. Students belonging to the socially and economically backward communities will continue to enjoy all the reservation benefits under autonomy also.

g) There is yet another wrong notion that autonomous colleges are self financing and that student fees will be hiked unjustifiably by them. Autonomy does not mean self-financing. The government can grant autonomy to aided, unaided and government colleges. Government aided institution will not be able to increase the fees as they like. Private self-financing autonomous colleges, if any, also would have to follow government / university guidelines in this regard.

h) It has been criticized that due to the non-availability of similar courses in other institutions and at higher levels, the mobility of students, both horizontally and vertically will be stifled. Further, the end-semester marks of students from autonomous colleges are some times not given proper consideration by other institutions, especially when admission to higher studies is sought. Though there is some truth in these criticisms, the problem is mitigated to a great extent by the recommendation of the UGC to the universities for adopting credit transfer among colleges in general and autonomous colleges in particular. Since the universities in Kerala have recently adopted the Choice Based Credit System, problems related to student mobility will not be a serious problem to deal with.

i) The major apprehension among the teaching community is that their workload will increase considerably without any additional remuneration. Some even think that many of the privileges and service conditions which teachers have achieved through organized agitations will be lost once autonomy is granted to the institutions where they work. In reality, the work load of the teachers regarding teaching hours in autonomous colleges will be on par with those in the non-autonomous colleges. Autonomy does not affect their service conditions either. It is true that their other responsibilities will increase marginally. But majority of the teachers in autonomous colleges are found to enjoy the new responsibilities in an atmosphere of greater academic freedom.

j) Some of the teacher organizations have raised fears that autonomy would give unlimited powers to the management and that they would use that power to victimize the faculty. In reality, the managements will not have more power under autonomy than what they have under the affiliating system. On the other hand, teachers of autonomous colleges will have greater administrative power and more freedom in introducing academic innovations than under the affiliating system.

k) Some of the detractors of autonomy wrongly believe that autonomous colleges have unbridled freedom to do what they want. However, autonomy does not mean open license to do anything. Autonomy brings with it responsibilities also. The working of the autonomous institutions is always monitored by the parent university as well as the UGC. The Governing Body and the Boards of Studies of the autonomous colleges include university nominees also. Further these institutions have to subject themselves to annual self-evaluation and two external evaluations by expert committees which include representatives of the university, state government and the UGC. In addition, autonomous colleges are required to get accredited by the NAAC at regular intervals as prescribed by the UGC.

l) There is a fear among those who oppose the introduction of the autonomous scheme that once autonomy is conferred, it will be difficult to withdraw the status. This is a baseless apprehension. Autonomy is initially conferred only for a period of six years and the institution will have to continually earn the status. If the institution is found to fail in maintaining the required standards, the autonomous status will be revoked. It is a Joint Expert Committee consisting of members of the parent university, state government and the UGC which will determine the continuance or revocation of the autonomous status of an institution.

m) Universities are generally reluctant to grant autonomy to affiliated colleges on the belief that they will lose control over some of its leading colleges and that they will be reduced to just degree-conferring institutions. Loss of revenue is yet another concern of the parent universities. At present under the affiliating scheme also the universities have become mere administrative bodies concerned with the syllabus, examinations and awarding degrees. Loss of revenue will not be significant as only a limited number of colleges will be eligible to attain autonomous status.

Some Guidelines for Introducing Autonomy in Kerala

As we have seen, academic autonomy has already been granted to affiliated colleges in 16 states since 1978. Broadly speaking, this academic experiment has been found to be successful in all these states. The UGC has also been actively encouraging the introduction of the scheme in more states. If the policy of the government of Kerala changes in favour of the scheme, Kerala will also have autonomous colleges. When that happens, colleges in Kerala should not be caught napping. Every aspiring college needs to start preparations much before applying for the conferment of autonomous status. The institutions as well as the authorities should have a broad idea about how to implement the scheme. The selection of a few colleges for the conferment of autonomous status will also not be an easy task. The concerned authorities in the state need to frame well-defined criteria in this regard on the basis of the UGC guidelines. Some of the important aspects related to the implementation of autonomy are discussed below in the light of the UGC Eleventh Plan Guidelines in this regard.

Selection of Colleges for Autonomy

Autonomy is granted by the parent university to the colleges which are permanently affiliated to it, with the concurrence of the state government and the UGC. Autonomy covers all the courses offered by a college and it includes UG, PG, Certificate, Diploma and M. Phil courses.

Aided, unaided, partially aided and self financing colleges which come under Section 2(f) of the UGC Act are eligible to apply for autonomous status. Though self–financing colleges which have completed 10 years are eligible to apply for autonomy, they are not entitled to receive autonomy grant. However, colleges that provide professional courses in Education, Engineering, Management, Physical Education, etc. are eligible to receive autonomy grants from the UGC.

The parent university needs to amend the university act and statutes in order to provide for the grant of autonomy to affiliated colleges.

According to the Eleventh Plan Guidelines of the UGC, the following criteria may be followed to identify institutions for the grant of autonomy.

i) Academic reputation and previous performance in university examinations and its academic / co-curricular / extension activities in the past.

ii) Academic / extension achievements of the faculty.

iii) Quality and merit in the selection of students and teachers, subject to statutory requirements in this regard.

iv) Adequacy of infrastructure, for example, library, equipment, accommodation for academic activities, etc.

v) Quality of institutional management.

vi) Financial resources provided by the management / state government for the development cf the institution.

vii) Responsiveness of the administrative structure.

viii) Motivation and involvement of faculty in the promotion of innovative reforms.

The selection procedure of the UGC is as follows. The UGC invites proposals from eligible colleges seeking autonomous status once every academic year. After receiving the applications, the UGC will constitute a screening committee to short-list the eligible colleges. Then another expert committee constituted by the UGC will visit these colleges and submit a report with its findings and recommendations to the UGC. The UGC will then send its recommendations to the parent university concerned for the conferment of autonomy to the selected colleges, initially for a period of six years. The UGC has been revising its guidelines for granting autonomy at least once in five years.

CONTINUOUS REVIEW AND MONITORING

The UGC Guidelines clearly states that the right of autonomy is not to be conferred once and for all. It has to be continuously earned by the college upon which autonomy has been conferred. An autonomous college will have to undertake a self-evaluation regarding its academic performance, improvement in standards, etc every year. Further, there will be two external evaluations. The first external evaluation will be conducted after four years and the second after completing six years. The external evaluation after six years is done by a Joint Expert Committee consisting of two representatives each from the affiliating university and the state government, and three representatives from the UGC out of which one will be the convenor of the Committee. This Committee will determine the extension or revocation of the autonomous status of the institution. All the autonomous colleges have to undergo accreditation by the NAAC within a period of two years from the date of conferment / extension of the autonomous status. If evidences clearly confirm a decline in standards in an autonomous college, the UGC and the university may revoke the autonomous status of that institution after careful scrutiny, mutual consultation and due notification to the management.

PREPARING A COLLEGE FOR AUTONOMY

According to the UGC Guidelines, all autonomous colleges need to adopt (i) semester system, (ii) continuous internal assessment, (iii) credit / grading system, (iv) student feedback and (v) self-appraisal by teachers. Comprehensive preparation is necessary for every section of a college, particularly the faculty, departments, students and the management for the effective implementation of autonomy. Adequate preparations should be started much before applying for the conferment of autonomous status.

a) Faculty Preparation

The success of an autonomous college primarily depends on its faculty. Therefore, involvement of the faculty from the thinking and planning stage itself is essential. Orientation classes, seminars and workshops need to be organized for the entire staff of the institution. This will make them familiar with the concept as well as the working of autonomy. It will also help them to have a sense of participation in decision making and motivate them to involve in the whole process from the very beginning. As the institution is required to perform many functions which were previously done by the university, it is imperative that both teaching and non-teaching staff of the college are trained to carry out the new responsibilities. Academic Staff Colleges also may organize special programmes to train and equip the faculty of the institutions which are going to become autonomous. Visits to established autonomous colleges by the faculty members will also help to bring about a change in their outlook and perception. Their interactions with the faculty members of the autonomous colleges could give them first-hand knowledge about the working of these institutions and the challenges faced by them.

b) Departmental Preparation

Under autonomy, the individual departments have the responsibility of designing the courses in the major and related subjects, introducing new courses of study, re-naming obsolete courses by changing their content, updating existing courses in each discipline and preparing course materials and human resources. These have to be done in the light of the general objectives of autonomy and the specific objectives of the education institution. Each department needs to chalk out a plan for developing new courses, new teaching methods and for providing new facilities. The departments must form different committees for effectively dealing with the new responsibilities.

c) Institutional Preparation

As an autonomous college is required to perform many of the functions that have been done hitherto by the university, it must study the academic, administrative, managerial and financial implications of such a changeover and prepare itself to discharge its new functions efficiently. The administrative structure of the college needs to be revamped and strengthened with adequate flexibility to ensure active participation of the faculty and students.

Governance of an Autonomous College

As per the UGC Guidelines, an autonomous college will have the following statutory committees to ensure proper management of academic, financial and general administrative affairs. They include: (i) Governing Body, (ii) Academic Council, (iii) Board of Studies and (iv) Finance Committee. The college will, in addition, have other non-statutory committees such as the Planning and Evaluation Committee, Grievances Appeals Committee, Examination Committee, Admission Committee, Library Committee, Student Welfare Committee, Extra-curricular Activities Committee and Academic Audit Committee.

A brief analysis of the composition and functions of the four statutory committees are given below. (For more details, see Appendix II : UGC Guidelines for Autonomous Colleges during the Eleventh Plan Period (2007-2012).

i) Governing Body

Subject to the existing provision in the bye-laws of the respective college and rules laid down by the state government, the governing body of the college shall have powers to fix the fees and other charges payable by the students of the college on the recommendations of the Finance Committee; to institute scholarships, fellowships, studentships, medals, prizes and certificates on the recommendations of the Academic Council; to approve institution of new programmes of study leading to degrees and/or diplomas; to perform such other functions and institute committees as may be necessary and deemed fit for the proper development, and to fulfil the objectives for which the college has been declared as autonomous. The Governing Body of the college consists of members from the side of the management and two faculty members nominated by the principal on seniority basis along with experts from outside including nominees of the UGC, state government and the university. The principal of the college will be an ex-officio member while chairman of the management will be the chairperson of the Governing Body.

ii) Academic Council

The Academic Council will be solely responsible for all academic matters, such as framing of academic policy, approval of courses, academic regulations, curricula, syllabi, instructional and evaluation arrangements and methods, admissions, sports and co-curricular activities, etc. The Academic Council, with the Principal as the chairman includes all the heads of departments and teacher representatives and experts from outside including representatives of the university and the state government. The decisions taken by the Council will not be subject to any further ratification by the Academic Council or other statutory bodies of the university.

iii) Board of Studies

The Board of Studies is considered to be the basic constituent of the academic system of an autonomous college. Its functions will include framing the syllabi for various courses, reviewing and updating syllabi from time to time, introducing new courses of study, suggesting innovative teaching and evaluation methods, determining details of continuous assessment, recommending panels of examiners under the semester system, coordinating research, teaching, extension and other academic activities, etc. The chairman of each Board of Studies is the head of the concerned department. The board includes the entire faculty of each specialization and experts nominated by the Academic Council, university and a meritorious alumnus nominated by the principal.

iv) Finance Committee

The Finance Committee will be an advisory body to the Governing Body on financial matters. It mainly deals with the budget estimates and audited accounts relating to the grants from the UGC and the income from fees, etc collected for activities concerned with the scheme of autonomy. The principal is the chairman of the Finance Committee. The Committee also includes the nominee of the Governing Body and a teacher representative nominated by the principal.

Starting of New Courses

As per the UGC Guidelines, an autonomous college has the freedom to start a new UG or PG course fulfilling the minimum standards prescribed by the University / UGC regarding the number of hours, curricular content and standards. It can also rename an existing course after restructuring / redesigning it. Further, an autonomous college is free to start diploma / certificate courses without the prior approval of the university. The university shall be duly informed of starting new courses or renaming an existing course. The university has the right to review new courses and ask the college to modify or even cancel such courses if found to be wanting in standards or quality.

Examination Cell

The Examination Cell of an autonomous college is headed by the Controller of Examinations who will be a permanent faculty member assisted by a team, the number of which will depend on the quantum of work in the examination cell. The principal will be the chief controller of examinations. All part time functionaries shall be paid honorarium for the extra work done by them and full time staff shall be paid salary. The Examination Cell has to conduct a minimum of two internal examinations per semester and one semester ending examination.

Awarding of Degree

The parent university will be awarding degree certificate to the students evaluated and recommended by an autonomous college. Though the degree certificates will be in a common format devised by the university, the name of the college will be mentioned in it.

Financial Assistance from the UGC

The UGC will provide financial assistance to autonomous colleges to meet their additional and special needs like guest / visiting faculty; orientation and re-training of the faculty; re-designing courses; examination reforms; office, library and laboratory equipments; books and journals; teaching aids; furniture for office, class rooms, library and laboratories; workshops and seminars; renovation and repairs; expenditure for governing body and committee meetings; honorarium for controller of examinations; extension activities; accreditation fees, etc. For multi-faculty arts / science / commerce autonomous colleges, UGC will provide up to Rs.15 lakhs per annum if they have only undergraduate courses and up to Rs.20 lakhs per annum for those colleges which offer both under graduate and postgraduate courses.

Every college which desires to become autonomous should be aware of the financial implications regarding the switch over from the affiliating system to the new scheme. Additional finance may be required to support the new curriculum, courses and examination systems, hiring human resources, providing physical facilities, record keeping, facilitating new bodies like Boards of Studies, etc. All the possible recurring and non–recurring expenditures in this regard need to be analysed and potential sources of funding identified by every aspiring institution well before it becomes autonomous.

Need for Proactive Initiatives and Planning

In order to ensure successful functioning of the autonomous scheme, there should be a healthy relationship among different agencies like the college, the parent university, state government and the UGC. Only a coordinated effort based on cooperation and mutual support will create a congenial atmosphere for the effective implementation of the scheme.

The state government needs to provide sufficient patronage to all the autonomous institutions in general and to government autonomous colleges in particular. A positive and encouraging attitude of the parent university is also essential. The parent university needs to render necessary guidance and permit adequate flexibility to the autonomous colleges for introducing innovative academic initiatives under the scheme. The parent university is expected to help them to develop their academic programmes, to improve the faculty and to provide necessary guidance by participating in the deliberations of the various bodies of the colleges. Autonomous colleges, in their turn, can make use of the expertise of the university departments in preparing their curricula, in starting new courses and in devising methods of teaching and evaluation. Nominees of both the state government and the parent university to the various bodies of the autonomous colleges need to be deputed on time.

However, the success of autonomy in a college mainly depends upon the factors which are internal to an institution. The role of the management, principal and the faculty are of utmost importance. If the management of the institution is progressive in its outlook and has the willingness to provide administrative as well as financial support for the implementation, the transition from the affiliating system to autonomy will be smoother and more successful, (*The Hindu*, Sept.23, 2007) The leadership and initiative of the head of the institution and his understanding of the concept of autonomy are crucial for the effective implementation of the scheme in any institution. According to the Report of the Expert Committee of the Kerala Government (1987), "The principal has to be an inspired person with a sense of mission. He should be able to inspire his colleagues and in turn ready to be inspired by the enthusiasm and zeal of his colleagues". The role of the faculty members in an autonomous institution is the single most important prerequisite for the success of autonomy. The active involvement of teachers at the college level as well as at the department level in the matter of planning, decision making and implementation are indeed crucial. They need to willingly undertake the additional responsibilities under the new system for its success.

Conclusion

Three decades have passed since the scheme of college autonomy was introduced in India. Different states in the country which have already implemented autonomy are going ahead with the scheme as they found it to be beneficial. Delinking of the colleges from the rigid affiliating structure is found to improve both quality and accountability in the higher education sector. It is paradoxical that Kerala which is renowned for its achievements in the field of education is yet to introduce the scheme. There seems to be a lack of awareness about the scheme in the state. Since the existing affiliating system has ceased to function effectively, autonomy should be viewed as an alternative or corrective to the affiliating system. Even though there may be several practical difficulties for the introduction of autonomy in Kerala, the scheme needs to be given a fair trial in the state. However, before the introduction of autonomy, all the stakeholders, particularly the teachers, students, parents and the society need to be made aware of the merits and possibilities of the scheme. There should not be any sort of compulsion or haste in the matter of introducing autonomy in any college as it can be counter-productive. Autonomy may be granted only to those institutions which have the willingness and potential to become autonomous.

Kerala has several colleges which have potential for the successfull implementation of the scheme. The state government should not deny this opportunity for such institutions to develop and grow to become centres of academic excellence at the national level. In order to start implementing the scheme in Kerala, the state government may think of conferring autonomy to reputed government and private aided colleges which have completed 25 years and which have been accredited with A-grade by the National Assessment and Accreditation Council (NAAC). If the scheme is found successful, it may be extended to more colleges.

Colleges aspiring to become autonomous need to start planning and preparation without further delay. The state government, the Kerala State Higher Education Council and the different universities in the state need to take up the case of autonomy seriously and make necessary amendments in the rules and statutes for its successful implementation. A proactive role of these agencies assumes great significance with regard to the introduction of autonomy in Kerala in order to bring about a qualitative transformation in the higher education sector of the state.

References

Abraham, Ninan (2004), *'College Autonomy – Policy, Practice and Prospects'*, Centre for Civil Society, New Delhi.

Alphonse, Xavier and Jacob, Mani (Ed.) (2000), *'Autonomous Colleges in India'*, Lokabodhan Kendra Publications, New Delhi.

Krishnakumar, G (2009), 'University to Tighten Autonomy Rules', *The Hindu*, January 22.

Mohandas, Poornima (2008), 'Autonomy out of Reach for Kerala's Colleges; Studnts Exits State', www.livemint.com

Muthukumaran, S (2007), 'Autonomy Promotes Academic Excellence', *The Hindu*, September 23.

Naha, Abdul Latheef (2006), 'Autonomy Under the Scanner', *The Hindu*. February 7.

Soundararaj, Francis (2009), 'Academic Autonomy for Change Towards Quality', *University News*, Vol.47, No.11.

University Grants Commission, 'Guidelines for Autonomous Colleges during the IX Plan Period (2007-2012).

Appendices

Appendix I

List of Autonomous Colleges in India (As on 23-03-2009)

S.No:	Name of State	University	No. of Autonomous colleges	Sub Total
1	Andhra Pradesh	Andhra University,	14	47
		Achraya Nagarjuna University,	12	
		Osmania University,	13	
		Sri Krishnadevarya University	05	
		Kakatiya University,	02	
		Jawaharwarlal Nehru Technological University	01	
2	Chhattisgarh•	Guru Ghasidas University,	04	10
		Pt.Ravi Shankar University	06	
3	Gujarat	Bhavnagar University	01	01
4	Himachal Pradesh	Himachal University	05	05
5	Jharkhand	Rachi University	04	04
6	Nagaland	Nagaland University	01	01

7	Karnataka	Banglore University,	11	41
		Gulbarga University,	03	
		Mysore University,	06	
		Mangalore University,	07	
		Karnataka University,	03	
		Kuvempu University,	03	
		Visvesvaraya Technological University	08	
8	Madhya Pradesh	A.P.Singh University,	04	31
		Barkatullah University,	06	
		Devi Ahilya University,	07	
		Dr.Hari Singh Gaur University,	03	
		Jiwaji University,	03	
		Rani Durgawati University,	06	
		Vikram University	02	
9	Maharashtra	S.N.D.T Women's Univeristy,	01	14
		Dr.Babasaheb Ambedkar University,	02	
		Shivaji University,	02	
		Pune University,	04	
		Swami Ramanand Teerth MarathwadaUniversity,	01	
		University of Mumbai,	01	
		Sant Gadge Baba Amravati University	03	

10	Orissa	Bherhampur University,	06	31
		Sambalpur University,	05	
		Utkal University,	14	
		North Orissa University,	02	
		Fakir Mohan University,	02	
		Biju Patnaik University of Technology	02	
11	Rajasthan	University of Rajasthan	02	02
12	Tamil Nadu	Bharthiar University,	19	116
		Bharathidasan University,	19	
		Mother Teresa Women's University,	02	
		Madras University,	28	
		Madurai Kamraj University,	18	
		Manonmaniam Sundaranar University,	08	
		Periyar University,	03	
		Alagappa University,	01	
		Anna University,	11	
		Thiruvalluvar University,	06	
		Tamil Nadu State Physical Education & Sport University	01	
13	Pondichery	Pondichery University	02	02
14	Uttar Pradesh	Allahabad University,	01	05
		U.P.Technical Univ,	01	
		LucknowV.B.S.Purvanchal University,	02	

		JaunpurUniversity of Lucknow	01	
15	West Bengal	Calcutta University	03	03
16	Uttrakhand	H.N.B.Garhwal University, Srinagar	01	01
			Total	314

State = 16
University = 58
Colleges = 314

STATE: ANDHRA PRADESH

Affiliated to Andhra University

S.No:	Name of the College	Autonomy first time given w.e.f	Autonomy valid upto. As per records of available with UGC
1	4	4	5
1	Chintelepati Satyavati Devi St.Therea's College for Women, Eluru (A.P)		1987-19882007-2008 to 2012-2013
2	D.N.R.Collee Bimavaram (A.P)		1987-19882006-2007 to 2012–2013
3	Shri Durga Prasad Saraf College of Arts & Applied Sciences, Sheeramnagar (A.P)		1987-19882006-2007 to 2012-2013
4	St.Joseph's College for Women Waltair (R.S.Visakhapatnam) (A.P)		1987-19882006-2007 to 2012-2013

5	Govt. Degree College, Rajah Mundry East Godavari Distt.	2000-2001	2007-2008 to 2012-2013
6	P.R.Govt.Degree College (Men) Kakinada East, Godavari Distt.	2000-2001	2006-2007 to 2013-2014
7	College of Engineering GITAM, Visakhapatnam	2003-2004	2007-2008
8	College of Management Studies, GITAM.Visakhapatnam	2003-2004	2007-2008
9	Maharajah's College, Vizianagaram-535002	2005-06	2010-2011
10	Sir.C.R.Reddy College, Eluru-534007	2006-07	2011-2012
11	Ideal College of Arts & Sciences Samalkot Road, Kakinada	2006-2007	2011-2012
12	Gayatri Vidya Parishad College for Degree & P.G.Course Sector-8,M.V.P, Colony, Visakhapatnam (A.P)	2007-2008	2012-2013
13	K.G.R.L. College, Bhimavaram, West Godavari Dist.534201 (A.P)	2007-2008	2012-2013
14	Sri Yerramilli Narayana Murthy College, West Godavari District Narsapur-534275 (A.P)	2007-2008	2012-2013

	Affiliated to Acharya Nagarjuna University	
15	Andhra Loyla College, Vijayawada-520008	1987-19882007-2008 to 2012-2013
16	P.B.Siddartha College of Arts & Science, Vijayawada-520010	1987-19882007-2008 to 2012-2013
17	Maris Stella College, Vijaywada-520 008 (A.P)	2003-04 2007-2008
18	Sri Durga Malleswara Siddartha Mahila Kalasala, Vijawada	2003-2004 2007-2008
19	V.S.R & N.V.R. College, Tenali-522201	2005-06 2010-2011
20	Montessori Mahila Kalasala, Punnammathota, Vijaywada	2005-06 2010-2011
21	J.M.J College of Women, Tenali	2005-2006 2010-2011
22	Noble College, Machilipatnam-521001	2005-2006 2010-2011
23	St. Joseph's College of Education for Women, Guntur-521001	2005-2006 2010-2011
24	Koneru Lakshmaiah College of Engineering, Vaddeswaram, Guntur-522502 (A.P)	2006-2007 2011-2012

25	V.S.R Siddhartha Engineering College, Kanuru, Vijayawada-520007 (A.P)	2006-2007 2011-2012
26	Jagarlamudi Kuppuswamy Choudary College, Guntur-522506 (A.P)	2006-20072007-2008 to 2012-2013
	Affiliated to Osmania University	
27	Anwar-ul-Uloom College New Mallepally, Hyderabad-500001	1988-1989 2008-2009
28	Loyola Academy, Alwal Secunderabad-500001	1992-1993 2007-2008
29	Nizam College, Gunboundry, Hyderabad-500001	1988-1989 2008-2009
30	R.B.V.R.R Womens' College Narayanguda, Hyderabad-500001	1988-1989 2008-2009
31	St.Francis College for Women Hyderabad, Bequmpet-500016	1988-1989 2008-2009
32	Osmania University College for Women, Koti, Hyderabad (A.P)	1988-1989 2008-2009
33	PGCollege, S.P.Road, Secunderabad , Osmania University	2004-2005 2009-2010
34	Girraj Government college, Nizamabad, AP	2004-2005 2009-2010

35	Government City College, Hyderabad	2004-2005	2009-2010
36	St.Ann's College of Education, Sarojini.Devi Road, Secunderabad 500003	2005-2006	2010-2011
37	Arts and Science College for Women, Andhra Mahila Sabha, Osmania university Road, Hyderabad	2007-2008	2012-2013
38	College of Teachers Education, Andhra mahila Sabha, Osmania University Road, Hyderabad	2007-2008	2012-2013
39	Nagarjuna Govt.College,Nalgonda (AP)	2007-2008	2012-2013
	Affiliated to Sri Krishnadevaraya University		
40	Sri.Sai Baba National Degree College, Anantpur	2005-2006	2010-2011
41	Osmania College, Kurnool	2005-2006	2010-2011
42	Silver Jubilee Government Degree College, Kurnool	2005-2006	2010-2011
43	Dri Ramakrishnan Degree College, Nandyal	2005-2006	2010-2011
44	G.Pulla Reddy Engineering College, Nandyal Road, Kurnool-518002 (AP)	2006-2007	2011-2012

	Affiliated to Kakatiya University	
45	Chaitnaya Degree College,# 5-11-43, Krishnapura, Hanamkonda, Warangal-506001 (A.P)	2007-20082007-2008 to 2012-2013
46	Chaitnaya P.G.College, # 5-11-43/1 Kishanpura, Hanamkonda, Warangal – 506001 (A.P)	2007-20082007-2008 to 2012-2013
	Affiliated to Jawaharlal Nehru Technological University	
47	Gayatr Vidya Parishad College of Engineering, Visakhapatnam (AP)	2008-2009 2013-2014
	STATE: CHHATISGARH	
	Affiliated to Guru Ghasidas University	
48	Govt.Science P.G College Bilaspur (CG)	1987–19882005-2006 to 2010-2011
49	Govt.P.G.College, Ambikapur (CG) 497001	1987-19882005-2006 to 2011-2012
50	K.G.Arts & Science College Raigarh (CG)	1987-19882005-2006 to 2010-2011
51	Govt.Girls P.G.College, Bilaspur (CG)	1987-19882005-2006 to 2010-2011
	Affiliated to Pt.Ravi Shankar Shukla University	
52	Govt.Science College Raipur (CG)-492 010	1988-19892007-2008 to 2012-2013
53	Govt.Arts & Science College Durg (CG) – 491 001	1988-1989 1992-1993

54	Govt.D.B.Girls College Raipur (CG)-492 001	1988-19892007-2008 to 2012-2013
55	Govt.Digvijai Mahavidyalaya Rajnandgaon (CG) 491 441	1988-1989 1992-1993
56	Govt.Degree College Jagdalpur, Bastar, (CG)	1988-1989 1992-1993
57	Kalyan Arts & Commerce College, Bhilai Nagar (Durg) CG	1988-19892007-2008 to 2012-2013
	STATE : GUJARAT	
	Affiliated to Bhavnagar University	
58	Lok Bharati Lok Seva Mahavidyalaya, Sanesra-364 230 Gujarat	19992-1993 2007-2008
	STATE: HIMACHAL PRADESH	
	Affiliated to Himachal Pradesh University	
59	Govt.College, Dharamshala (Kangra) H.P-176215	1995-1996 1999-2000
60	Govt.College, Solan, Himachal Pradesh-173 212	1995-1996 1999-2000

61	Govt.College, Bilaspur Distt.Bilaspur-174 001	1995-1996	1999-2000
62	G.B.Pant Memorial Govt.College, Rampur Bhushaher, Shimla-172 001	1995-1996	1999-2000
63	Vallabh Govt.College, Mandi, Distt.Mandi, H.P – 175 001	1995-1996	1999-2000
	STATE : NAGALAND		
	Affiliated to Nagaland University		
64	Patkai Christian College, Dimapur, Nagaland	2005-2006	2010-2011
	STATE : KARNATAKA		
	Affiliated to Bangalore University		
65	Christ College, Hosur Road, Bangalore-560029	2004-2005	2009-2010
66	Jyoti Niwas College, Bangalore-560 095	2004-2005	2009-2010
67	St.Joseph's College, 36 Lalbagh Road, Bangalore-27	2004-2005	2009-2010
68	St.Joseph's Evening College, 35, Museum Road, Bangalore-560025	2004-2005	2009-2010
69	St.Joseph's College of commerce, 163, Bridge Road, Bangalore-25	2004-2005	2009-2010

70	Mount Carmel College, Bangalore	2005-2006	2010-2011
71	NMKRV College for Women, Jayanagar, Bangalore	2005-2006	2010-2011
72	The National College, Basavangudi, Bangalore	2005-2006	2010-2011
73	The National College, Jayanagar, Bangalore	2005-2006	2010-2011
74	College of Fine Arts, Karnataka Chitrakala, Parishath, Bangalore	2005-2006	2010-2011
75	CMR Institute of Management Studies #2, 3rd Cross, 6th A Main HRBR Layout, Kalyan Nagar, Bangalore-560043	2009-2010	2014-2015
	Affilitated to Gulbarga University		
76	Sh. Sharanabasaveshwar College of Science, Gulbarga-583103	2004-2005	2009-2010
77	Sh. Sharanbasaveshwar College of Arts, Gulbarga-585103	2004-2005	2009-2010
78	Godutai Dudduppa Appa Arts & Commerce College for Women, Gulbarga	2004-2005	2009-2010
	Affiliated to Karnataka University		
79	K.L.E. Society's Lingaraj College, elgaum (Karnataka)	2005-06	2010-11

80	K.L.E. Society's P.C.Jabin Science College, Vidyanagar, Hubli (Karnataka)	2005-06	2010-2011
81	A.S.Patil College of Commerce, Solapur Road, Bijapur	2007-08	2012-2013
	Affiliated to University of Mysore		
82	All India Institute of Speech and Hearing, Manasagangotri, Mysore	2005-06	2010-2011
83	Yuvaraja's College, Mysore	2005-06	2010-2011
84	JSS Law College, Kuvempunagar, Mysore	2005-06	2010-2011
85	JSS College of Arts, Commerce and Science, Mysore	2005-06	2010-2011
86	JSS College for Women, Saraswathipuram, Mysore	2005-06	2010-2011
87	Government College for Boys, Mandya	2005-06	2010-11
	Affiliated to Mangalore University		
88	St.Ann's College of Education (Women's College) Mangalore	2005-06	2010-11
89	School of Social Work, Mangalore	2005-06	2010-11
90	St.Aloysius College, Mangalore	2005-06	2010-11
91	St Agnes College, Mangalore	2005-06	2010-11
92	Sri Dharmasathala Manjunatheshwara,	2005-06	2010-11

	College, Ujire (Karnataka)		
93	Bhandarkars Arts and Science College, Kundapura, (Karnataka)	2005-06	2010-11
94	Mahatma Gandhi Memorial College, Udupi, Karnataka	2005-06	2010-11
	Affiliated to Kuvempu University		
95	Sahyadri Science College, Shimoga	2005-06	2010-11
96	Lal Bahadur Arts, Science and S.B., Solabanna Shetty Commerce College, Sagar, Shimoga (Karnataka)	2005-06	2010-11
97	Shrishaila Jagadguru Vageesha,		
	Affiliated to Visvesvarya Technological University		
98	Maland College of Engineering, P.B.No:21, Hassan-573201	2008-09	2013-2014
99	Shri Jayachanarjajendra College of Engineering, Mysore	2008-09	2013-2014
100	B.V.Bhoomaraddi College of Engineering & Technology, Vidynagar, Hubli	2008-09	2013-2014
101	NMAM Institute of Technology, Nitte, Udupi (Karnatak)	2009-2010	2014-2015
102	PDA College of Engineering Gulbarga	2009-2010	2014-2015

103	RV College of Engineering Bangalore	2007-2008	2012-2013
104	Siddaganga Institute of Technology, B.H.Road, Tumkur-572103	2009-2010	2014-2015
105	Sri Siddhartha Institute of Technology, Kunigal Road, Maralurm Tumkur-572105	2007-2008	2012-2013
	STATE MADHYA PRADESH		
	Affiliated to A.P.Singh University		
106	Govt.P.G.College, Satna (MP)	1995-1996	2000-2001 to 2014-2015
107	Govt.P.G College Shahdol (MP)	1995-1996	1999-2000
108	Sanjay Gandhi Samriti Shaskiya Mahavidyalaya Sidhi (MP)	1995-1996	1999-2000
109	Thakur Ranmat Singh Arts college, Rewa (MP)	1995-1996	2000-2001 to 2014-2015
	Affiliated to Barkatullah University		
110	S.N.Govt.Girls Degree College Shivaji.Nagar, Bhopal (MP)	1985-1986	2005-2006 to 2010-2011
111	Govt.Maharani Laxmibai Girls P.G.College, Bhopal (MP)	1985-1986	2006-2007 to 2011-2012
112	A.E.C.Training College & Centre, Panchamarhi (MP) – 461 881	1985-1986	2008-2009 to 2012-2013

113	Institute for Excellence in Higher Education (IEHE), Kaliasot Dam, Kolar Road, Bhopal-16	2007-2008	2007-2008 to 2012-2013
114	Career College, Govindpura, BHEL, Bhopal-462023	2009-2010	2014-2015
115	Govt.Geetanjali Girls College Berasia Road, Bhopal-462038	2009-2010	2014-2015
	Affiliated to Devi Ahilya University		
116	Holkar Science College Indore (MP)-45201	1987-1988	2006-2007
117	Kasturbagram Rural Institute, Kasturbagram, Indore-452020 (MP)	1987-1988	2006-2007
118	Shri.G.S.Institute of Technology & Science, 23 M.Visvesvaraya Marg, Park Road, Indore-452003 (MP)	1989-1990	1993-1994
119	Govt.Girls P.G.College, Moti Tabela, Indore (MP)	1996-1997	2000-2001
120	Govt.Arts & Commerce College, Indore (MP)	1996-1997	2000-2001
121	Govt.P.G.College, Dhar (MP)	1996-1997	2005-2006 to 2010-2011
122	Prestige Institute of Management & Management, Indore-452010 (M.P)	2006-2007	2011-2012

	Affiliated to Dr.H.S.Gour University		
123	Govt.Post-graduate College Chhindwara (MP)	2006-2007	2008-2009 to 2013-2014
124	Government Maharaja P.G College, Chhattarpur	2005-2006	2006-2007 to 2013-2014
125	Government P.G.Girls College, Sagar (M.P)	2007-2008	2008-2009 to 2013-2014
	Affiliated to Jiwaji University		
126	Ambah P.G.college, Ambah (Morea) MP	2007-2008	2008-2009 to 2013-2014
127	Govt.P.G.College, Datia (MP)	1995-1996	2007-2008 to 2010-2011
128	Kamla Raja Girls Degree College, Gwalior (MP)	1995-1996	2007-2008 to 2012-2013
	Affiliated to Rani Durgwati University		
129	College of Material Management Jabalpur (MP) 482 001	1990-1991	2007-2008 to 2012–2013
130	Govt.Model Science College Civil Lane Jabalpur Dist Jabalpur (M.P)	1988-1989	2007-2008 to 2013-2014
131	Govt.M.H.College of home Science for Women, Jabalpur (MP)	1988-1989	2007-2008 to 2012-2013
132	Govt.Mahakoshal Arts & Commerce College for Women, Jabalpur (MP)	1988-1989	2007-2009
133	Govt.Mankunwarbai Arts & Commerce	1990-1991	2007-2009

	College for Women, Jabalpur (MP)		
134	St.Aloysius College, 1 Ahilya Bai Marg, Sadar, Jabalpur-482001 (M.P)	2007-2008	2012-2013
	Affiliated to Vikram University		
135	Madhav Vigyan Mahavidyalaya Ujjain (MP) – 456 010.	1989-1990	1993-1994
136	Govt.Girls P.G.College, Ujjain (MP)	2005-2006	2010-2011
	STATE : MAHARASTRA		
	Affiliated to Sndt Women's University		
137	S.V.T.College of Home Science, Juhu, Mumbai (Maharashtra)	1995-1996	2005-2006 to 2010-2011
	Affiliated to Dr.Babasaheb Ambedkar Marathwada University		
138	Govt.College of Arts & Science, Aurangabad-431 001	1997-1998	2001-2002
139	Govt.College of Engineering, Station Road, Osmanpura, Aurangabad-431005	2007-2008	2007-2008 to 2012-2013

	Affiliated to Shivaji University		
140	Chhatrapati Shahu Central Institute of Business Education & Research, Kolhapur (Maharashtra)	1995-1996	2005-2006 to 2010-2011
141	Walchand College of Engineering Sangli (Maharastra)	2007-2008	2012-2013
	Affiliated to Pune University		
142	Government College of Engineering , Shivaji Nagar, Pune-411 005	2007-2008	2007-2008
143	Indian Instt. Of Cost & Management Studies & Research (lnd Search85/1, Law College Road, Erandavane, Pune	2007-2008	2007-2008 to 2012-2013
144	St.Mira's College for Girl's 6, Koregaon Road, Pune-411 001	2007-2008	2007-2008 to 2012-2013
145	Bansilal Ramnath Agarwal Charitable Trust's Vishwakarma Institute of Technology, 666, Upper Indiranagar, Bibwewadi 411 037	2008-2009	2013-2014
	Affiliated to Swami Ramanand Teerth Marathwada University		
146	Shri Guru Gobind Singhji Institute of Engineering and Technnology, Vishnupuri, Nanded, Maharashtra	2005-2006	2010-2011

	Affiliated to University Of Mumbai		
147	H.R.College of Commerce & Economics, 123, Dinshaw Wachha Road, Churchgate, Mumbai	2007-2008	2012-2013
	Affiliated to Sant Gadge Baba Amravati Univeristy, Amravati		
148	Vidya bharati Mahavidyalaya, C.K.Naidu Road, Camp, Amravati	2007-2008	2007-2008 to 2012-2013
149	H.V.P.Mandal's Degree College of Physical Education, Hanuman Vyayam Nagar, Amaravati	2007-2008	2007-2008 to 2012-2013
150	College of Engineering, Amravati		2008-2009 2013-2014
	STATE : RAJASTHAN		
	Affiliated to University of Rajasthan		
151	International College of girls Gurukul Marg, Mansarover, Jaipur – 302020 (Rajasthan)	2007-2008	2007-2008 to 2012-2013
152	Ovt. (P.G) R.R College, Alwar – 301001 (Rajasthan)	2007-2008	2007-2008 to 2012-2013

STATE : ORISSA

	Affilitated to Bherhampur University		
153	Khalikote College Berhampur (Orissa)	1989-1990	2001-2002 to 2005-2006
154	S.K.C.G.College, Paralakhemundi, Gajapati-761 200 (Orissa)	2002-2003	2006-2007
155	Vikram Dev College, Jeypore-764 001 (Orissa)	2004-2005	2009-2010
156	Govt.College, Phulbani-762 001 (Orissa)	2004-2005	2009-2010
157	S.B.R.Govt.Women's College Berhampur-760001	2006-2007	2011-2012
158	Rayagada College Rayagada-795001	2006-2007	2011-2012
	Affilitated to North Orissa University		
159	Dharanidhar College, Keonijhar, (Orissa) – 758001	2004-2005	2009-2010
160	Maharaja Puran Chandra College Baripada, Orissa	2004-2005	2010-2011
	Affilitated to Fakir Mohan University		
161	Fakir Mohan College Balasore (Orissa)	1999-2000	2003-2004
162	Bhadrak College, Bhadaak-756100 (Orissa)	2002-2003	2006-2007

	Affilitated to Sabalpur University		
163	Gangadhar Maher College, Sambalpur, Dist.Sambalpur – 768 004	1989-1990	2001-2002 to 2005-2006
164	Government College, Rourkela (Orissa)	2002-2003	2006-2007
165	Rajendra College, Boloangir, Distt.Bolangir-767 002 (Orissa)	2002-2003	2006-2007
166	DAV College Titilagarh, PO Bhatipada, (Orissa)	2009-2010	2014-2015
167	Government College, Bhawanipatna, Kalahandi (Orissa)	2002-2003	2006-2007
	Affilitated to Utkal University		
168	Ravenshaw College Cuttack (Orissa)	1989-1990	2001-2002 to 2005-2006
169	Samanta Chandra Sekar College Puri (Orissa)	2004-2007	2007-2008 to 2012-2013
170	B.J.B.College, Bhubaneshwar (Puri) Orissa	2004-2007	2007-2008 to 2012-2013
171	Ramadevi Women's College, Bhubaneshwar (Puri)	2004-2007	2007-2008 to 2012-2013
172	Narsingha Choudhury College, Jaipur, Orissa	2004-2007	2007-2008 to 2012-2013
173	Dhenkanal College, Dhenkanal (Orissa)	2006-2007	2007-2008 to 2012-2013
174	Kendrapara College, Kendrapara, Cuttack (Orissa)	2006-2007	2010-2011

175	Banki, CoolegeBanki Cuttack, (Orissa)	2006-2007	2010-2011
176	Nayagarh College, Nayagarh, Puri (Orissa)	2006-2007	2010-2011
177	Prananath College, Khurda-752 057 (Orissa)	2006-2007	2010-2011
178	S.V.M.College, Jagat Singhpur	2006-2007	2010-2011
179	Govt. College Angul. Orissa	2006-07	2011-2012
180	Udaya Nath College of Science and Technology, At-Prachi-jnanapitha, Post Adaspur District-Cuttack (Orissa)	2009-2010	2014-2015
181	Vyasanagar College Jaipur Road, Jaipur-755019 (Orissa)	2009-2010	2014-2015
	Affilitated to Biju Patnaik University Of Technology		
182	University College of Engg. Burla, Sambalpur-768018	1989-1990	2011-2012
183	Regional College of Management Bhubaneswar	2009-2010	2014-2015
	STATE : TAMILNADU		
	Affilitated to Bharthiar University		
184	Erode Arts College, Rangampalyam, Erode-638009	1987-1988	2005-2006 to 2010-2011
185	Gobi Arts & Science College	1987-1988	2011-2012

	Gobichettipalayam-638453		
186	Govt.Arts College, Arts College Road, Coimbatore-641018 (TN)	1987-1988	2011-2012
187	Nallamuthu Gunder Mahalingam College Pollachi-642001 (TN)	1987-1988	2005-2006 to 2010-2011
188	P.S.G College of Arts & Science Civil Aerodrome, Post Coimbatore-641 014	1978-1979	2011-2012
189	Sri.Ramakrishna Mission Vidyal Arts & Science College Coimbatore (TN)	1986-1987	2011-2012
190	Sri Ramakrishnan Mission Vidyalaya College of Education Perianaickenpalayam Coimbatore-641 020 (TN)	1996-1997	2001-2002 to 2005-2006
191	G.V.G.Visalakshmi college for Women Sri Venkatesa Mills Post, Udulmatpet	1995-1996	2005-2006 to 2010-2011
192	SNR Sons College, SNR Road, Coimbatore	2004-2005	2009-2010
193	Kongunadu Arts and Science College, Gnanambikai Mills P.O.,Coimbatore-641 029	2004-2005	2009-2010
194	R.V.S.College of Arts & Science, Coimbatore	2004-2005	2009-2010
195	PSGR Krishnammal College for Women, Coimbatore	2004-2005	2009-2010
196	Dr.G.R.Damodaran College of Science, Civil Aerodrome Post, Avanashi Road, Combatore-641014	2004-2005	2009-2010

197	Karpagam Arts & Science College, Eachanari Post, Coimbatore-641021	2006-2007	2011-2012
198	Nirmala College for Women, Coimbatore	2007-2008	2012-2013
199	CMS College of Science and Commerce, Chinnavedampatti, Coimbatore	2007-2008	2012-2013
200	Vellalar College for Women, Thindal, Erode-638009, Erode, Distt.	2007-2008	2012-2013
201	Park's College, Chinnakkarai, Tirupur, Tamilnadu	2007-2008	2012-2013
202	Sree Saraswathi Thyagaraja College, Palani Road, Pollachi (TN)	2008-2009	2013-2014
	Affilitated to Manonmaniam Sundaranar University		
203	St.Xavier's College Palayhankottai Tirunelveli 627002	1987-1988	2011-2012
204	S.P.College for Women Courtallaim-627402 (Tirunelveli)	1978-1979	2010-2011
205	Scott Christian College, Nagercoil-629 003	2005-2006	2010-2011
206	St.Xavier's College of Education, Palayankottai, Tirunelveli (T.N)	2006-2007	2011-2012
207	Sadakathullah Appa College, Rahamath nagar, Tirunelveli 627011 (T.N)	2006-2007	2011-2012
208	Sarah Tucker College,	2006-2007	2007-2008 to 2012-2013

	Tirunelveli 627007 (T.N)		
209	Holy Cross College, Nagercoil-629004 (TN)	2006-2007	2007-2008 to 2012-2013
210	St.Mary's College Thoothukudi-628001	2009-2010	2014-2015
	Affilitated to Bharathidasan University		
211	A.V.C.College Mayiladuthurai-609 305	1987-1988	2007-2008 to 2012-2013
212	A.V.V.M.Sri Pushpam College, P.O.Pondi-613503 , Tanjavur Dist (TN)	2002-2007	2008-2009 to 2013-2014
213	Govt.Arts College Khumbakonam-612 001 (TN)	2004-2007	2007-2008 to 2012-2013
214	Holy Cross College Tiruchirapalli 620 002 (TN)	1987-1988	2011-2012
215	Regional Engg. College Tiruchirapalli 620 015 (TN)	1978-1979	1998-1999
216	St.Joseph's College Tiruchirapalli – 620 002 (TN)	2005-2007	2007-2008 to 2012-2013
217	Setha Lakshmi Ramaswami College, Tiruchirappalli – 620 002	1987-1988	2011-2012
218	Periyar EVR Govt.Arts College, Iruchirappalli – 620 023	1998-1999	2011-2012
219	H.H.The Raja's College, Pudukottai – 622 001	1998-1999	2002-2003

220	Jamal Mohamed College, Khajanagal, Tiruchirappalli	2004-2005	2009-2010
221	Bishop Heber College, Tiruchirappalli Palkalaiperur – 620 024	2004-2005	2009-2010
222	Nehru Memorial College, Pathupatti -621 007 (TN)	2004-2005	2009-2010
223	Raja Serfoji Govt.College, Thanjavour-613005 (Tamil Nadu)	2004-2005	2009-2010
224	Govt.Arts College for Women, Pudukkottai	2004-2005	2009-2010
225	ADM College for Women, Nagpathnam	2004-2005	2009-2010
226	Kundaivai Nachiyar Govt.Arts College for Women, Thanjavur	2004-2005	2009-2010
227	Govt.Arts College, Karur	2006-2007	2006-2007 to 2011-2012
228	Govt.college for Women, Kumbabakonam	2006-2007	2006-2007 to 2011-2012
229	Poompuhar College Melaiyur (TN)	2009-2014	2014-2015
	Affilitated to Madras University		
230	Loyola College Nungambakkam, Madras (TN)		
231	Madras Christian College Tambaram East, madras-59 (TN)	1989-1990	2005-2006 to 2010-2011
232	Women's Christian College, College Road Madras-600 006	2002-2003 to 2007-2008	2008-2009 t0 2013-2014

233	Y.M.C.A College of Physical Education Nandanam, Madras-600 035 (TN)	1988-1989	2005-2006 to 2010-2011
234	Stella maris College 17, Cathedral Road, Madras-86 (TN)	2002-2003 to 2007-2008	2008-2009 to 2013-2-14
235	Presidency College Triplicane, Madras-600 005 (TN)	1987-1988	2002-2003 to 2007-2008
236	Queen Mary's College Mylapore, Madras-600 004 (TN)	1987-1988	2002-2003 t0 2007-2008
237	N.K.T.National College of Education for Women Triplicane, Madras-600 005 (TN)	2003-2004 to 2007-2008	2008-2009 to 2013-2014
238	St.Christoper's College of Education, 63, E.V.K.Sampath Road, Madras-600 007 (TN)	1989-1990	2008-2009 to 2009-2010
239	Technical Teacher's Training Institute Madras-600113 (TN)	1987-1988	1996-1997
240	Dr.Ambedkar Govt. Arts College, Vyasarpadi, Chennai	2006-2007	2006-2007 to 2011-2012
241	Bharathi Women's College, North Madras, Madras-600 108	1998-1999	2004-2005 to 2009-2010
242	Ethiraj College for Women Chennai-600 105	1998-1999	2007-2008 to 2012-2013
243	Meenakshi college for Women, Chennai-600 024	1998-1999	2008-2009 to 2013-2014
244	Govt.Arts College (Men), Chennai	2004-2005	2009-2010

245	MOP Vaishnav College for Women, Nungambakkam, Chennai	2004-2005	2009-2010
246	Ramakrishna Mission Vivekananda College, Mylapore, Chennai	2004-2005	2009-2010
247	Quaid-E-Millath Government College for Women, Chennai	2004-2005	2009-2010
248	Stella Matutina College of Education, Chennai	2005-2006	2010-2011
249	Institute of Advanced Study in Education, Saidapet, Chennai	2005-2006	2010-2011
250	Meston College of Education, 10/33, West Cott Road, Royapettah, Chennai-600014	2006-2007	2011-2012
251	Dhanraj Baid Jain College, Jothinagar, Thoraipakkam, Chennai-600096	2006-2007	2011-2012
252	Lady Willington Institute of Advanced Study in Education, Chennai-600005	2006-2007	2011-2012
253	The New College No.87, Peters Road, Royapettah, Chennai-600014	2007-2008	2011-2012
254	SDNB Vaishnav College for Women, Chroniepet, Chennai	2006-2007	2011-2012
255	Justice Basheer Ahmed Sayeed College	2006-2007	2011-2012

	for Women Chennai-600018		
256	The Madras School of Social Work, 32, CASA Major Road, Egmore, Chennai-600008	2006-2007	2011-2012
257	Dwaraka Doss Goverdhan Doss Vaishnav College, Chennai (TN)	2008-2009	2013-2014
	Affilitated to Thiruvalluvar University		
258	Sacred Heart College Tirupattur-635601 (TN)	2007-2008	2012-2013
259	Muthurangam Government Arts College, Otteri Road, Bagayam, Vellore-632002	2005-2006	2010-2011
260	St.Joseph's College of Arts & Science, Cuddalore, Tamil Nadu	2005-2006	2010-2011
261	Auxillium College, Gandhi Nagar, Vellore-632001	2007-2008	2012-2013
262	Dhanabagiyam Krishnaswamy Mudaliar College for Women Vellore-632001 Vellore, District	2007-2008	2012-2013
263	Theivanai Ammal College for Women, Villupuram-605602 (TN)	2009-2010	2014-2015
	Affilitated to Alagappa University		
264	Thassim Beevi Abdul Kader College for Women, kilakarai-623 517	2005-2006	2010-2011

Affilitated to Madurai Kamaraj University			
265	Lady Doak College Maduri-625 001 (TN)	1989-1990	1999-2000 to 2003-2007
266	Madura College Madurai-625 011(TN)	1978-1979	1999-2000 to 2003-2007
267	The American College Tallakulam, Madurai-625002	1978-1979	1999-20000 to 2003-2007
268	Arul Anandar College Karamathur, Madurai-626 514 (TN)	1987-1988	2005-2006to 2010-2011
269	Thiagarajar College, Madurai-625 009 (TN)	1987-1988	1997-1998 to 2010-2011
270	Vivekanand College Thiruvedakam West P.O (Via) Sholavandan Dist.Madurai-624 217	1987-1988	2005-2006 to2010-2011
271	Ayya Nadar Janaki Ammal College Sivakasi-626124(TN)	1987-1988	2005-2006 to 2010-2011
272	Fatima College Madurai-625018(TN)	1990-1991	1999-2002 to 2003-2007
273	Sree Meeakshi Govt. College for Women, Madurai-625002	1998-1999	2002-2003
274	The Standard Fireworks Rajaratnam college for Women, Sivakasi6261	2005-2006	2010-2011
275	Yadava College Madurai-625014	2006-2007	2011-2012
276	EMG Yadava Women's College, Madurai-625014	2006-2007	2011-2012

277	Subalakshmi Lakshmipathy College, of Science Madurai-625022	2006-2007	2011-2012
278	Devanga Arts College, Aruppukottai (TN)	2006-2007	2011-2012
279	Saraswathi Narayanan College, Madurai	2007-2008	2012-2013
280	Nadar Mahajana Sangam S. Vellaichamy, Nadar College, Theni Main Road, Madurai	2007-2008	2012-2013
281	Madurai Institute of Social Science Madurai	2009-2010	2014-2015
282	Sri Ramasamy Naidu Memorial College Sattur-626203 (TN)		Since the teaching faculty wanted more time to implement autonomy, a committee may be sent to the college during 2009-2010
	Affilitated to Mother Theresa Women's University		
283	Arulmigu, Palariandavar Arts College for Women, Chinnakkalayamputhur, Palani-624615 Dindigul district (TN)	2004-2005	2009-2010
284	Jayaraj Annapackiam College for Women, Periyakulam	2004-2005	2009-2010
	Affilitated to Anna University		
285	Thiagarajar College of Engg..., Madurai-625015 (TN)	1987-1988	1996-1997
286	Coimbatore Institute of Tech Civil Aerodrome Post Coimbatore-641014(TN)	1987-1988	1996-1997

287	P.S.G.College of Technology Peelamedu Coimbatore-641004	1978-1979	1998-1999
288	Govt.College of Technology Coimbatore-641013	1986-1987	1995-1996
289	Sri.Ramakrishna Engineering College, Vattamalaipalayam, NGGO Colony, Coimbatore	2007-2008	2012-2013
290	Bannari Amman Institute of Technology, Sathyamangalam-638401 (TN)	2007-2008	2012-2013
291	Kongu Engineering College, Perundurai. R.S.Road,Perundurai, Erode-638052	2007-2008	2012-2013
292	Kumaraguru College of technology, Coimbatore	2007-2008	2012-2013
293	K.S.Rangasamy College of technology, K.S.R.Kalvi Nagar, Tiruchengode (TN)	2007-2008	2012-2013
294	Adhiyamaan College of Engineering, Dr.M.G.R.Nagar, Hosur, Krishnagiri District (Tamilnadu)	2007-2008	2012-2013
295	Karpagam College of Engineering, Coimbatore	2010-2011	2015-2016

	Affilitated to Periyar University		
296	Sri Sarada College for Women, Fairlands, Salem-636016 (TN)	1989-1990	2001-2002 to 2005-2006
297	Sri Sarada College of Education, Fairilands, Salem-636016 (TN)	1988-1989	2001-2002 to 2005-2006
298	Govt.Arts College,Salem-636007 (T.N)	2007-2008	2007-2008 to 2012-2013
	Affilitated to Tamilnadu State Physical Education & Sport University		
299	Sri Ramakrishna Mission Vidyalaya Maruthi College of Physical Education, Coimbatore	2007-2008	2012-2013
	STATE : PONDICHERRY		
	Affilitated to Pondicherry University		
300	Bharthidasan Government College for Women, Mahatma Gandhi road, Pondicherry-605003	2004-2005	2009-2010
301	Kanchi Mamunivar Centre for P.G.Studies, lawspet, Puducherry-605008	2007-2008	2012-2013

STATE : UTTAR PRADESH

	Affiliated to Allahabad University		
302	Ewing Christian College Allahabd-211003 (UP)	1989-1990	2007-2008 to 2012-2013
	Affilitated to U.P. Technical University		
303	Harcourt Butlar Technological Institute, kanpur-208002(UP)	2000-2008	2008-2009 to 2013-2014
	Affilitated to Purvanchal University		
304	Udai Pratap College Varansai (UP)	2005-2007	2007-2008 to 2012-2013
305	Sri Agersen Kanya Post-Graduate College. Bulanala, Varanasi-221001(U.P)	2005-2007	2007-2008 to 2012-2013
	Affilitated to University Of Lucknow		
306	National P.G.College, 2 Rana Pratap Marg, Lucknow	2009-2010	2014-2015
	Affilitated to H.N.B.Garhwal University		
307	Pt. L.M.S.Govt.P.G.College, Rishikesh District, Dehradun (Uttarakhand)	2008-2009	2013-2014

STATE : WEST BENGAL

	Affilitated to University of Calcutta			
308	St.Xavier College Park Street, Kolkata	2006-2007		2011-2012
309	Ramakrishna Mission Sikshanamandira (A Residential College of Teacher Education), PO. Belur Math, District. Howrah Pin:7110202	2008-2009		2013-2014
310	Ramakrishna Mission Residential College, P.O.Narendrapur, kolkata (West Bengal)	2008-2009		2013-2014

STATE : JHARKHAND

	Affilitated to Ranchi University			
311	St.Xavier's College, Ranchi	2005-2006		2010-2011
312	Jamshedpur Women's College Jamshedpur	2008-2009		2013-2014
313	Ranchi College, Ranchi	2009-2010		2014-2015
314	Marwari College Ranchi		2009-2010	2014-2015

Appendix II

University Grants Commission Guidelines for Autonomous Colleges During the Eleventh Plan Period (2007-2012)

UNIVERSITY GRANTS COMMISSION
ELEVENTH PLAN GUIDELINES

SCHEME OF AUTONOMOUS COLLEGE

1. Introduction

Highlighting the importance of autonomous colleges, the UGC document on the Eleventh Plan profile of higher education in India clearly states that: "The only safe and better way to improve the quality of undergraduate education is to the link most of the colleges from the affiliating structure. Colleges with academic and operative freedom are doing better and have more credibility. The financial support to such colleges boosts the concept of autonomy". It is proposed to increase the number of autonomous colleges to spread the culture of autonomy, and the target is to make 10 per cent of eligible colleges autonomous by the end of the Eleventh plan period.

Need for Autonomy

The affiliating system of colleges was originally designed when their number in a university was small. The university could then effectively oversee the working of the colleges, act as an examining body and award degree on their behalf. The system has now become unwieldy and it is becoming increasingly difficult for a university to attend to the varied needs of individual colleges. The colleges do not have the freedom to modernize their curricula or make them locally relevant. The regulations of the university and its common system, governing all colleges alike, irrespective of their characteristic strengths, weaknesses and locations, have affected the academic development of individual college. Colleges that have the potential for offering programmes of a higher standard do not have the freedom to offer them. The 1964-66 Education Commission pointed out that the exercise of academic freedom by teacher is a crucial requirement for development of the intellectual climate of our country. Unless such a climate prevails, it is difficult to achieve excellence in our higher education system With students, teachers and management being co-partners in raising the quality of higher education, it is imperative that they share a major responsibility. Hence, the Education Commission (1964-66) recommended college autonomy, which, in essence, is the instrument for promoting academic excellence.

2. Objectives

a) *The National Policy on Education (1986-92) formulated the following objectives for autonomous colleges. An autonomous college will have the freedom to:*

   i) Determine and prescribe its own courses of study and syllabi; and restructure and redesign the courses to suit local needs; and

   ii) Prescribe rules for admission in consonance with the reservation policy of the state government;

   iii) Evolve methods of assessment of student's performance, the conduct of examinations and notification of results;

   iv) Use modern tools of educational technology to achieve higher standards and greater creativity; and

   v) Promote healthy practices such as community service, extension activities, projects for the benefit of the society at large, neighbourbood programmes, etc.

b) *Relationship with the parent university, the state government and other edu cational institutions*: Autonomous colleges are free to make use of the expertise of university departments and other institutions to frame their curricula, devise methods of teaching, examination and evaluation. They can recruit their teachers according to the existing procedures (for private and government colleges).

The parent university will accept the methodologies of teaching, examination, evaluation and the course curriculum of its autonomous colleges. It will also help the colleges to develop their academic programmes, improve the faculty and provide necessary guidance by participating in the deliberations of the different bodies of the colleges.

The role of the parent university will be:

i) To bring more autonomous colleges under its fold;

ii) To promote academic freedom in autonomous colleges by encouraging introduction of innovative academic programmes;

iii) To facilitate new courses of study, subject to the required minimum number of hours of instruction, content and standards;

iv) To permit them to issue their own provisional, migration and other certificates;

v) To do everything possible to foster the spirit of autonomy;

vi) To ensure that degree /diplomas/certificates issued indicate the name of the college;

vii) To depute various nominees of the university to serve in various committees of the autonomous colleges and get the feedback on their functioning; and

viii) To create separate wings wherever necessary to facilitate the smooth working of the autonomous colleges.

The state government will assist the autonomous colleges by:

i) Avoiding, as far as possible, transfer of teachers, especially in colleges where academic innovation and reforms are in progress, except for need-based transfers;

ii) Conveying its concurrence for the extension of autonomy of any college to the Commission within the stipulated time of 90 days after receipt of the review committee report, failing which it will be construed that the state government has no objection to the college continuing to be autonomous; and

iii) Deputing nominees on time to the governing body of government colleges and other bodies wherever their nominees are to be included.

iv) All three stake holders, the parent University, the State Govt. and UGC have to play a very harmonious and pro active role as facilitators in letter and spirit.

c) *Conferring autonomous status*: Autonomy granted to the Institution is Institutional and covers all the courses at U.G., P.G., Diploma, M.Phil. Level, which are being run by the Institution at the time of conferment of autonomous status? Also, all courses introduced by the Institution after the conferment of autonomous status shall automatically come under the purview of autonomy. Partial autonomy cannot be given to any Institution.

Autonomous status covers certificate, diploma, undergraduate, postgraduate and M.Phil. programmes offered in colleges that are autonomous and those seeking autonomous status. The parent university will confer the status of autonomy upon a college that is permanently affiliated, with the concurrence of the state government and the University Grants Commission. Once the autonomy is granted, the University shall accept the students of autonomous college for award of such degrees as are recommended by the autonomous college. The Act and Statutes of the universities ought to be amended to provide for the grant of autonomy to affiliated colleges. Before granting autonomy, the university will ensure that the management structure of the applicant college is adequately participatory and provides ample opportunities for academicians to make a creative contribution.

3. Target Group and Eligibility Target Group

All Colleges under Section 2 (f), aided, unaided, partially aided and self-financing which are or are not covered under 12(B) of the UGC Act are eligible to apply for autonomous status. This includes Engineering Colleges also.

Criteria for Identification of Institutions for Grant of Autonomy:

a) Academic reputation and previous performance in university examinations and its academic/co-curricular/ extension activities in the past.
b) Academic/extension achievements of the faculty.
c) Quality and merit in the selection of students and teachers, subject to statutory requirements in this regard.
d) Adequacy of infrastructure, for example, library, equipment, accommodation for academic activities, etc.
e) Quality of institutional management. (f) Financial resources provided by the management/state government for the development of the institution.
f) Responsiveness of administrative structure. (h) Motivation and involvement of faculty in the promotion of innovative reforms.
g) Self-Financing colleges can also apply for autonomy after they have completed minimum 10 years of existence. However, conferment of autonomy will not entitle them to receive autonomy grant. They will have to follow the same procedure as applicable to other colleges.
h) Colleges that provide professional courses in Education, Engineering Technology Management and Physical Education, etc. will also be eligible to receive grants from the Commission. The sanction of such grants will depend on the size and stage of development of these colleges after attaining autonomous status.

4. Preparation Prior to Applying for Autonomy

Preparing a College for Autonomy

There are several areas where proper preparation is necessary if college autonomy is to be implemented successfully. These are: faculty preparation, departmental preparation, institutional preparation, and preparation of students and the local community. Such multi-pronged preparation should be completed well before autonomy is sought and conferred upon a college so that no part of the college community is found unprepared for the new responsibility which it is called upon to shoulder.

Faculty Preparation

It is essential to get the staff of the college involved in the thinking and planning processes from the very beginning. Seminars, workshops and consultations may be organized to make the staff familiar with the concept, objectives and rationale of autonomy. (This will help them have a sense of participation in decision making and motivate them to get involved in the entire exercise). This could form part of the academic calendar of the college.

Departmental Preparation

An important responsibility of the department is that of designing suitable courses in the major and related subjects, introducing new courses of study, renaming obsolete courses by changing their content, updating existing courses to match the current state-of-the art in each discipline, and preparing course materials and human resources.

These will be done in the light of the general objectives of autonomy and the specific objectives of the education institutions.

Common programmes to be adopted are:

a) Semester pattern of study
b) Continuous internal assessment
c) Credit/grading system
d) Student feedback
e) Self-appraisal by teachers

Institutional Preparation

Since an autonomous college is called upon to perform many of the functions that the university has hitherto performed, it must study the academic, administrative/management and financial implications of such a changeover and prepare itself to discharge its new functions efficiently.

5. Procedure for Applying

The UGC will invite proposals from eligible colleges seeking autonomous status, once in an academic year in September/

October. The individual university can also send circulars asking the colleges to apply.

6. Procedure for approval by the UGC

The approval for the grant of autonomous status will be done in two stages. At stage I a screening committee will be constituted by the UGC. The composition of the committee will be as follows:

a) Three to five experts nominated by the UGC (One of the experts will be nominated as convener).
b) Principal Secretary of higher Education of the respective State or his/her nominee.
c) Chairman, State Council for Higher Education or his/her nominee (wherever constituted).
d) Commissioner/Director of Collegiate Education or his/her nominee.
e) Vice-Chancellor or his/her nominee.
f) Joint Secretary, UGC In-charge of Autonomous Colleges-Member Secretary.

At stage II short-listed colleges will be visited by another expert committee constituted by the UGC. This committee will submit its report with its findings and recommendations to the UGC. Thereafter, the UGC may send its recommendation to the university concerned for conferment of autonomy.

The university will notify the colleges concerned. Autonomy will be conferred initially for a period of six years.

7. Nature of Assistance

Pattern of Financial Assistance and Other Enabling Provisions

The Commission will provide assistance under this scheme to autonomous colleges to meet their additional and special needs.

a) Guest/visiting faculty
b) Orientation and re-training of teachers.
c) Re-designing courses and development of teaching/learning material
d) Workship and seminars
e) Examination reforms

f) Office equipment, teaching aids and laboratory equipment
g) Furniture for office, classrooms, library and laboratories
h) Library equipment, books/journals
i) Expenditure on meetings of the governing body and committees
j) Honorarium to Controller of Examinations (full-time) not exceeding Rs.8,000 p.m.
k) Accreditation (NAAC) fee
l) Renovation and repairs not leading to construction of a new building
m) Extension Activities

Following shall be the guiding principles for utilization of autonomy grant.

a) Autonomy grant cannot be used for creation of posts, payment of salary to any of the college staff, payment of honorarium (except clause (x) above) to existing staff, to meet normal college contingency requirement or to subsidies.
b) Examination fee should be fixed so that income from fee can meet the expenditure on examinations and other staff appointed in examination cell.
c) The ceiling of normal assistance will be as follows:

Sl.No:	*Nature of Institution*	*Amount of Grant in Rs.*
a	Only Under Graduate:	
	1. Arts/Science/Commerce-one faculty only	9,00,000
	2. Arts/Science/commerce More than one faculty:	15,00,000
b.	Both Undergraduate and Postgraduate levels:	
	1. Single faculty	10,00,000
	2. Multi-faculty	-20,00,000

8. Governance of an Autonomous College

The college will have the following committees to ensure proper management of academic, financial and general administrative affairs.

The following are statutory bodies:

a) Governing Body

b) Academic Council

c) Board of Studies

d) Finance Committee

The composition and functions of the above committees are given in Annexture-III to VII. The college will, in addition, have other non statutory committees such as the Planning and Evaluation Committee, grievance Appeal Committee, Examination Committee, Admission Committee, Library Committee, Student Welfare Committee, Extra-Curricular Activities Committee and Academic Audit Committee.

*Governing Body**

The constitution of this body will be according to the structure given in Annexure-III.

Academic Council

The Academic Council will be solely responsible for all academic matters, such as, framing of academic policy, approval of courses, regulations and syllabi, etc. The Council will involve faculty at all levels and also experts from outside, including representatives of the university and the government. The decisions taken by the Academic Council will not be subject to any further ratification by the Academic Council or other statutory bodies of the university. The composition and functions of the Academic Council are given in Annexure IV.

Board of Studies

The Board of Studies is the basic constituent of the academic system of an autonomous college. Its functions will include framing the syllabi for various courses, reviewing and updating syllabi from time to time, introducing new courses of study, determining details of continuous assessment, recommending panels of examiners under the semester system, etc. The composition and functions of the Board of Studies are given in Annexure V.

(*The Governing Body is different from Trust Board/Board of Management/ Executive Committee/Management Committee).

Finance Committee

The Finance Committee will advise the Governing Body on financial matters and shall meet at least twice a year. The constitution and functions of the Finance Committee are given in Annexure.

9. Procedure for Monitoring/Evaluation and Release of Grant

a) The right of autonomy may not be conferred once and for all. It has to be continuously earned by the college. The status of autonomy will be granted initially for a period of six years.

b) Each autonomous college will, with the approval of its Academic council, formulate an appropriate mechanism to evaluate its academic performance, improvement of standards, and assesses the extent and degree of success in the utilization of autonomy. Self-evaluation will be made annually. In addition, there will be two external evaluations, the first after four years and the second after six years. The latter will determine the continuance or revocation of autonomous status.

A Joint Expert Committee consisting of two representatives each from the affiliating University and the concerned State Government and three representatives from the UGC out of which, one shall be the Convener of the Committee to examine the proposal of the colleges for extension of autonomous status after completion of first and subsequent tenures of autonomy.

To avoid hardship to existing autonomous colleges, provision of 80% of the admissible grant will be released to such autonomous colleges by the Regional Offices as an " On Account" grant, in case the review of the autonomous colleges is delayed beyond the expiry of tenure of autonomy.

Also in the event of delay in the review report and renewal of autonomy, the college will continue to enjoy autonomy with the entitlements of benefits, fiscal or otherwise so conceived under the scheme, unless the government or parent university by a special order withholds such continuation.

In the event of the availability of evidence confirming decline in standards in an autonomous college, it shall be open to the UGC and the university to revoke the autonomous status of that college after careful scrutiny, and mutual consultation and due notification to the management. In such cases the students already admitted under the autonomous scheme would be allowed to complete the course under autonomous status. An autonomous college should get themselves accredited by the NAAC within a period of two from the date of conferment/extension of autonomous status.

Procedure for Release of Autonomy Grant by UGC

Following procedure is laid down for release of autonomy grant to Autonomous Colleges enjoying autonomy in the tenure period.

a) Autonomous College should hold meeting of Finance Committee in the month of April 1st week to take stock of the utilization of autonomy grant of coming year. A detailed Blue Print of budget should be duly approved by the Finance Committee in this meeting.
b) Only those items should be included, which are admissible as per clause 7 of these guidelines. No expenditure other than these items shall be accepted for utilization.
c) The budget so prepared and approved by the Finance Committee will be submitted to the Governing Body for final approval before 25th of April every year.
d) The budget duly approved by the Finance Committee and the Governing Body should be submitted to the concerned Regional Office of the UGC on or before 30th April. In case the meeting of the Governing Body is not held before 30th April due to unavoidable reasons, the Principal in the capacity of Member Secretary f Governing Body, may submit the budget to the concerned Regional Office of the UGC under approval of the Chairman of the Governing Body.

General Matters Starting of New Courses

An autonomous college is free to start diploma (undergraduate and postgraduate) or certificate courses without the prior approval of the university. Diplomas and certificates shall be issued under the seal of the college.

An autonomous college is free to start a new degree or postgraduate course with the approval of the Academic Council of the college. Such courses shall fulfill the minimum standards prescribed by the university/UGC in terms of number of hours, curricular content and standards, and the university shall be duly informed of such courses.

An autonomous college may rename an existing course after restructuring/redesigning it with the approval of the college Academic Council as per UGC norms. The university should be duly informed of such proceedings so that it may award new degrees in place of the old.

The university should have the right to review all new courses of an autonomous college. Where there is evidence of decline in standards or quality, the university may, after careful scrutiny, and in consultation with the UGC, either help modify them, wherever possible, or cancel such courses.

Award of Degrees through Parent University

The parent university will award degrees to the students evaluated and recommended by autonomous colleges. The degree certificates will be in a common format devised by the university. The name of the college will be mentioned in the degree certificate, if so desired. Autonomous colleges that have completed three terms can confer the degree under their title with the seal of the university

10. Special Features of an Autonomous College

Starting of New Courses

An autonomous college is free to start diploma (undergraduate and postgraduate) or certificate courses without the prior approval of the university. Diplomas and certificates shall be issued under the seal of the college.

An autonomous college is free to start a new degree or postgraduate course with the approval of the Academic Council of the college. Such courses shall fulfill the minimum standards prescribed by the university/UGC in terms of number of hours, curricular content and standards, and the university shall be duly informed of such courses.

An autonomous college may rename the existing course after restructuring/redesigning it with the approval of the college Academic Council as per UGC norms. The new nomenclature should be as specified by UGC under section 22 of UGC Act. The university should be duly informed of such proceedings so that it may award new degrees in place of the old.

The university should have the right to review all new courses of an autonomous college. Where there is evidence of decline in standards or quality, the university may, after careful scrutiny, and in consultation with the UGC, either help modify them, wherever possible, or cancel such courses.

Procedure to Introduce a New Course by Autonomous College

Step 1

The concerned department of the college should conceive the idea of introducing new course and it should be well discussed in the Board of Studies of that subject. The Board of Studies will formulate the idea into a proposal with all necessary details such as objectives, eligibility, course content and fees structure. Such proposal will be forwarded to the Academic Council. The proposal will be in the shape of an ordinance.

Step 2

The Academic Council will discuss such proposal in its meeting and shall approve the proposal in case the Council finds the proposal appropriate. The Academic Council shall have the right to send back the proposal to the Board of Studies for revision/modification or may reject the proposal giving suitable reasons. The proposal can be resubmitted to the Academic Council for reconsideration after the necessary modifications are made.

Step 3

The proposals approved by the Academic Council will ultimately be submitted to the Governing Body of the college for final approval and for permission to execute the proposal.

Step 4

Autonomous college shall send all proposal approved by the Governing Body of the college to the University for information.

University may ask clarification regarding the issues in the proposal from the college. The college is bound to give such clarification with an understanding that the university shall accept the students for award of degree under such newly proposed courses.

11. Meetings of the Statutory Bodies

Introduction of a new course should be executed after due preparation and large scale participatory discussions.

a) Preparation for a course to be introduced in the next academic session should start in the month of October of the preceding session with meetings of Board of Studies.
b) Academic Council meeting should be held twice, once in the month of January to discuss proposals for the next academic session and again in the month of August to monitor status of newly introduced courses. Academic Council shall propose ways and means to maintain quality norms.
c) Governing Body meetings should follow the meetings of Academic Council. In the month of August the Governing Body should pass the budget of the autonomous fund including the autonomy grant received from UGC.
d) Finance committee should meet at least twice in a financial year. The meetings can be organized in the month of April and September of every year. The meeting in the month of April shall be the budget meeting for autonomy grant and in September it will be another budget meeting for autonomous fund created by the college through examination and other relevant fees.

12. Examination Cell & System

Autonomous College shall have an Examination Cell headed by Controller of Examination who will be a permanent faculty nominated by the Principal on the basis of potential of the person. The Principal of the college shall be the Chief Controller, Examinations.

The Controller of Examination will create his/her own team with the approval of the Principal of the College. The team shall consist of Deputy Controllers/Assistant Controllers, the number of persons to be nominated shall depend on the quantum of work in the Examination Cell. Teachers working in the college shall be nominated in the Examinations Cell for tenure of 3 years. They will continue doing their teaching work as scheduled by the college.

There shall be a team of Office Assistants, Computer Programmers, Data Entry Operators and other helpers in the Autonomous Cell.

Examination Cell will have appropriate printing unit also for printing of question papers and other relevant confidential material.

All part-time/full time functionaries of the Examination Cell shall be paid honorarium for the extra work being done by them apart from their usual work. Such honoraria shall be proposed by the Finance Committee and shall be approved by the Governing Body.

Governing Body may also approve appointment of full time office staff in the examination cell on contractual basis on the recommendation of Finance Committee. The salary of such staff will also be decided by the same mechanism.

There shall be continuous, comprehensive evaluation of students through internal and external examination. At least 2 internal examinations per semester and 1 semester ending examination should be conducted.

In order to motivate students to be free of rot learning, various mechanism of internal evaluation should be adopted such as group discussion, paper reading, home assignments and viva voce.

Remuneration for examination work should be decided by the finance committee and should be approved by the Governing Body. In no case it should be less than that paid by the parent university.

13. Award of Degrees

Through Parent University

The parent university will award degrees to the students evaluated and recommended by autonomous colleges. The degree certificates will be in a common format devised by the university. The name of the college will be mentioned in the degree certificate, if so desired.

14. Few General Issues

a) All recruitments of teaching staff will be made by the Governing Body/state government in accordance with the policies laid down by the UGC and state government.

b) Universities shall consider both internal and external assessment of students in autonomous colleges for admitting them to higher-level courses.

c) Organisation of special need-based short-term courses under the colleges department of continuing education may be an important activity of an autonomous college. Such courses ought to benefit the students of the college besides outsiders who may enroll for them.

d) The time spent by teachers on projects and extension work shall be counted for reckoning their workload as prescribed by the Commission.

e) An autonomous college should prepare a calendar for meetings of various bodies to ensure that the implementation of the recommendations made by them is not unduly delayed for reasons of non-convening of such meetings.

f) A wide variety of courses may be evolved in modules so that students may opt for them according to their convenience. Such courses may help them acquire additional credits.

g) Teacher evaluation in autonomous colleges may include periodical self evaluation, institutional assessment of teacher performance, student feedback, research appraisal and other suitable forms of teacher appraisal.

h) Autonomous colleges in a given region may form a consortium for mutual cooperation/collaboration in chosen areas such as management skills, national services, entrance examinations, services projects, intercollegiate/intra-collegiate sharing of expertise and human resources for teaching programmes.

i) Credit system and credit transfer among colleges in general and autonomous college in particular may be suitably adopted.

j) Autonomous colleges to be involved in recurrent academic innovative activities which are carefully designed keeping the interest of the students and quality of education at non compromising end.

k) Autonomous colleges due to their permanent affiliation with the university need not apply for affiliation for new subjects at the time of introduction. Any new subject to be started by an autonomous college shall be covered under autonomous scheme.

l) The Principal of the government autonomous college will be empowered to make purchases from UGC fund without prior approval/permission of the State Government.

m) Autonomous college need not pay affiliation fees to the Parent University every year. One time fees can be paid at the time of conferment of autonomous status. Such fees can be decided by the Executive Council of the Parent University.

n) The UGC will provide VSAT to each autonomous college for Internet connectivity.

o) Autonomous colleges are free to institute medals for meritorious students. The value and other terms of reference may be decided with the approval of appropriate bodies in the college.

Annexure I.

Format for Submission of Proposal for Autonomous Status

The proposal should be submitted to the UGC in the following format:

Part I: Background of the Institution

Part II: Supply of Information Based on Criteria

1. Academic reputation ad provisions (performance in university examinations and other academic activities)
2. Academic attainments of the staff
3. Mode of selection students and teachers
4. Physical facilities, i.e., library, accommodation and equipment

5. Institutional management
6. Financial resources the management can provide for the development of the institution
7. The responsiveness of the administrative structure to the views of staff and students.
8. Extent of freedom enjoyed by the staff for advanced scholarship, research and experimentation and involvement in educational innovation and reforms.

Part III: Implementation of Autonomy

1. Aims and objectives
2. Management of the college
3. Academic Council: Structure & functions
4. Boards of Studies: Structure & functions
5. Other committees
6. Admission eligibility
7. Curricular programme
8. Student feedback
9. Internal assessment
10. External assessment
11. Financial implications
12. Course contents
13. Co-curricular and extra curricular activities

Part IV: Basic Information

1. Name of college:
2. Name of Principal:
3. Telephone/fax/email:
4. Year of establishment:
5. Whether private/government/university maintained:
6. Year of grant of permanent affiliation:
7. Courses offered:

   U.G

   P.G

   M.Phil

8. Student enrolment during last three years:

   U.G

   P.G

   M.Phil

9. Faculty strength category-wise: (Please enclose list of faculty with their qualifications/papers/books/monographs if published)
10. Administrative, laboratory and library staff:
11. Results during the last five years: percentage of:

	1st Division	2nd Division	Overall Pass
UG			
PG			

12. Number of M.Phil/Ph.D..s produced during the last three years:

Subject	Year	M.Phil	Ph.D.

List of journals in the library:

List of major items of equipment in the college (costing more than Rs.50,000/- each):

13. Whether college has been accredited by NAAC, mention the rating

Signature of Registrar of Affiliating University (With Seal)

Signature of Principal

Annexure II.
Proforma for Extension of Autonomy

1. Name of college:
2. Name of Principal:
3. Telephone/fax/email:
4. Year of establishment:
5. Whether private/government/university maintained:
6. Year of grant of permanent affiliation:
7. Courses offered:

   U.G

   P.G

   M.Phil
8. Student enrolment during last three years:

   U.G

   P.G

   M.Phil
9. Faculty strength category-wise: (Please enclose list of faculty with their qualifications/papers/books/monographs if published)
10. Administrative, laboratory and library staff:
11. Results during the last five years: percentage of:

	1st Division	2nd Division	Overall Pass
UG			
PG			

13. List of journals in the library:
14. List of major items of equipment in the college (costing more than Rs.50,000/- each):
15. Physical facilities added during the last six years:

    a. Accommodation:

b. Equipment

c. Library

16. Academic Council:

    a. Involvement of members of faculties of the college at all levels:

    b. Whether the students are represented in the Academic Council and if so their contribution:

17. Board of Studies

    a. Please indicate how many Boards of Studies have been constituted:

    b. Whether the Boards of Studies have external experts, including an expert nominated by the university:

18. Curriculum:

    a. Whether annual or semester system is adopted:

    b. Innovative aspects and experiments introduced by the college since obtaining autonomy:

    c. Please give a note on curriculum development under autonomy:

19. Research activities:

    a. Research programme/research activities undertaken in the departments during the last five years:

    b. Research activities/programme on hand:

20. Evaluation/examination patern:

    a. Examination reforms if any introduced during the period of autonomy:

    b. Question paper setting for final examinations (Internal/External/Combined).

    c. Evaluaion (Completely internal/completely external/partly external and partly internal):

    d. Proportional weightage of continuous internal assessment and final examination:

       (Also indicate break-up for assignments, tests, etc. for a awarding continuous internal assessment)

    e. Criteria for passing and classification:

    f. Is a grading system adopted? If yes, indicate the method of awarding grades:

g. Is there any qualifying board to declare the results? If yes, indicate the constitution and function:

h. While declaring the results, is any moderation done? What are the criteria adopted for moderation?

i. Is there provision for improvement?

j. For practical examinations are the examiners internal or one external and one internal?

k. Has any question bank been set up? If yes, give the subject:
1. Has a credit system been introduced?

21. Examination results (past six years, branch-wise):
   a. Number appeared:
   b. Number passed:
   c. Percentage of passes:
   d. Number passed in first class and with distinction:

22. Re-evaluations:
   a. Is there provision for re-evaluation?
   b. Fee for re-evaluation:
   c. Number applied for re-evaluation and number passed by such re-evaluation during the last five years:

23. Scope of getting admission into postgraduate courses and employment opportunities for the graduate coming out of college:

24. Expenditure
   a. Annual additional expenditure to the college (last six years):
      – Salary to staff
      – Stationery
      – Remuneration for examiners, TA & DA for various authorities, etc.
      – Equipment
      – Other contingency expenditure, If any
   b. Sources from which this expenditure is met: (last six years)
      – Salary to staff
      – Annual recurring and non-recurring grants

available from the UGC, central government and state government:

- Grant from any other source
- Contribution by the Management

25. Has any evaluation of the autonomous functioning been made? If yes, give a summary of the outcome:
26. Whether college has been accredited by the NAAC. If yes, give the rating:
27. Whether the University has conducted the review as per the guidelines. If yes, please enclose the report.
28. Number of times meeting of Governing Board, Academic Council, Board of Studies, and Finance Committee during the tenure of autonomous status. Date/Year.
29. Any other relevant details:

Signature of Registrar of Affiliating University (With Seal) — Signature of Principal

Annexure III.

Recommended Composition and Functions of Board of Governing Body

A. Constitution of Governing Body of Private Management Autonomous College

Number	*Category*	*Nature*
5 members	Management	Trust or management as per the constitution or byelaws with the chairman or President/Director as the Chairperson
2 members	Teachers of the college	Nominated by the Principal based on seniority
1 member	Educationist or industrialist	Nominated by the management
1 member	UGC nominee	Nominated by the UGC
1 member	State Government nominee	Academician not below the rank of Professor or state government official of Directorate of Higher Education/State Council of Higher Education.

1 member	University nominee	Nominated by the university
1 member	Principal of college	Ex-officio

B. Constitution of Governing Body of Government Autonomous College

Number	Category	Nature
3 members, one of them to be chairperson	Educationist, industrialist, professional	Nominated by the state government. Persons of proven academic interest with at least PG level qualification
2 members	Teachers of the college	Nominated by the Principal based on seniority
1 member	Educationist or industrialist	Nominated by the Principal based on seniority for two years
1 member	UGC nominee	Nominated by the UGC
1 member	State government nominee	Nominated by the state government
1 member	Principal of college	Ex-officio.

Table C. Constitution of Governing Body of University Constituent Autonomous

Number	Category	Nature
3 members, one of them to be chairperson	Educationist, industrialist, professional	Nominated by the state government. Persons of proven academic interest with at least PG level qualification
2 members	Teachers of the college	Nominated by the Principal based on seniority
1 member	Educationist or industrialist	Nominated by the Principal based on seniority for two years
1 member	UGC nominee	Nominated by the UGC
1 member	State government nominee	Nominated by the state government
1 member	Principal of college	Ex-officio.

Term: Two years, except for the UGC nominee whose term will be a full six years. Meeting: At least twice a year.

Functions

Subject to the existing provision in the bye-laws or respective college and rules laid down by the state government, the governing body* of the above colleges shall have powers to:

a) Fix the fees and other charges payable by the students of the college on the recommendations of the Finance Committee.
b) institute scholarships, fellowships, studentships, medals, prizes and certificates on the recommendations of the Academic Council
c) Approve institution of new programmes of study leading to degrees and/or diplomas
d) Perform such other functions and institute committees, as may be necessary and deemed fit for the proper development, and fulfill the objectives for which the college has been declared as autonomous.

*Governing Body/Governing Board/Board of Management/Executive Committee/ Management Committee, as may be named.

ANNEXURE IV.

RECOMMENDED COMPOSITION OF THE ACADEMIC COUNCIL AND ITS FUNCTIONS IN AN AUTONOMOUS COLLEGE

I. Composition

1. The Principal (Chairman).
2. All the heads of department in the college.
3. Four teachers of the college representing different categories of teaching staff by rotation on the basis of seniority of service in the college
4. Not less than four experts from outside the college representing such areas as Industry, Commerce, Law, Education, Medicine, Engineering etc., to be nominated by the Governing Body.

5. Three nominees of the university
6. A faculty member nominated by the Principal (member secretary)

II. Terms of Members:

The term of the nominated members shall be two years.

III. Meetings:

The Principal shall convene a meeting of the Academic Council at least once a year.

IV. Functions:

Without prejudice to the generality of functions mentioned, the Academic Council will have powers to:

a) Scrutinise and approve the proposals with or without modification of the Boards of Studies with regard to courses of study, academic regulations, curricula, syllabi and modifications thereof, instructional and evaluation arrangements, methods, procedures relevant thereto etc., provided that where the Academic Council differs on any proposal, it will have the right to return the matter for reconsideration to the Board of Studies concerned or reject it, after giving reasons to do so.
b) Make regulations regarding the admission of students to different programmes of study in the college
c) Make regulations for sports, extra-curricular activities, and proper maintenance and functioning of the playgrounds and hostels.
d) Recommended to the Governing Body proposals for institution of new programmes of study.
e) Recommend to the Governing Body institution of scholarships, studentships, fellowships, prizes and medals, and to frame regulations for the award of the same.
f) Advise the Governing Body on suggestions (s) pertaining to academic affairs made by it.
g) Perform such other functions as may be assigned by the Governing Body.

ANNEXURE V

RECOMMENDED COMPOSITION OF THE BOARD OF STUDIES AND IT'S FUNCTIONS IN AN AUTONOMOUS COLLEGE

I. Composition:

1. Head of the department concerned (Chairman).
2. The entire faculty of each specialization.
3. Two experts in the subject from outside the college to be nominated by the Academic Council
4. One expert to be nominated by the Vice-Chancellor from a panel of six recommended by the college Principal.
5. One representative from industry/corporate sector/ allied area relating to placement.
6. One postgraduate meritorious alumnus to be nominated by the Principal. The chairman, Board of Studies, may with the approval of the Principal of the college, co-opt:

a) Experts from outside the college whenever special courses of studies are to be formulated.

b) Other members of staff of the same faculty.

II. Term

The term of the nominated members shall be two years.

III. Meeting

The Principal of the college shall draw the schedule for meeting of the Board of Studies for different departments. The meeting may be scheduled as and when necessary, but at least once a year.

IV. Functions

The Board of Studies of a department in the college shall:

a) prepare syllabi for various courses keeping in view the objectives of the college, interest of the stakeholders and national requirement for consideration and approval of the Academic Council;

b) suggest methodologies for innovative teaching and evaluation techniques;

c) suggest panel of names to the Academic Council for appointment of examiners; and

d) coordinate research, teaching, extension and other academic activities in the department/college.

Annexure VI.

Recommended Composition of the Finance Committee and It's Functions in an Autonomous College

I. Composition:

a) The Principal (Chairman).

b) One person to be nominated by the Governing Body of the college for a period of two years.

c) One senior-most teacher of the college to be nominated in rotation by the Principal for two years. The Finance Committee will be an advisory body to the Governing Body, and will meet at least twice a year to consider:

d) Budget estimates relating to the grant received/ receivable from UGC, and income from fees, etc. collected for the activities to undertake the scheme of autonomy; and

e) Audited accounts for the above.

Place:

Date:

Signature :

Name :

Designation: (Principal)

Annexture VII.

Progress Report of College (Autonomous) (To be furnished in duplicate by the Principal of the college)

Progress Report for the Academic Year

1. Date when autonomy was first given by UGC:
2. Year in which last external evaluation was done
   a. By managing society:
   b. By university
3. Annual evaluation done by the college during the year under review
4. Number of courses modified, stopped or started during the year (Give names of courses):

5. If external evaluation done during the year, attach report:
6. Progress of expenditure:

Item	Unutilised grant available from previous Year	Grant received from UGC during the year	Expenditure during the year	Unspent balance	Remarks
Building guest faculty					
Orientation of teachers					
Redesigning of courses					
Workshops /seminars, others					
Office/teaching					
Laboratory equipment furniture, library					
Meeting of overning & other bodies					

Place:

Date:

Signature :

Name :

Designation: (Principal)

ANNEXTURE VIII
UTILISATION CERTIFICATE

It is certified that the amount of Rs. .... (Rupees) out of the total grant of Rs........... (Rupees.............)sanctioned to ....by the University Grants Commission vide its letter number.........................dated..................towards........................ ....under..............................scheme has been utilized for the purpose for which it was sanctioned and in accordance with the terms and conditions as laid down by the Commission.

If, as a result of check or audit objection, some irregularities are noticed at a later stage, action will be taken to refund, adjust or regularize the objected amount.

Signature
Principal with seal

Signature
Statutory Auditor of the College with seal/
Charted Accountant with seal and Registration No.